Contemporary Selling

Contemporary Selling

Richard Cummings
College of Lake County

Rand McNally College Publishing Company/Chicago

To Jan, my wife, and Ian, my son.

Sponsoring Editor, Edward Jaffe
Project Editor, Theresa M. Ludwig
Designer, Gene Rosner
Cover, Kathleen Sullivan
Illustrator, Ted Carr

79 80 81 10 9 8 7 6 5 4 3 2 1

Contents

Contents

Contents

Preface

The selling field is undergoing extensive changes. Over the past several years a new age of sales sophistication has emerged. *Contemporary Selling* is written in response to the changing face of the sales profession.

Contemporary Selling is a unique package. It contains a textbook, an instructor's manual, and a separate adoptor's kit. These components have been carefully integrated and will provide a considerable amount of pedagogy for the students as well as additional instructional tools for the teacher.

The textbook provides a current and practical discussion of the sales profession. To achieve this objective, the publisher edited extensively, and, in some cases, rewrote sections of the textbook. The text emphasizes the standard topics covered in this course: the selling process; psychological factors in selling; buyer decision making; and so on. In addition, there are several features that differentiate this text from the majority of sales texts on the market.

One of the basic differences is that the five basic types of selling are thoroughly integrated into each chapter. This includes examples of selling retail goods, retail services, commercial goods, commercial services, and industrial goods. Another important feature of the book is the extensive coverage of sales support. Chapters on the use of the telephone and mail as sales support, visual materials, and electronic sales support cover many of the key trends in sales.

A career perspective is emphasized throughout the book. Chapters 16, 17, and 18 examine career issues that a salesperson might encounter. In Chapter 16, the discussion of sales management is approached from a career perspective rather than emphasizing sales management techniques.

This textbook contains numerous pedagogical features. At the beginning of each chapter, key concepts are identified and are defined in the chapter in the margins. At the end of each chapter there are homework assignments based on the key concepts. Additionally, there are class exercises interspersed throughout each chapter. These exercises are in the form of discussion questions or simple activities that can be solved in the classroom. At the end of each chapter there is also a mini-case to facilitate further student involvement.

Contemporary Selling also contains five appendices: an excerpt from Robert Molloy's book *Dress for Success;* an excerpt from Molloy's book *Women's Dress for Success Book;* an original appendix on pricing policies; an excerpt from the Dartnell publication *Sales Manager's Handbook;* and a listing of various business directories.

The text contains more illustrative material than most texts on the market. There are approximately 50 photographs which are closely keyed to the text. Each chapter begins with a cartoon that was specially designed for this text.

The instructor's manual also is quite innovative. It contains standard types of instructional assistance by providing chapter outlines and test questions for each chapter. Besides this, it contains a resource guide that indicates where media and print materials can be obtained as well as listing organizations that can provide additional teaching materials. The media guide only includes those resources favorably rated by a media service. Also included is a review of instructional techniques—lecture outlines, cases, classroom presentations, field trips, speakers, and so on. This section is designed to provide additional instructional tools and for the instructor who might have several different teaching preparations each semester.

The adoptor's kit will provide the instructor with additional tools. When *Contemporary Selling* is adopted, an adoptor's kit will be provided to the department. This kit includes five booklets from the widely read *Sales & Marketing Management.* These booklets contain articles written by practitioners on the subjects of prospecting for the sale, opening the sale, closing the sale, sales motivation, and telephone sales. There will be six sales games to facilitate further role playing in the classroom. Additionally, there will be course development worksheets that relate to section B (instructional techniques) in the instructor's manual. These worksheets can be used for all of your courses. The final premium item is an attractive pocketplanner for your personal use.

May we have your order?

I would like to acknowledge the help and assistance of my editor, Ed Jaffe, and Eleanor McConnell, who helped in the development of this text.

R. C.

To the student

This course and textbook are based on experience. You and I are involved in selling every day therefore most of the information and skills presented in this text can be put to practical use right away. As a personal benefit, you should be better able to sell yourself and your ideas, including getting a job, a promotion, or a higher grade in this course.

Our focus, however, is on *professional* selling—that is, selling a product or a service for profit. Because there are many different products and services, the business world requires a wide range of skills and talents to fill selling positions. For instance, selling real estate and selling computers are similar but require different skills and strategies.

With this in mind, the text is primarily concerned with those aspects of professional selling common to the majority of selling situations. You must apply the principles and concepts to your situation. In the classroom this application is most easily accomplished through role playing, cases, and class discussion of problems.

In order to get the most out of these classroom exercises, you should select some area of selling as a possible career. By applying the lessons to a practical situation, depth will be added to your experience. The text will not only be more meaningful to you, but it will make a you a stronger candidate when you apply for a job.

This text is meant to be used with either of the two different approaches used in teaching professional selling—the more theoretical, "about selling" selling approach and the more practical, "how to" approach. *Contemporary Selling,* which includes both theoretical and practical materials for the instructor, can be used with either approach. While the text is primarily "about selling," it also covers the "how to" approach. It includes basic information necessary for you to develop both your knowledge and skills. I hope you find the reading enjoyable and beneficial. I also hope this text will introduce you to new fields of opportunities and will expand your horizons.

Best of luck.

R. C.

Background 1

1 The rewards of professional selling

Key terms

in-home selling
direct marketing
outside sales
wholesaler
rack jobber
route sales
agent
broker
merchandise mart
manufacturer's
   representative
team selling
merchandiser
missionary sales

Overview

Many people have unclear or mistaken impressions about careers in selling. They fail to see the wide range of opportunity that exists. Careers in professional selling do in fact offer a variety of situations and rewards. Your sales career may involve any kind of product or service. Your rewards include the education and experience received by trainees and the financial benefits and personal satisfaction attained by a successful salesperson. This chapter will survey the job market in order to help you set a career goal if you do decide to pursue a sales career. This book is designed to serve the wide range of interests of men and women who seek careers in any phase of sales, and this chapter will help you gain a perspective for the following chapters. Finally, this chapter will discuss how the adoption of sound selling concepts extends beyond business to your personal life.

Professional selling: myths and reality

Relatively few college students sign up for a sales course with the intention of pursuing a career in sales. A course in sales is, for many at the community college level, simply a required course in the curriculum. Other students take the course because they are already selling and have found that their firm does not offer sound training. It is estimated that the community college night programs now account for 40–50 percent of the business training acquired by full-time workers.

At four-year colleges and universities the situation is slightly different. Many students at these institutions anticipate that their first job will be either in sales or in a sales-related area. They see the course in selling and the resulting first job as the first stepping stones to management positions. As with many of their community college counterparts, few students intend to pursue a sales career.

And yet, rewarding sales opportunities are everywhere. By 1980, as Figure 1–1 shows, the number of people in sales jobs may reach six million. How can we explain the discrepancy between attitudes and reality?

Part of the reason is that most young people do not know what professional selling is. The fictional image of the salesperson as a "huckster" persists and seems very slow to die. TV and movie performances as well as comic-strip characters reinforce the myths and lend credibility to them. Furthermore, the unpleasant sales encounters we have are the ones we tend to remember; we forget the professional salespeople who meet our needs cordially and effi-

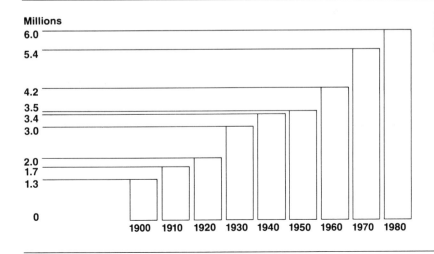

Millions

6.0
5.4
4.2
3.5
3.4
3.0
2.0
1.7
1.3
0

1900 1910 1920 1930 1940 1950 1960 1970 1980

**Figure 1-1.
Salesworkers in the U.S.
Labor Force, 1900-80**

Robert Preston in *The Music Man* is an example of the "huckster."

Courtesy of the Museum of Modern Art, New York

A more realistic view of professional selling is illustrated in this photo of traders at the Chicago Mercantile Exchange.

Courtesy of the Chicago Mercantile Exchange.

ciently. After the completion of a transaction, we concentrate on our satisfaction, not on the salesperson's role in delivering it.

Four myths exploded

The stereotypes also persist because few people are conscious of the wide variety of selling required in our economy. People continue to cling to myths built around the stereotypes. In this section we will examine four of these myths involving work, environment, personal habits, attitudes of others, and the self-image of the salesperson.

1. Salespeople spend most of their time on the road at the expense of their family. This statement is false. The vast majority of selling jobs allow the salesperson to be at home in the evenings, particularly in the sale of retail goods, consumer services, wholesale goods, and commercial services. Where extensive travel is required, modern transportation has reduced overnight stays. Increased use of the telephone will continue to decrease travel requirements.

2. Salespeople keep a hectic pace — they wear themselves out before their time. This statement is also false. Although the hours may be long and somewhat more irregular than a typical, nine-to-five factory or office job, most salespeople set their own activity level. Their selling may be done during business hours, as with most commercial sales, or during evening hours, as with some in-home sales. It is always possible to become a "workaholic," but that is a matter of professionalism. Skilled, well-trained salespeople probably do not experience any more job related stress than other professional people do.

3. Salespeople are not respected. This attitude is relative. The question is, whose respect do you wish to have? More and more people seem to be losing respect for doctors and lawyers as well as other professionals. In a highly technological society such as ours, the professional salesperson is an educator. Those who are successful as educators have the respect of their clients as well as of their peers. Respect is something that one must earn, both as an individual and as a professional person. It is based on trustworthiness and reliability, no matter what career path is chosen.

4. Salespeople have to take too much abuse. This statement may be true of those who lack the necessary knowledge and skills, but it is certainly not true of the able professional. In the majority of selling situations the salesperson deals with established accounts or customers, and repeat business; mutual respect grows out of satisfactory transactions. Even where the turnover of customers is high the customer tends to seek out the salesperson as an educator and problem solver. Abuse may occur when an inept or pushy salesperson tries to sell a product to someone who has no real need for it. In view of the total amount of goods and services bought and sold daily, such cases are extremely rare, although they may be widely publicized.

A code of professional ethics

Professional selling should be guided by a set of ethics or a creed. An ethical code sets down guidelines for honesty and decency in dealing with other people. One such code, developed by Sales and Marketing Executives International, is reprinted here. Memorize it. Cut it out and frame it. Hang it on a wall where you can read it frequently. This set of principles can guide you throughout your professional sales career. It places on you the responsibility to put these basic principles into action.

Table 1-1.
SMEI Code of Ethics

SMEI shall support and preserve the highest standards of professional conduct in the field of sales and marketing management. Toward this end, its members should reflect this objective in their individual activities at all times under this code:

1. It is the responsibility of SMEI and its entire membership to maintain honesty and integrity in all relationships with customers, and to put first emphasis upon quality of product and service, with accurate representation to the public.

2. SMEI recognizes the basic marketing principle that there must be mutuality of benefit and profit to the buyer and seller in order to insure true economic progress, and thus to fulfill the inherent responsibility of marketing to advance our country's standards of living.

3. SMEI is keenly alert to the need for constant advancement and protection of individual and corporate rights in the entire marketing concept. It is therefore inherent that SMEI shall always crusade to protect the freedoms of choice and competition which are a fundamental part of the free enterprise philosophy.

4. SMEI shall always strive for constructive and effective cooperation with governmental agencies in areas of appropriate interest, always with the objective of supporting and maintaining the free enterprise system.

5. SMEI shall ever be dedicated to the information and education of the public, in all its segments and age levels, to the true values and advantages of the free enterprise system.

Source: Sales & Marketing Executives International.

1. Make a list of your negative feelings about a career in professional selling. Which can be supported facts and which are perpetuated by myths?

The retail sector

Since we are all consumers, the majority of our contacts with salespeople are in the retail goods sector. For reasons stated above, we tend to remember the negative encounter and forget the positive encounter. Because of the negative image, few young people seriously consider a professional career in retail sales. Yet the jobs number in the tens of thousands, and turnover is relatively high; most people at some time in their lives have been engaged in a retail selling job, by chance, if not by choice. If they are poorly trained they may carry unpleasant memories of the experience.

Types of selling jobs

When we talk of retail sales, most people form a mental picture of over-the-counter sales in a retail store setting, but these encounters form only a small portion of total annual retail sales. In truth, the retail sector offers many desirable alternatives for professional sales-people. One area often overlooked is **in-home selling.** This form of selling occurs when the salesperson visits the customer's home and is called **direct marketing.** Tupperware, Avon, Sarah Coventry, and many other companies use this technique successfully. Some firms have actively recruited husband and wife teams to sell full time and to develop new salespeople. Sales may be made on a one-to-one basis or at a party held in someone's home for the purpose of showing the merchandise to several people.

Another method of in-home selling, often called **outside sales,** is used by established retail firms such as department stores when the presentation is delivered more effectively in the home. The range of job opportunities and income potential is quite large. Items commonly sold by this method include home improvements, garages, carpeting, interior design services and home furnishings, appliances, heating and air conditioning, blacktop driveways, draperies, and many other goods. Since this type of selling deals

in-home selling
selling consumer goods in the customer's home.

direct marketing
sales made in a customer's home or place of business. The sales may be brought about through customer response to advertisements, telephone solicitation, or placement of an order in a catalog.

outside sales
in retailing, sales made in the customer's home by an established firm such as a department store.

An outside sales presentation in the customer's home.

Courtesy of Charles Beseler Company.

primarily with high-priced items that entail one-time sales with delivery or installation, it differs significantly from the clientele-building practices associated with home parties and consultive selling, such as Avon or Tupperware sales.

Attitudes

Contrary to popular belief, consumers do not regard in-home selling negatively. Surveys have shown that most buyers are satisfied with the services they have received from in-home salespeople, and sales in the home have been increasing steadily. This increase can be attributed to an increase in the number of firms doing business in this manner, but a significant factor is the acceptance of these salespeople by consumers impatient with sales clerks in retail stores. Catalog sales have also increased significantly in the past few years, and many say this reflects two factors: consumers' desire for wider variety and their dissatisfaction with the level of personal service in retail stores. Excellent opportunities in in-home selling are waiting for those willing to prepare themselves properly.

The two major differences between the selling of retail merchandise in the home and in a store are prospecting and environment. The first difference, *prospecting,* is the seeking out of potential customers, or *prospects.* The in-store salesperson relies on the firm's location, advertising, and reputation to draw customers. To a degree, the types of customers are predetermined by these factors. In in-home selling, on the other hand, the salesperson usually seeks out the customer.

The second difference, *environment,* refers to both the psychological and physical surroundings in which the sale takes place. Selling in a retail store has the advantages of a controlled environment, a wide range of merchandise that can be shown and demonstrated, and the availability of support materials and people. In-home selling lacks these advantages, but the customer experiences a familiar and comfortable environment, which is also an advantage.

Commissioned sales

Retail salespersons may be paid on the basis of hourly salary, straight commission, or some combination of both. In food service locations, tips represent a significant portion of the total income. The most lucrative opportunities probably lie in *commissioned sales,* in which the salesperson is paid a percentage of the total sales. While many find this idea frightening at first, they soon find it desirable to see their efforts directly reflected in their incomes.

Many of the items mentioned in the section on in-home selling are also sold on commission in retail locations. Examples are furniture and carpeting; vans and pickups; stereo systems and other electronics including CB radios, sporting goods, and recreational equipment; tires, batteries, and auto accessories; fashions—including furs, jewelry, and accessories—and on and on. The opportunities are abundant. Incomes over $20,000 a year can be earned entirely on commission by those who have learned to sell effectively. Competition is not especially keen since few salespeople have adequate training for this type of selling.

2. List two or three hobbies, sports, or recreational activities you actively pursue. What opportunities do you see in the retail sector to sell the merchandise and supplies associated with each? Find out what the top salespeople earn each year. Report.

Consumer services

Until this point we have been discussing the selling of *tangibles*—manufactured products the consumer can use in finished form or put into production to manufacture something else. In the next section we will introduce the sale of *intangibles*—services or entertainment facilities that are used over and over again, with no actual, physical product involved. Instead of presenting a long list enumerating the many possibilities in this area, we will discuss specific examples as we come to them.

The area of intangibles is lucrative for several reasons. First, in an affluent society such as ours the demand for services tends to increasesat a faster rate than the gains in the standard of living. Second, people have an almost limitless capacity for intangibles such as entertainment and other services. Finally, the field is lucrative because both profit-based and nonprofit firms such as political campaigns and colleges are involved in selling services, and both sectors are growing.

New opportunities

With few exceptions, consumer service firms have become actively customer oriented only recently. The exceptions are insurance, real estate, and a few small industries, and even these firms are stepping up their activities. Real estate franchises are selling rapidly. Insurance companies are moving toward full service, offering a complete line of property, life, auto, and other insurance to meet consumer needs.

Private and even public colleges are now using selling concepts to recruit students. Utilities, especially the electric companies, employ people to sell installations of electric heat. Bell Telephone uses

Illinois Bell "phone store."

salespeople to encourage the sale of additional phones, extension jacks, and decorator telephones in both new and established institutions. Bell has recently opened "phone stores," retail outlets to sell telephone instruments.

People are out selling lawn maintenance, home maintenance, and house cleaning. Many automobile dealerships also deal in leasing, complete with maintenance, insurance, and licensing. Selling is occurring in travel agencies, beauty and barber shops, photography studios, caterers, figure salons, dance studios, and health resorts. There is a big market in selling tennis lessons, driving lessons, skiing lessons, music lessons, and on and on. It's a virtually unlimited field.

The range of opportunities
As the size and scope of consumer services expands, so does the range of opportunities. There are a few factors you should take into account before choosing the selling of services as a career. Many services are more of a luxury than a necessity and, therefore are subject to great changes in demand; in a bad economy, consumer buying of some services may cease almost entirely. In good times, sellers may flood the market because little money is required to establish a business. For example, in one city in Illinois, one adult in three holds a real estate sales license.

The need for training
There is an advantage to selling consumer services, however, and you are benefiting from it right now. As in retail sales, few consumer salespeople have formal training in effective selling techniques.

Real estate salespeople offer the best example. With the exception of those either employed by major firms or involved with a franchised network, only a very small percentage of real estate salespeople pursue formal study in selling after receiving their brokers licenses. At one community college in Illinois, over 200 students complete the real estate licensing course each year, but less than 5 of those 200 actually enroll in the selling course.

There is another aspect to selling consumer services. The person who sells the service also produces it: production and use occur at the same time. Those not schooled in effective selling often do not produce good services because they remain unaware of the customers' needs. Some estimates state that 80 percent of the sales and earnings go to only 20 percent of those actively selling services. Service selling, then, tends to be either feast or famine. With proper preparation in sales techniques, you will be able to enjoy the feast.

3. What services have you purchased recently from a salesperson? Would you consider the services more a necessity or a luxury? Evaluate the performance of the salesperson.

Wholesale and export/import sales

Retail sales of the type we have been discussing involve sales of goods or services directly to the ultimate user or consumer. **Wholesalers**, on the other hand, sell products to industry or agriculture for use in production, to retail stores for resale, or to government institutions. We will discuss in the following pages several types of wholesale activities, an area that has undergone many changes in the three decades since World War II. We will also discuss a huge market of growing importance, that of import and export sales.

wholesaler
a firm that buys and stores goods for the purpose of reselling them to other businesses.

Supplying the wholesale market
In the past, a wholesale seller was merely an order-taker with a huge catalog. Today the salesperson's role has changed to that of consultant. Many people find this type of selling very attractive, since the primary focus is on servicing existing accounts. Prospecting and developing new accounts is minimal in this field. Selling activities tend to have less pressure than in some other fields. A client who does not buy anything this week will still return to you when the need to buy arises. This is not to imply that the job opportunities are not diverse, for they are.

One group of wholesalers includes **rack jobbers**, the people who restock the racks of bread, milk, panty hose, and magazines, to

rack jobber
in route sales, salespeople who restock racks in local retail stores. They often own both the merchandise and the display rack.

name only a few lines commonly serviced in this way. While new accounts must often be solicited, most of the selling activity is concerned with the location and size of the assigned selling space, the addition of new products, the discontinuing of old products, and the use of attention-getting sales materials such as banners, signs, displays, and similar devices.

Similar jobs are found in wholesaling firms that serve commercial and industrial clients. Tools, cleaners, grease and oil, janitorial supplies, office supplies, and fasteners (nuts, bolts, strapping) are commonly sold by *route sales*; salespeople have assigned routes and regular accounts. While part of the salesperson's job is suggesting new materials that may be more cost effective, the main emphasis is on inventory control—providing neither too much nor too little. Prospecting for new accounts takes on more importance for these route people than for rack jobbers because the volume they can sell to any one customer is usually limited by the customer's sales. An account may also grow when new products are added to the sales line.

Full-service salespeople are also needed by wholesalers who carry a wide range of products for a particular use. Your local auto parts store's wholesaling activities fit in this category. Other such operations in the consumer goods area include food and hardware products. Some of the largest operations in the commercial-industrial area are in health care supplies and equipment.

Salespeople who sell for these firms are primarily concerned with inventory supply and control, although in recent years they have also become coordinators for consulting services. For the retail market these services would include store design and layout, advertising planning, accounting services, and management training, as well as computer support. The person who deals with both retail goods and commercial-industrial goods needs a strong background in finance. While some salespeople for these firms still function as order takers, their numbers seem to be diminishing.

Selling for exporters/importers

In the rapidly growing export/import area, job opportunities fall into two main categories. One group functions primarily as manufacturers' agents or as brokers who bring buyers and sellers together. The other group is composed of those who run the wholesaling operations. The day-to-day activities of people in these two groups differ considerably.

An *agent* is one who does the actual selling to clients. A *broker* serves more as a mediator in arranging transactions overseas, and is used primarily by firms who cannot afford a full-time salesperson

route sales
sales made by people who have assigned routes and regular accounts.

agent
a person with authority to represent another person in conducting business. Commonly used by firms that do not have enough volume to support their own salesforce.

broker
a person who arranges transactions between two parties. Real estate and stocks are sold in this manner.

Courtesy of the Drupa Exposition, Frankfurt, West Germany.

Exposition selling is international in scope.

in a given foreign sales market. Agents and brokers tend to concentrate in major market centers or **merchandise marts** such as the New York World Trade Center, the Chicago Merchandise Mart, and the Dallas Market Center. Many agents and brokers operate out of their homes or small offices, since many of their contacts are made by phone and the mail. The key to success is a thorough knowledge of the market of potential buyers and sellers. Personal contacts and foreign travel are often extensive.

merchandise marts *market centers where many competing firms maintain sales and display offices. In essence, it is a shopping center for retailers.*

The other group in the export/import sector consists of those who run wholesale operations, not unlike those previously discussed. While some sell directly to retailers and other businesses, many sell to local and regional wholesalers. They may buy from domestic producers and sell overseas, or buy from foreign markets and sell in the United States. A great many specialize in only a few merchandise lines, such as linens or crystal, although they may buy from many countries.

Preparation for a selling career within this vast foreign-related market should include language, history, and anthropology as well as the normal business curriculum. Of great importance is a very good understanding of the culture and customs of the people with whom you will be working. In foreign trade, seemingly small offenses may not only kill a sale, but cut off any future dealings with that client.

Sales in the manufacturing sector

Manufacturers sell their product lines in several different ways. They may use full-time sales and support personnel, staffed by their own

manufacturer's rep
a person or company that sells for a manufacturing firm that does not wish to maintain its own full time salesforce.

employees and reporting to the sales department. Or they may sell through agents known as **manufacturers' representatives (reps)**. In this section we will look at the types of sales personnel employed by manufacturers; then we will look at the functions of manufacturers' reps.

Types of selling

Many manufacturers in basic industries or highly technological fields use *sales engineers* to sell the product and educate the buyer in its use. Whether in the basic industries such as steel or chemicals or in such complex areas as medical technology, the individual should have a thorough knowledge of both the users' needs and the technology involved in producing the item. Selling frequently involves the use of teams of specialists. Considerable coordination of support people is required in **team selling**; other support people are needed for installation and in-service training. Since these sales may run into the hundreds of thousands and even millions of dollars, the sales activities differ from the traditional type. Pre- and post-sale activities occupy most of the team's efforts.

team selling
sales presentations made by several specialists to provide thorough coverage of benefits offered. It is usually coordinated by a sales engineer or an account executive.

Another more traditional group of sales personnel calls on wholesalers and retailers: most of their time is spent serving established customers. Those serving the wholesale sector may also call on retail or other wholesale accounts on behalf of the wholesaler, acting as **merchandiser** for them. Some firms assign people to do this type of merchandising on a full time basis. They serve mainly to coordinate cooperative advertising efforts, in which cost is split between the retailer and the manufacturer. They also see to displays, new product introductions, and other promotional activities, and therefore usually do not sell in the traditional sense.

merchandiser
a sales support person who aids several salespeople in servicing existing accounts. Main function is to allow the salesperson more time to sell.

A more difficult type of selling is **missionary selling**. On the frontier of the market, these people face the task of introducing a company or a line of products to new markets or different distribution channels. Once customers are established they are turned over for servicing to a person who operates in a specific limited geographical area or territory. Some firms employ missionary salespeople to call on chain-store accounts at the national level, such as J. C. Penney, Sears, Walgreen's, A & P, with local representatives servicing individual stores in the chain.

missionary sales
the introduction of a new company or new product line to new markets or to different distribution channels.

Many manufacturers are too small to employ a field service force. Volume in any given territory is too small to support such personnel. Thousands of agents known as manufacturers' representatives (reps) make their living selling for these small firms. They sell compatible but not competitive lines, often the output of 50 to 75 different firms, and they do it in a protected, specified geographical territory.

The product is shipped directly to the buyer by the manufacturer. These people are widely used in fashion, furniture and decorative accessories, notions and gifts, and advertising specialties such as calendars, pens, pennants, or key chains. While an order written for any one firm with a customer may be small, the total amount of goods sold for that firm to various customers will result in enough sales to earn a very good commission.

4. Select one of the various selling positions in either wholesaling or manufacturing that has some appeal to you. Secure an interview with a salesperson doing that kind of selling. What occupies the majority of his or her time? The least?

Commercial services

The field of business services, like that of consumer services, has been expanding greatly in recent years. Unlike consumer services, the seller often does not deliver the service but functions primarily as coordinator. The account executive who sells the services of an advertising agency, for instance, will consult with artists, photographers, media planners, copywriters, and many others who work to produce the service. The same is true for those selling advertising space for newspapers, magazines, and advertising time on radio and television stations.

Business needs a great many services, like those of accountants, bankers, lawyers, consultants, and other professionals. These services must be sold, and although this selling activity is normally kept at low key, it is selling, nevertheless. Businesses need insurance, employee fringe benefits, janitorial and building maintenance services, and equipment maintenance and repairs. They also consume a great deal of paper in the form of sales order forms, catalogs, call reports, letterheads, business cards, and brochures. Design and production of forms for internal records and reports is a major industry by itself.

Many firms who manufacture and sell equipment that will need repairs have set up separate divisions for that service. They sell service contracts, train the repair personnel, and maintain inventories of replacement parts. They are also responsible for guarantee or warranty commitments.

Hotels, convention centers, training services, fleet rental cars and trucks, air, land, and water freight movers, private warehouses, and assorted financial services all have to sell their products. The computer industry has created the need for many service-oriented firms as well. The range of opportunity is great.

Of importance to those interested in a career in the service industry is the ability to work well with a diverse group of people. The diversity of people is often significant both in one's own firm and within the customers' businesses. There is a need for people who can direct and motivate others while being able to handle conflicts. Because services are intangible, they offer the additional challenge of adapting to changes in demand as the business climate changes.

5. Visit with a salesperson selling the services of an employment agency. To what degree is income determined by the local economic climate? How does one deal with ethics questions typical of industry?

Interpersonal relationships

After surveying the wide range of selling opportunities, you may have decided that a professional sales career is not for you. Should you continue to read this text? Yes, because it has a lot to offer. Selling is very much a part of everyone's daily life. We sell ideas to others, sell ourselves to employers, and we are consumers (buyers). An understanding of the selling-buying process will make you more effective in your relationships with others. By using the basics of selling in your everyday social relationships, conflicts may be minimized and advantages gained.

Whatever your job may be, selling will have an effect on promotions and in-office relationships. Those who have customer contact in a nonselling capacity will better appreciate their role in meeting their firm's objective and their role in supporting the firm's salesforce. We hope that the course will introduce you to the wide range of nonselling jobs in sales support—areas of training, sales promotion, advertising, display, trade shows and exhibits, and audiovisual materials.

We have yet to meet the student who completes the selling course and then says he or she felt the time was wasted.

6. Review the selling jobs discussed in the chapter. Select two that seem the most interesting as a career. Interview a sales manager working in each area to discover the requirements for an entry level position. Or spend a day with a salesperson in each of the two areas. Report.

"Business needs two types of salespeople—those who *take* orders and those who *get* orders!"

    What is the difference between the two?

    In each job sector what kind of positions are there for order takers?

    How can the course be of value to both types of salespeople?

Mini-case

agent	merchandiser	route sales
intangible product	missionary sales	sales engineer
manufacturers'	outside sales	tangible product
representative	professional selling	wholesaler
merchandise mart	rack jobber	

**Define these
key concepts**

2 Professional selling, sales promotion, and advertising

Key terms

marketing
market segmentation
marketing mix
promotion
market research
synergism
advertising
promotion mix
sales promotion

Overview

Over the past thirty years, business has developed the marketing concept, a philosophy that has expanded slowly to reach all segments of commerce. This chapter explores the marketing concept and its relationship to the professional salesperson.

Because selling is becoming increasingly a team activity, we will explore the kinds of jobs held by other members of the team—both technical support people and others in the firms who sell. We will provide insight into alternative career paths and develop an appreciation and understanding of the roles of others in team selling.

The marketing concept

Until recently, American business has been production oriented: most company efforts were devoted to producing a good or service. Areas such as finance, personnel, and sales functioned with minimal direction. The message given to the salesforce was: "Here is the product: go out and sell it." Most of the time that concept was sufficient to sell a moderate amount of goods. Following the hardships of World War II especially, an eager public gobbled up most of the consumer goods produced. When that demand was satisfied, however, manufacturers found themselves with expanded production facilities and a shrinking market. The next logical step for them was to work with the growing advertising industry to identify consumers' wants and needs and, if possible, to create new demands for consumer goods.

These new strategies reflected the development of the marketing concept. **Marketing** starts with the idea that, in order to build long-run profits, a business enterprise must understand its customers and their particular needs. Studies were undertaken to divide or segment the market—the total population of consumers—and to determine the needs of each segment or group of consumers. Although the first **market segmentation** studies were done by advertising firms that wanted to be sure of reaching their audiences, the concept is now used by sellers in all areas: commercial, industrial, and retail. Firms define their own objectives concerning which market segment they want to reach, concentrating their production, advertising, and selling efforts on that segment.

marketing
the flow of goods and services from producer to consumer to satisfy wants and needs. Profit oriented, the process begins from the consumer's viewpoint.

market segmentation
division of a market into submarkets; each is different from the other in one or more significant factors.

Changes in the organization

Putting the marketing concept into practice required many changes in the structure of the manufacturing firm. Figure 2-1 shows the organization of a firm before and after adoption of the marketing concept. As Figure 2-1 shows, the sales area was immediately affected. In the past, the sales manager reported directly to the company president. Now a new individual, the director of marketing, has been placed between these two positions. The addition of the director of marketing has the effect of lowering the sales manager's position on the corporate ladder. The responsibilities of the marketing executive are discussed next.

The marketing mix

The function of the marketing executive is to determine the allocation of the company budget and time to the four elements of the

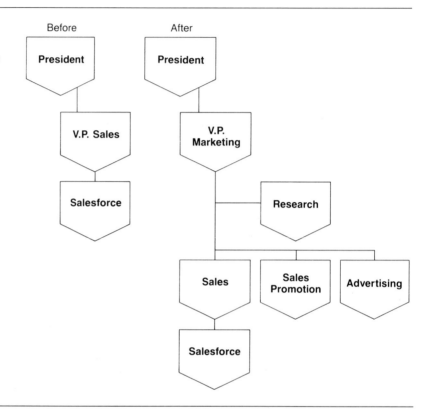

Figure 2-1.
A firm's structure before and after adoption of the marketing concept

Before

After

marketing mix
the elements of product, price, promotion, and distribution planned together to meet the needs of a particular market segment.

promotion
all activities used by a firm to stimulate sales; activities of the salesforce, advertising, sales promotion, and publicity.

marketing mix: product, price, distribution, and promotion. We will define these elements more fully in later chapters. **Promotion**, as we will use the term, refers to all activities a firm uses to stimulate sales. The marketing executive must plan the means, or strategy, by which the company will develop this mix to achieve the objectives.

While the changes we have discussed relate to a production firm, which manufactures a product for sale, similar changes have been made in other types of businesses as well. In the retailing field, buying has been centralized, with the local department managers primarily responsible for selling. Banks have adopted marketing techniques to sell their services. In real estate, division by product areas (commercial, residential, leasing) has resulted in a restructuring of real estate selling and an emphasis on developing special skills and marketing mixes for each type.

To achieve this balance and successfully coordinate all these activities requires close communication between departments. This need has been filled in many cases by the addition of the *marketing communications specialist*. The addition of this position, which removes the sales manager's position one more step from the president, has been met with understandable resistance. The structuring of marketing activities is illustrated in Figure 2–2.

This figure shows that the communications group has been expanded from three members to five. Some firms add a sales training manager (not shown) who may also relieve part of the sales manager's burden of recruitment and personnel selection. In addition, the firm's advertising agency may share in market research, public relations, sales promotion, and sales support. Events stemming from the adoption of the marketing concept have produced many changes in the role of the salesforce.

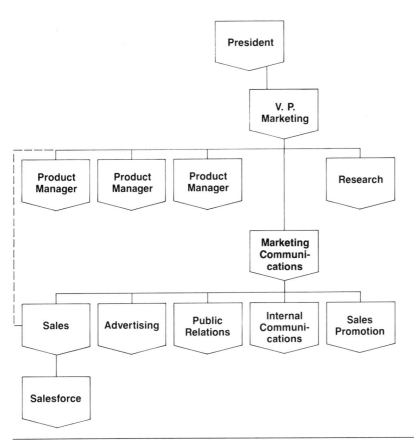

**Figure 2-2.
Recent changes in the structure of a firm**

1. **Assume you have two selling job offers. One is from a small firm organized as shown in Figure 2–1, "Before." The second firm is larger and is organized similarly to that shown in Figure 2–2. Both sell similar products to the same market. Which sales job would you prefer, and why?**

Nonmarketing activities

As firms grow in size and scope, communication becomes more and more important. Each member of a salesforce needs to develop an understanding of internal relationships as they relate to both formal and informal communication. This knowledge is especially important as the salesperson enlists the help of others within the firm to solve problems. While the salesperson may be filling out all the right forms (formal communication) to get assistance, the timing of such requests or the salesperson's attitude toward the person being asked (informal communication) may block cooperation. A different kind of selling job is required here since many nonmarketing personnel who have not been exposed to the marketing concept remain production oriented. Their main concern is their own priority schedule, and they may see requests for help as an unwanted intrusion on their time. This is true of managers as well as their workers. In order to deliver what has been promised to a customer, the salesperson may have to make a second sale within the firm.

Emphasis on finance

As we have seen, the prestige given earlier to production has begun to shift to marketing, and currently we are seeing a shift toward finance. Objectives relative to the growth of the firm are determined by finance. These objectives will ultimately influence production and marketing decisions. With this change comes the requirement of the salesforce to be a producer, not of sales, but of *profits*. This is true in more and more areas of business, as attention is devoted to a firm's investment in an operation and to the return on that investment. You will recall that the marketing concept was developed in an attempt to build long-run profits.

Many of these financial decisions affect the salesforce directly. The trend is toward commissions being tied to profit, not merely to volume. Even in selling to other firms the focus may be on methods to raise their profits, not merely their volume. With this outlook, finance people within the company may be called upon to support the salesperson's efforts. It is easy to see the importance of an understanding of the principles of finance, especially the relationships between investment, costs, and profits.

market research
the collection and analysis of data concerning attitudes, opinions, and buying behavior that are relevant to the marketing mix.

Consumer research

Selling is also based on **market research**, often separated into several specializations in medium and larger firms. While most people associate research with technology and engineering, market research has expanded into the gathering and analyzing of data relevant to consumer behavior, store design and layout, packaging, advertising response, and even selling. In fact, most major business decisions today are based upon market or consumer research in some form.

From the salesperson's point of view selling should be based on research findings. In medium and larger businesses, research information will be obtained from several sources. Some research data will be included in presentations to support product benefits. Research in psychology will help you make better presentations, using its findings in areas such as word psychology and body language, for instance.

The personnel area

In the past, the personnel area has usually been far removed from contact with the sales department. Even today, many sales managers prefer to do their own recruiting, selecting, and training, independent of the personnel office. That this situation is changing is most evident in larger firms that have signed Affirmative Action plans administered by the federal government. These agreements require that women and members of minority groups be recruited and trained for management positions.

The direct effect on the salesforce has been that many firms are viewing the sales area as a managerial training ground. As a result, the personnel department and the sales manager have closer ties. But with these events have come problems. Some salespeople, in selling areas long restricted to men, are reluctant to welcome women into their ranks. Others feel that when underqualified people are hired the degree of professionalism is diminished. These personnel policies, in the long run, may create two conflicting groups: managerial trainees temporarily assigned to sales, and career sales professionals.

Other changes in the personnel area relate to compensation and fringe benefits, an area long controlled by the sales manager. Today sales employees seek fringe benefits similar to those paid to other employees. Union recruitment activity is also growing; the Retail Clerks International has made many gains. As unionism grows in professional areas among doctors, teachers, and engineers, for instance, one can look for sales to follow. With it comes closer ties to the personnel area.

The legal department

Sales' relationship with the legal staff has been growing. Federal and state laws increasingly regulate sales activities. Sears signed an agreement to discontinue misleading advertising in which a very cheap product was advertised, but customers attracted by the advertisement were discouraged from buying it; instead salespeople aggressively pushed a more expensive and better quality alternative. Levi Strauss signed an agreement concerning the limiting and controlling of who may resell its merchandise. All states now have laws governing in-home selling, providing for a *cooling-off period* during which the customer may cancel a sale.

Also covered by laws are land sales and schemes known as *pyramid selling,* in which the thrust of the selling is toward distributorships, not the good or service listed. Real estate is under investigation for *block busting* or *panic peddling*—using the racial change of neighborhoods to solicit sales at a price advantageous to the real estate dealer. Home mortgage lenders face regulation concerning *redlining*—the practice of denying mortgage or improvement loans to applicants in specific areas of cities. Manufacturers have seen changes in their cooperative advertising plans. Bribes and kickbacks, which some buyers have come to expect, can lead to serious legal consequences. The legal department must be viewed as a support area.

As we have seen, individuals and firms must develop and practice *high ethical standards*. Without this outlook, more and more legislation will be sought to control the daily activities of the salesforce, and the number of government agencies policing sales activities will continue to grow.

The need for communication

As business becomes more complex, an ever-increasing share of the market is shifting to the medium and large firms. Every management area within a firm has a relationship with the salesforce. While the salespeople are rarely involved in the decision-making process, beyond providing an information input, an understanding of the function and problems of each area is essential. Few firms have adopted the marketing concept. Fewer still have conveyed that philosophy to their nonmarketing personnel. Much internal selling needs to be done, and some of that burden will fall on the salesforce.

2.   After selecting a business within your career interest, rank the following departments in importance to you as sales support. Assume your firm is at least medium in size.

Legal	**Data Processing**	**Warehousing and**
Personnel	**Research**	**transportation**
Financing	**Production**	**Purchasing**

What is the rationale for your decisions?

Marketing structure and sales support activities

Earlier we defined some of the ways in which various aspects of marketing are becoming more specialized. One highly visible example is McDonald's, the hamburger chain, which uses two advertising agencies—one for advertising and one for sales promotion items such as calendars, coupons, and contests. The public can see the results of the two agencies' close cooperation with their client. Much of McDonald's TV and newspaper advertising is concerned with the current promotion, producing a synergism few firms have been able to duplicate. **Synergism** results when closely coordinated activities produce a greater response than those activities would generate if pursued independently.

Marketing is primarily a team effort today; the activities of advertising, sales, and sales promotion must be closely coordinated. People involved in these activities are sometimes called the *marketing team*. More specialists are being employed and coordination of these support activities is important to the salesforce. The nature of the activities and the reporting structure within the organization vary in different selling areas. While all these activities are designed to make the sales job easier, they also serve to make it more complex.

Retail sales support

In retailing, the salesforce must rely on many sales support activities. Probably the most important one is **advertising**, which we can define as any paid, nonpersonal communication by an identified sponsor. The effectiveness of the advertising program has a direct bearing on traffic—people visiting a store or contacting a firm—and traffic has a direct relationship to the amount of sales generated. With a trend toward *centralized advertising units*—advertising by the parent company or a manufacturer, rather than by an individual store—using mass media, especially television, there have been significant improvements in the quality of retail advertising. Even so, the advertising support given many retail salespeople today is relatively poor.

Another important area of retail sales support is display, including fixtures. Just as traffic affects volume, so does the way the merchandise is exposed to that traffic. Recently research has been devoted to creating a selling environment using the new concept called *psychographics*. This means the store's interior design, display, and merchandise assortment is compatible with a specific market segment to which the store wishes to sell. People in this segment feel secure and comfortable in the environment and respond by purchasing.

synergism
closely coordinated activities produce a greater response than those activities would produce if pursued independently.

advertising
any paid form of nonpersonal communication by an identified sponsor.

**The design of shopping
centers includes the use of
applied psychographics
both within individual stores
and the mall area.**

Photo courtesy of The Taubman Company, Inc., developer.
Photographer: Balthazar Korab.

Use of computers or *electronic data processing (EDP)* as sales support on the retail level is on the increase. Many stores have limited inventory. Computers can now communicate directly with the warehouse for immediate inventory access. Out-of-stock items can be replenished either from the warehouse or from other stores. Slow-moving items can be transferred or marked down and cleared out. In addition, the computer is used for credit checks, electronic fund transfers (the transfer of "money" from one account to another with no cash, checks or credit forms), and other activities that directly touch the salesforce. We will see more about how computers operate in business in Chapter 13.

Perhaps the biggest organizational difference between the retail sector and other businesses is the separation of buying from the selling function. Chains and franchises continue to take a bigger slice of the retail dollar. With them comes centralized buying, more pressure on manufacturers to advertise, demands for cooperative advertising money, emphasis on point-of-purchase sales aids, and self-service. The mass merchandising concept that started in discount houses has moved to full-line department stores. Even furniture and appliance stores, long a major commissioned sales area, are moving to self-service. Some believe the automobile market, with huge dealerships showing acres of cars, will move in this direction too.

Many of these activities are already having a negative impact on professional retail selling. If other promotional activities (advertising, created environment, point-of-purchase materials, and display) can move goods faster and at a lower price, they will be used. However, a strong desire for personalized service may be reappearing and could reverse this trend.

Manufacturing sales support

Manufacturers will continue to use a salesforce to move goods. In the consumer goods area, however, there seems to be a shift from selling to servicing. One sales call on the buyer for a major chain or national mass merchandiser may yield a large order for hundreds or thousands of stores with automatic reorders to fill shelves in the retail outlets.

The function of the territory sales force is to provide point-of-sale materials in each store and to control inventories. This has led to the forming of *merchandising companies* that employ local people on a part-time basis to check stock levels, initiate replacement orders, and maintain attractive displays. This has been highly effective in reducing out-of-stock situations and increasing sales.

The role of the salesperson is changing in these areas, and many salespeople find themselves acting more as consultants than as salespeople. As automated physical distribution systems move merchandise from the manufacturer through the wholesaler to the retailer, the sales relationship between wholesaler and retailer becomes closer as they seek mutually higher profits. Automation of production and distribution is having similar effects on commercial and industrial goods manufacturers. Technology has shifted the emphasis from selling to servicing of accounts.

Perhaps the most difficult job for a manufacturer's salesforce is introducing new products, which are being developed at an ever-increasing rate. Support is usually provided by advertising directed at wholesalers and retailers as well as the ultimate consumer for consumer goods. With commercial and industrial goods, advertising directed at the end user supports the field sales staff.

Manufacturers also have stepped up significantly their support in the sales promotion area. (See Chapter 15 for more details.) Trade shows and exhibits are used heavily to reach new customers, for instance. There are also signs that in the future manufacturers' salespeople will be equipped with some sophisticated selling aids. Preparation of audiovisual materials to support the sales presentation is a rapidly growing market.

More than any other group, manufacturers have adopted the marketing concept; they led the way in developing a coordinated promotional plan. On the whole, manufacturers' salespeople receive more and better sales support than those in other selling areas.

Sales support for services

Services are only beginning to assimilate the marketing concept. The number of support people in these firms is often small, but it is growing. Since service areas are by definition the selling of intangibles, personal contact is essential. Services are the fastest growing segment of our economy, and demand for both sales and sales support personnel for the service industry will continue to grow.

The fastest growing areas of sales support in services are sales training and support materials. When selling goods, samples can be shown, the product can be demonstrated, and technical data can be provided. This is not true for intangibles. To make up for this deficiency in sales support, many firms are now using media to illustrate more dramatically their unique services (see Chapter 14). Only recently have salespeople in the services area been given training comparable to those selling in the manufacturing area.

Many service areas are becoming more technical. Salespeople working in these areas are becoming coordinators, combining the talents of several service areas within the firm. This is true in advertising, data processing, architecture, and engineering. In advertising, for instance, the *account executive* is the person who sells a "package" of services—copywriters, artists, researchers, media schedulers, and other specialists who provide services for the client.

Service selling is one area that has been using more team selling to make presentations to groups. Much preparation is required in the form of typed detailed proposals, visual presentation materials, and use of specialists. Using a team to make a presentation is becoming more common. The salesperson functions as a *moderator* during the presentation and *coordinator* before and after.

Personal relationships

Organizational differences are significant in retailing, manufacturing, and service firms. The common link is the significant trend to use both sales support people and nonmarketing personnel in aiding the salesforce. This means the salesforce must develop many personal relationships within the firm with people whose performance directly affects sales volume or income. This places a premium on salespeople with outstanding human relations skills.

3. You have been hired to sell advertising by a local weekly newspaper. What services would you supply your accounts? What services would you expect from other employees within the firm?

4. You are a senior salesperson in one store of a ten-unit furniture chain. Since the stores are scattered, each manager handles both local advertising and sales management. The chain owner plans to hire a sales promotion person to aid the salesforce to produce greater sales. He or she would serve all ten stores. What would you like this person to do for you? Write a brief job description.

The promotional mix: the role of sales

Earlier in this chapter we introduced the four elements of the marketing mix: product, price, distribution, and promotion. In this section we will consider the **promotion mix**: the tools a firm uses to sell its products. A well-managed firm will carefully balance all three elements in this mix: advertising, sales promotion, and personal selling. In most firms all three areas can contribute to total sales; the big decision is where to place the emphasis. When the advertising department is selling bacon, the sales promotion department is running a contest to sell canned hams, and the sales manager pays the largest commission on lunchmeat, there can be no promotional *synergism*. *Synergism* is the combined effect of many efforts to achieve a goal. It can occur only when all areas are coordinated in support of each other and in support of the company's objectives.

For a salesperson to understand fully his or her role in a firm's promotion mix requires knowledge of how the company defines that mix and defines its own sales and marketing objectives. It also requires an awareness of the roles of advertising and sales promotion as they relate to the company's objectives.

promotion mix
the balance of elements of sales promotion, advertising, and personal selling used by a firm to sell its products.

Advertising's role

The relationship between sales and advertising should be coordinated and complementary. For some firms, the performance of the salesforce is crucial and advertising is merely supportive of their efforts. In others, advertising is much more efficient and productive than personal selling. The salesperson should know how he or she figures in this relationship.

It is also important for the salesperson to know about the firm's advertising plans and themes. A firm's advertising should be used in selling, and the sales presentation should reinforce the advertised message as often as possible.

Advertising can be effective in overcoming sales resistance at a much lower cost than personal selling. Problems of sales resistance should be communicated to the advertising people. A potential result would be campaigns designed to reduce the resistance prior to the personal presentation. As the cost of face-to-face selling mounts, more firms are willing to increase advertising to support selling efforts. Wherever personal selling is involved, advertising should be viewed as a part of the total promotional plan.

Sales promotion's role

This category includes all short-term activities to support the salesforce, including contests, coupons, display materials, and pre-

sales promotion

short-term activities to support and enhance the activities of the salesforce and advertising campaigns; includes use of contests, coupons, exhibits, displays, premiums, and so on.

miums. The role of **sales promotion** in supporting sales activities is increasing greatly. Some believe these activities are more efficient than any other promotional effort. In the majority of firms, however, sales promotion is not a planned, continuing activity, but is only used to bolster sales when they are down. In small firms, this attitude will probably continue because small firms cannot afford a full-time person in this capacity, but tend to use an agency to handle promotion. Also, sales promotion activities are by nature "one-shot" productions. We will consider this area further in Chapter 15. One sales promotion area, however, that tends to be ongoing in most firms is materials to support the salesforce. These include catalogs, price lists, technical specifications, and other materials that improve presentations. With no full-time person assigned to this task in the majority of businesses, outstanding support is lacking.

As the cost of personal selling increases, this situation must change. Firms are beginning to improve the quality of the print support materials and are moving into audiovisual materials as well. Media-based selling will be covered more fully in Chapter 14.

Although the voice of the salesforce tends to be weak in determining the advertising message, it is fairly strong in requesting better selling tools. Part of the knowledge required to become a professional salesperson lies in sales support materials. This area is so important today that Part 4 of this text is devoted to the wide range of sales support activities, of which sales promotion is only one part.

To summarize, each salesperson must be able to answer the question, "What is the promotion mix of my firm?" If it cannot be answered, a discussion with the sales or marketing director or one's immediate supervisor would be advised. The range of personal selling is so great today that it includes those who are aggressively opening new territories or markets as well as those whose primary function is to provide customer services. The promotion mix varies even among firms selling similar products to similar markets. An understanding of the promotion mix and its relationship to the professional selling role is essential.

5. Most automobile dealerships have separate sales and service divisions. How would the promotion mix be different for each? How would you coordinate the mixes to maximize sales of both product and service? How would you organize the personnel?

6. You work for a small firm with no formal research department. What kinds of research activities would you expect to perform for your management? Other than customers, to what sources would you have easy access?

7.   In your community you can identify firms that are still oriented toward production rather than marketing. How does this affect their sales force?

8.   Select three service firms—consumer or commercial—selling to the same market. Analyze their local advertising for similarities and differences from a sales support viewpoint.

Mini-case

John sells labels, primarily to retail accounts. They are custom printed for each store in long rolls. The most common variety are those peeled from a paper backing for statements, boxes, and customer packages.

He is supplied with samples, sales literature, and other sales aids to make an effective presentation. However, his firm uses no advertising or other sales promotion since he calls on most accounts just once a year. He will spend from one to three days in each town or city, essentially going from door to door.

Yet John feels he could sell more and sell faster if these people knew more about the variety of labels he sold and their many uses before he called.

Question: Is there an economical way John or his company can use either advertising or sales promotion to support the personal selling effort?

**Define these
key concepts**

account executive
advertising
consumer research
market segmentation
marketing mix
marketing team
merchandising company
promotion mix
psychographics
pyramid selling
sales promotion
synergism

Basic knowledge 2

3 Psychology and sociology in selling

Key terms

consumer behavior
demography
Maslow's hierarchy
extraverted
introverted
self-concept
Gestalt
empathy
cognitive dissonance

Overview

Students bring to this course varied backgrounds in the social sciences. Courses in marketing, consumer behavior, applied psychology, management, and personnel cover essentially the same material, but from different perspectives. This chapter will provide review and reinforcement for students who have completed these courses.

Students who have not taken psychology or sociology courses will benefit from the application of these subjects to marketing. They will discover that basic psychological concepts are commonly and profitably used in selling. They will recognize the importance of controlling the psychological environment in which the sale takes place. As we shall see, sales are made in the mind.

Sociological factors affecting purchasing decisions

The basic purpose for the marketing concept, as we discussed in Chapter 2, is to segment the market—the total population of potential consumers—and to identify the needs of each segment or part. We'll turn our attention now to the social and economic features that characterize these separate market segments and to the changing sociological factors that affect *consumer behavior*—the buying patterns of purchasers.

Demographic factors

The most commonly used classifications are based on sociological theory and research defining factors of *demography*—that is, such economic and social factors as age, sex, income, place of residence, and type of employment. U.S. Census Bureau statistics and studies by private research agencies are compiled and compared in order to sort out these factors. The market was first segmented in this way by producers of consumer goods, but commercial and industrial research is also relevant.

Analysis of the figures not only identifies existing markets but predicts future needs as well. The increase of purchasing power among the black and Latino segments was predicted by demographic methods.

Although demographics are usually used to select new prospects with high potential, sociological studies have also contributed to knowledge about consumer behavior: how people buy. They have found a considerable general increase in large purchases made without prior planning. Notable examples of goods formerly considered planned, but now bought on impulse, are furniture and automobiles.

Conformity and upward mobility

Sociologists are able to analyze and predict buying patterns on the basis of social trends. Perhaps the greatest pressures on purchasing are the conflicting pressures for *conformity*—the desire to be like others—and *upward mobility*—the desire to raise one's income and social status. We live in an increasingly impersonal world, where people are packed into major urban metropolitan markets; the need to belong—to conform—leads to purchases that others can see. Visible items reflect one's relative position, or status, in a society.

Expectations of upward mobility also affect the use of *credit*. Slowly but surely credit has become a major purchasing factor.

consumer behavior
the decision making process exhibited in buying goods and services.

demography
the analysis of population by age, sex, income, education, occupation, and so on.

Retail sales are closed on the basis of the amount of future monthly payments rather than the total cost of the item. There appears to be widespread indifference to the true cost of that credit despite efforts by the Federal Trade Commission and the Truth-in-Lending Act.

Changes in shopping habits

At the retail level *shopping behavior* has changed over time. Families shop together in major malls. Women have a greater voice in hard-line purchases today and many more men are doing grocery and other convenience buying. The great increase in the number of married women who work (55 percent is the latest estimate) and the increase of working single women means increased economic power for women.

Income is a major determinant of buying behavior, and a second income in a household frequently is used to purchase products formerly considered luxuries. Even the way these products are purchased has changed. Luxuries have traditionally been purchased after some planning and saving. As more people begin to consider these purchases part of their expected standard of living, the purchases are more informal and more frequently are made on impulse.

There is a further consideration based on income level. Different income groups perceive a given product differently. A professional salesperson should determine what income group the prospect is in and then use this information to decide which selling points to emphasize and which to ignore.

Importance of the social image

Similar sociological factors are at work in commercial and industrial purchasing as well. Firms have a need to put on the appearance of being successful. This is most commonly reflected in office furnishings, decor, and dress codes. Other sociological factors include membership in certain professional, business, and fraternal organizations. One of the major determinants of a person's social class is type of employment. A given position then requires some purchasing by the company for the employee in order to maintain an expected role. Luncheon meetings, country club memberships, use of automobiles, and other benefits are purchased to meet the social needs of employees.

The influence of reference groups

Three different groups of people influence both business and personal buying behavior. These reference groups are the groups an individual looks at to know how to act in a situation. They provide a

standard of behavior. Those who exert the greatest influence are
membership groups such as the family, work, recreational, or avocational interests; and social groups. The power of these groups varies
with different purchases, but in almost all cases they do have an
impact.

Two other reference groups that are infrequently discussed also
influence purchases. One set is those groups that one would like to
be a member of. Purchases such as tennis, golf, and similar club
memberships are often made by those assimilating behavior associated with given social or economic groups, even though they
are not group members. Housing in certain sections of a town, sport
or luxury cars, and other highly visible items are used to differentiate
social and economic groups and thereby to influence purchasing.

A third group may be considered a negative reference group; it is
a group one does not wish to be associated with. One of the representatives of this attitude is the motorcycle. In the past, the motorcycle has been associated with leather jackets, heavy boots, and
warring gangs: this image was supported by several motion pictures. Honda's TV advertising dramatically changed this association
and improved the image, which had to change before the motorcycle could be sold to the mass market. Using images of grand-

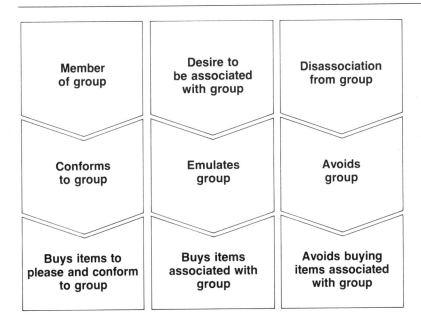

Figure 3-1.
Effect of reference
groups on purchasing
behavior

mothers, businessmen in three-piece suits, and fathers and sons on motorcycles, Honda successfully built a positive environment for selling. The image-building campaign was expensive and required several years to accomplish, as will most situations where negative pressures restrict sales.

People involved in professional selling must look at the effect all three kinds of reference groups have on individual purchases. Sociological factors are always at work in all three environments— consumer, commercial, and industrial. Some feel the limited suc- cess of minority-owned businesses in selling can be traced to nega- tive group influence. Figure 3 – 1 represents graphically the ways in which reference groups affect purchasing behavior.

1. Identify one or more groups you definitely do not want to be associated with. What purchases do they make that you avoid for fear of association? Use visible items like clothing, cars, housing, and furniture.

2. Interview salespeople selling primarily items with a price over $1,000. Find out to what degree the credit terms affect the sale of these items. How often are sales lost because of the credit terms?

Psychological needs motivate purchases

Psychological theory can yield important insights into the reasons for people's buying behavior. In this section we will review briefly some theories of personality that are applicable to the buying and selling process. *Personality* can be defined here as the sum of one's attitudes and beliefs as they are reflected in behavior. Bear in mind we have drastically oversimplified the theoretical material in order to extract and apply the most important principles.

Most people, with the possible exception of hermits and a few recluses, are not entirely satisfied with their present situation. If satis- faction is achieved, it is only temporary. We are all surrounded by items we would like to have—bigger, sportier, or more luxurious cars: a finer or more stylish wardrobe; a larger office with more impressive furniture; perhaps an estate with a pool and tennis courts. No matter what our current position, something better is always worth striving for. Furthermore, we live in a society that places value on possessions as evidence of material success.

Maslow's five levels of needs
Abraham Maslow, a humanistic psychologist, developed a ladder or pyramid in which he arranged five levels of needs and wants that he

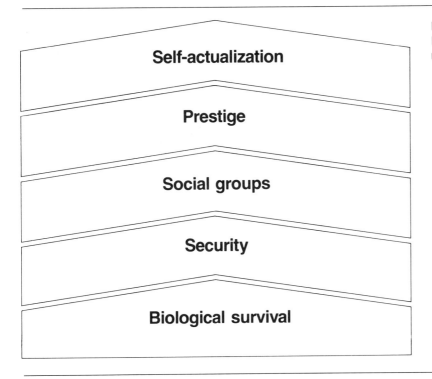

**Figure 3-2.
Maslow's hierarchy of
needs**

identified. (You will find this concept defined more fully in A.H. Maslow, *Motivation and Personality,* New York: Harper Bros., 1954).
Briefly, Maslow stated that individuals are motivated to satisfy
needs. At each level, needs do not become activated until those at
the previous level have been satisfied. The illustration in Figure 3–2
is a graphic representation of **Maslow's hierarchy** of needs and *need
satisfaction.*

The levels of needs range from basic physical needs, through
social needs, to psychological needs. In what Maslow referred to as
a *hierarchy,* these levels relate to survival, safety, belonging to social groups, prestige or esteem, and the highest level of needs,
which Maslow calls self-actualization.

At the basic, essential level are those needs dealing with *biologi-
cal survival;* they include the need for food, water, air, and shelter.
Clearly someone who has not satisfied the basic needs for survival
will not be in the market for luxury goods.

Safety and physical security needs are next to be satisfied. Their
relationship may best be observed by comparing the actions of two
animals. An animal that has just eaten will take no risks to obtain

*Maslow's hierarchy
classification of human
wants and needs as a
basis for analyzing
behavior—developed by
Abraham Maslow.*

food; safety has become more important. One that is starving, however, will take risks, with the degree of risk increasing as hunger becomes more severe. Security is less important than immediate survival. In humans, a parent who has difficulty earning enough to feed a family will have minimal shelter needs; an apartment in a slum building will suffice. If income becomes stabilized and first-level needs are met, however, an individual may start to look for a dwelling in a better neighborhood, safer places for children to play, and so on.

The need for *social relationships* becomes activated after the individual has satisfied needs on the two basic levels. Maslow's term *belongingness,* implies a more social or psychological nature to denote this level. Many authorities suggest that these needs have the most positive effect on purchases, since group activities require better clothing, sporting equipment, or other related material goods. Party selling, as discussed in Chapter 1, takes advantage of this kind of need.

On the next level are the needs for *prestige or esteem.* These needs are associated most often with an individual's choice of car, country club, school, or neighborhood. An individual can attempt to raise his or her status in the eyes of others by being promoted to a position of greater authority, winning a citation for outstanding achievement, being elected to office in a club or organization, or becoming the author of a textbook.

At the top of Maslow's ladder are the needs for *self-actualization.* In today's affluent society, as people find their material and external needs being met, more and more people are seeking to attain higher satisfaction and to express themselves fully.

What is the relevance of all this information to sales? How can you use it to motivate people to buy your products? Let's take as an example a tour or cruise being sold by a travel agent. The agent who is in tune with the clients' needs will be able to distinguish clearly between those traveling because others in their social groups are travelers (level three); those traveling because it will give them prestige in the eyes of others (level four); and those who choose to travel simply for their own satisfaction (level five). Desire for accommodations, gifts, services, and even destinations will be vastly different in each of these groups.

Need satisfaction and selling objectives
Maslow and others who have followed him have used his theory as a basis of research to determine how each need level relates to individual behavior, including purchasing. In fact, the marketing con-

cept, as discussed in Chapter 2, is based on the principle of identifying the needs of people in the various market segments, and Maslow's hierarchy can be useful in fully defining these needs.

For the salesperson, awareness of the need hierarchy Maslow developed can be an important tool in identifying the level that one's immediate prospect has reached. It applies most obviously in the retail or consumer services sector, but can also be used by the commercial or industrial salesperson to identify and control the *psychological environment.* For example, a purchasing agent who has worked the last 36 hours taking a warehouse inventory cannot be expected to be receptive to your best sales pitch. One who has just overeaten at another supplier's luncheon may not be too receptive either, but for different reasons.

On the next level (level two), the needs are obvious. Individual families as well as retail and commercial establishments need devices for protection against theft or vandalism. Burglar alarms, smoke detectors, and shoplifting precautions are items they want and need. Less obvious are the elements of the psychological environment. The transaction will be less than satisfactory if the purchaser senses hostility in the air.

Social group membership, as we have said, may be the impetus for many consumer purchases, and most people belong to several groups with varying degrees of attachment. The group may include family, school, work, athletic, professional, and avocational ties. If a purchasing agent will buy only from other members of his professional group, the salesperson should be aware of that fact. These reasons for purchasing will be explored further in Chapter 4.

3. In what social groups that you are a member do you have some level of status or prestige? What purchases, goods, or services, helped you attain that prestige? What have you purchased recently to maintain or increase that status?

4. Select a product, good, or service, to be sold to a commercial business. Which of Maslow's five levels would be of highest concern to the buyer? Why?

Personality influences purchases

While many authors have tried to classify or scale personality traits and apply them to professional selling, none have been greatly successful. Consequently, few sales textbooks deal with personality and its relationship to successful selling. This is unfortunate since any face-to-face relationship between people, whether a selling situation or not, involves personalities. In groups, the personality problem is multiplied.

Extravert or introvert

In their general style of behavior, people may be classified as extraverts or introverts. Some people tend to be more **extraverted** than others; that is, they are more outgoing, people oriented, desire the company of others, and may tend to be aggressive or even "pushy." They like to see things done their way and tend to be more dominant in personality. Other people may be more **introverted** or shy, preferring to be alone or with few people, liking concerts rather than dances, and so on. These people might be seen as submissive in a personal encounter.

Individual outlook may vary at all points along a scale that may be seen as going from extreme extroversion at one end to extreme introversion and fear of human contact at the other. Further, any individual may adopt various shadings of behavior depending on the situation. In a personal relationship between two people, one will be more dominant, the other more submissive. Where two people are primarily introverted and submissive, decisions are slow and uncomfortable.

Applications to selling

The applications to selling should be obvious. You will have to sell to both kinds of people, and they will be introverted or extraverted to varying degrees. Exhibitions of introverted or extraverted behavior will be determined in part by a person's personality, in part by the situation, and in part by the personalities of those with whom one is communicating.

One's own situation in a selling environment can be controlled to some degree. Personality must be flexible but also controlled. A key characteristic of successful salespeople is their ability to adjust their personality to be compatible with those to whom they are selling. A very extroverted customer (one who is aggressive and even domineering) can be successfully dealt with by the salesperson who takes a submissive role but who skillfully leads the customer to a positive decision. It is a case of the follower actually leading the leader.

Countless sales are lost through lack of understanding of this basic concept. Hard aggressive selling will cause very introverted customers to cringe and cower, actually creating a negative psychological environment. The same approach with very ex-

extraverted
warm and outgoing person; at the extreme the person is aggressive and domineering.

introverted
opposite of extraverted; at the extreme, withdrawn from contact with people.

traverted customers often produces arguments, not mutually satisfying sales. Fortunately, few people are at the extremes. Most are
either slightly one or the other, and frequently they switch roles
depending on the situation. Except for those who are very extroverted, a skillful salesperson can develop a leader role, with the
buyer as a follower. The buyer must be comfortable with the role, not
threatened by it.

**5.   In recent confrontations with salespeople that turned you off,
identify extraverted or introverted behavior that led to either an
argument or a rapid retreat.**

**6.   How would you build a positive supportive environment to sell
to a very introverted customer? Contrast your approach selling to a
very extraverted person.**

Self-concept influences purchases

Psychologists have developed many theories in an effort to understand personality. One such theory has been indentified as the
self-concept theory. This theory holds that each individual is not one
person, but four. None may be truly real, as they are all in the mind.
The four views of oneself are illustrated graphically in Figure 3–3.

self-concept
*the image a person has of
oneself and one's
relationships with other
people.*

**Figure 3-3.
Four views of self**

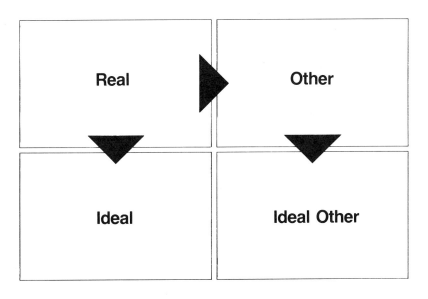

Four views of the self

The first inner person we will call the real self. It is the one you see as yourself, with all your aspirations and inadequacies, hopes, and fears. Few people are able to present all aspects of the real self to the world, but instead keep it a carefully guarded secret.

The second view of the self develops when the person is not entirely satisfied with the real self. It is the *ideal self:* the person he or she would like to be. This vision leads one to develop new skills, to learn self-discipline, and generally to take steps to improve the self-image.

Third is the mental picture of the self as we think others see us. We call this self the *other self.* Purchases to satisfy this part of the self are motivated not by the question, "Do I like it?" but by the question, "Will they like it?"

The final part of this four-dimensional mental image is called the *ideal other*, or how we would like others to see us. Unlike the ideal self, which is concerned with feelings and attitudes, the ideal other is more visible and material. It is the basis for most people's purchasing patterns, involving the physical image one presents to the outer world.

Impact on selling

The types of purchases motivated by each part of the self-image are represented graphically in Figure 3-4.

**Figure 3-4.
Purchases motivated by
views of self**

Real Food Clothing Shelter Entertainment Vacations	**Other** Cosmetics Clothing
Ideal Self-Improvement Education Books	**Ideal other** Housing Automobile Country Club Luxury Goods

As Figure 3–4 shows, the self that probably has the most impact on purchase decisions is the *ideal other*. The concept of conspicuous consumption has been applied to purchases of this nature. Our material purchases speak loudly about us both at home and in business. Most of us are reluctant to make dramatic changes in purchasing patterns—moving rapidly from *other* to *ideal other*—because to do so would require significant changes in our social relationships. Many who have gone rapidly from obscurity to fame have not been able to adjust to a new image and have fallen victim to alcoholism, drug addiction, psychological problems, and even suicide.

The primary application of the self-concept theory to selling is in understanding the basis of a person's motivational drives. The need to develop a better self-image, to maintain an image with some peer groups, and to change that image over time are very powerful. Sales that are not compatible with these needs end in failure.

7. Evaluate your recent major purchases with respect to your self-image. Which are primarily directed at either your *other* or your *ideal other* self?

Gestalt psychology: four factors that shape personality

Another line of inquiry into personality formation is taken by the theorists of **Gestalt** psychology. From the German word meaning total or whole, the Gestalt theory holds that a person's attitudes and behavior are shaped by four factors of experience and environment: past experiences, immediate past activities, current environment, and future expectations. We shall examine each of these in turn, and then explore the influence of each factor in purchasing decisions.

*Gestalt
psychological term
meaning "whole" or "total";
looking at all the factors
involved in a decision.*

The first factor is the sum of a person's *past experiences,* such as education, religion, family life, and social experiences. Since each person has a different set of experiences to draw upon, each person will view a given buying situation in a unique way. Many feel that television viewing, especially by those under 25, has moderated this effect by making everyone's experiences similar. Others point to equally strong differences in rural, urban, and suburban lifestyles, which contribute to maintaining significant individual differences.

A second factor is a person's *immediate past* activities. When shopping for food, for instance, a person who has not eaten for some time buys more than one who shops right after eating. Students who have breakfast before going to school do better in their studies. While these are physical examples, a recent experience that was psychologically satisfying or disappointing will produce the same effect. A call on a purchasing agent who has just tossed out a very rude or inept salesperson may prove unsatisfactory just because it is poor timing. On the other hand, a couple after an afternoon of love-making could be potential purchasers of a vacation plan or a floral arrangement. One cannot ignore a person's psychological frame of mind just prior to your presentation.

A third factor is *current environment*. Students in a classroom that is too warm, with comfortable chairs, a ticking clock, and an instructor lecturing in a monotone, frequently respond by falling asleep. Lighting can have a noticeable effect. For instance, to cut costs of maintenance, K-Mart replaces all fluorescent lights in a store at regular intervals. Those that burn out in the interim are left dark. After each relighting, sales jump significantly. The fashion industry has found that both the color of the dressing rooms and the color of the light in them have an effect on sales. Muzak Corporation has researched the effect of music on people's work and shopping behavior, and will provide taped music designed for a particular situation.

At the retail level, sellers have greater control of the environment than those in the commercial or industrial sectors. Car dealers, among others, use *closing rooms* designed to eliminate distractions and focus the prospect's attention on the presentation. This may not be possible for the person making outside calls, but many have been successful by having the prospect come to the seller's showroom. NCR, for example, uses this method to sell minicomputers and other equipment best sold with a demonstration. The more opportunity a salesperson has to control the environment of the presentation, the more opportunity one has for success.

The final factor is the prospect's *future planned activity*. Much of our activity is goal directed, as we discussed in relation to Maslow and the self-concept; goals will influence each situation. Much purchasing is for future use, as determined by past experiences. A young couple may favor a three- or four-bedroom house if they plan to have a family. To allow for later expansion, firms buy more land than they need and more equipment than current demand requires. Retirement and annuity plans are a prime example of a type of purchase based on expected future financial needs rather than current ones.

All four of these factors affect a given selling situation and although the prospect often is not consciously aware of them, the salesperson should be.

Using psychology to build sales

Developing empathy

People have often tried to identify what it is that differentiates a "natural" salesperson from one who cannot sell. Many factors can probably be identified but in this section we will discuss the function we consider most important—empathy.

Empathy is sensitivity to other people's wants and needs. People with empathy are interested in other people and their activities. They can develop a relationship that makes others feel good about themselves, and they provide a positive, supportive atmosphere that enables people to reconfirm attitudes and opinions they have. It has been stated that those who are successful in selling are able to "stand in the buyer's shoes."

empathy
the ability to understand another person's feelings and situation.

To build empathy, training workshops use role-playing activities. Salespeople take turns playing different buyer roles. Others use sensitivity training or consciousness raising programs that strive to help trainees become aware of themselves as well as their relationships with others. Consultants offer a variety of these seminars and workshops to business and industry. Colleges and universities have offered programs in Transactional Analysis (TA), sensitivity training, and other programs directed toward improving communications with others.

A question often asked is, "Can people be trained to sell"? *Yes they can.* While many people are gifted with a natural empathy, others can develop it with work. In fact, if business had to rely on those people with natural empathy, the shortage of salespeople would be extreme.

Some research has been conducted to identify characteristics of those who are very successful in selling. While not conclusive, it shows that many successful salespeople actually do not like people, but very much enjoy selling, and they are able to change their personality to fit each situation. Their goal of closing sales and acquiring wealth is realized. At the same time their customers are satisfied with their purchases and frequently return for more, and thereby their companies make money and prosper.

One should never lose sight of the fact that *sales are made in the mind.*

8. In your relationships with others, do you have a high or low level of empathy? What can you do to raise your level of empathy? Explain.

9. **Select a selling situation of your choice. Describe the physical environment factors you would design into the setting that would lead to a prospect being both physically and psychologically comfortable. Would any of these factors actually stimulate the prospect to buy? Explain.**

10. **Contrast the perspective a retail store buyer and a purchasing agent may have for a common item like ballpoint pens—the first for resale, the second for company use. Do they have similarities?**

Avoiding cognitive dissonance

cognitive dissonance
conflicting feelings about a purchasing decision.

To earn a good living as a professional salesperson one must have satisfied customers to make repeat sales to. Even in those areas where the second purchase may be a few years away, current satisfied customers are needed to secure more prospects. After the ink is dry on the paper one must keep selling. But often, after a sale is concluded, the customer becomes unsure of the wisdom of the purchase. This conflict is called **cognitive dissonance,** and many factors can cause it.

The first factor that can cause cognitive dissonance is the *value of the purchase.* As the dollar value goes up, so does the amount of dissonance that may occur. Another is the *social significance* of the purchase. Automobiles, furniture, and clothing have high social meaning in that they reflect a person's social role, self-concept, social class, and/or group memberships. People need assurance that the purchase is compatible with their role and will be approved by their peers.

A third factor has more selling significance. It applies when there are a number of *alternative choices* the customer sees as being relatively equal, yet only one item can be purchased. Here the cognitive dissonance can be so disturbing that the purchase is delayed or abandoned altogether. It is the salesperson's function to recognize dissonance and to reduce it in order to close the sale and to ensure that the customer is satisfied today, tomorrow, and the next day.

This kind of cognitive dissonance occurs not only among alternative products that are similar, but in other choices as well; for instance, among different, equally attractive choices that have similar dollar value. Examples may be purchasing a second car or remodeling the kitchen. Purchasing one means forgoing the other, so the salesperson may have two problems—two cars of equal attraction and separate purchases of equal attraction.

These same problems occur in business as well. Retailers are concerned whether they bought the correct merchandise and in the right quantity. There are many vendors of display fixtures, computers, office equipment, machinery, and real estate. Dissonance may require *post-sale assurance*. Follow-up telephone calls, letters, personal visits, warranties, and service visits by others can provide this assurance. Sales and satisfaction are in the mind.

11. **Select a product that would likely have high cognitive dissonance, with high unit value, social significance, and with many alternative choices. Identify those factors related to this product that would cause post-sale dissonance. What specific measures would you take to reduce it?**

12. **Referring back to question 7, how will the dissonance for this product be different than an appliance that has been on the market for several years? Will your post-sale activities be different? How?**

Mini-case

Sue has been working since graduation from college six months ago selling the services of a data processing service bureau. Most of the firms she calls on are small manufacturers, wholesalers, and a few retailers.

Sue is black and grew up in a ghetto; she senses a "psychological climate" in her selling that works against her. With few exceptions her customers are white males over 40 years old with very strong success drives ("bull-headed," in her words).

This type of selling is mostly consultive. First, she must assess the firm's needs and come back at a later time for a formal proposal. For those accounts she sells she functions as a liaison and trouble-shooter. A warm and friendly relationship is needed, but in most cases it is more cool and aloof.

Question: What can Sue do to work subtle changes in the psychological climate of her selling?

Define these key concepts

cognitive dissonance
conformity
empathy
Gestalt
Maslow's hierarchy
need satisfaction

personality
reference group—list three
self-concept theory
shopping behavior
upward mobility

4 Buyer decision making

Key terms

need recognition
impulse buying
P.O.P. materials
demand creation
frame of reference
closing
product life cycle
adoption factors
target group
rational motive
emotional motive
appeals
detail selling

Overview

Buying decisions are complex. Some of the factors that affect them are within the salesperson's control, but many are not. Professional salespeople must know how to identify a buyer's needs, how new ideas are adopted, and how social and psychological pressures influence buying. It is also important to know how to deal with the conflicts leading to cognitive dissonance. Involved in this knowledge are areas of anthropology, economics, and sociology. Understanding the buyer decision process is crucial to successful selling.

Need recognition

People's needs are many and ever changing. Identifying these is known as **need recognition**. Some of these needs are *self-generated,* something one decides one wants in response to basic physical and psychological requirements. Other needs are *latent,* stimulated by the purchases of other people or by the advertising appeals of the producer. Although much of advertising, promotion, and display are specifically designed to stimulate needs, most purchasing is probably the result of viewing the purchases of others. The portrayal of "real people" using the product in TV commercials is designed to take advantage of buyers' desire to conform.

need recognition awareness of an unsatisfied need.

The influence of others on purchasing is often seen in the rapid spread of fads. Word-of-mouth "advertising" greatly controls the total amount of buying, as well as the relative amounts spent for goods such as food, recreation, and transportation. Social structure and cultural pressures place people in various roles, and purchasing decisions are made according to those roles. These reactions are strongest on the most visible items such as clothing, furniture, and automobiles. The reaction is always present, however, either consciously or subconsciously, and it must be considered. The important thing to remember is that these buying pressures are often quite strong, and sales presentations with an opposing view will fall on deaf ears. Because producers have learned to use these human tendencies to sell more products we have seen a great increase in the amount of **impulse buying** —purchases made without prior planning. Stores stock a much larger variety of goods today than formerly, and self-service is no longer the exception, but the rule. **Point-of-purchase (P.O.P.)** displays and packaging are designed to trigger this type of buying, that is, they are designed to create a desire to buy when the customer sees them.

impulse buying purchases made without prior planning.

point-of-purchase (P.O.P.) materials displays and packaging designed to create in the customer a desire to buy.

In the past impulse buying was looked upon as irrational or nonrational behavior and was usually associated with small convenience purchases. This is no longer true. Impulse buying now has spread to automobiles, homes, and other areas still employing a salesperson to complete the sale. There is some evidence this buying is not confined strictly to consumer goods and services; industrial and commercial purchasing are experiencing similar changes. The perceptive salesperson recognizes when buying decisions have been made *in advance* of the personal contact. This selling requires primarily the job of matching customer perceptions with available products and using a different type of presentation. Millions of dollars in sales are lost each year because too many salespeople do not recognize the customer's decision.

Demand creation

Firms cannot rely on individuals recognizing their own needs either through self-discovery or through observation and social relationships. Therefore different means are used to effect **demand creation** — developing a desire for a product or service. Advertising and sales promotion are widely used to make people aware of needs. Advertising is usually employed to reach large numbers of people at a very low cost per person. Sales promotions, usually targeted at a more precisely defined market, cost more per person; normally, however, it produces more sales per advertising dollar spent.

demand creation
using advertising and sales promotion to create or increase demand for a product or service.

All selling efforts are designed to lead the buyer through these five steps in the purchase decision:

1. Awareness or attention
2. High level of interest
3. Desire to purchase
4. Action
5. Need satisfied

Where advertising and sales promotion are used in the selling effort, a decision must be made as to which steps they will lead the purchaser through and which steps the salesperson is directly responsible for.

The use of outdoor advertisements is a means of creating and maintaining demand and supporting the salesforce.

Courtesy of Lake-to-Lake Dairy Cooperative.

A direct response firm will use advertising, good products, and prompt delivery to accomplish all of the steps. At the retail level advertising may achieve the first, point-of-purchase materials the second, and the salesperson the last three. In most commercial and industrial selling advertising or sales promotion will achieve only the first one or perhaps two steps. In some sectors of selling the salesperson must take the buyer through all five steps, although the number of these firms are declining. This approach is still used in two kinds of selling: where the product is unique and the customer has no **frame of reference** by which to evaluate it, and in firms dealing in highly sophisticated technologies.

When any of these responsibilities can be shifted to advertising or sales promotion, however, the salesforce is permitted to concentrate on presentations (steps 2 and 3), closing (step 4), and servicing the sale (step 5). The five step process is illustrated in Figure 4–1.

Closing is the completion of a sale, when money changes hands or a purchase order is written. It is the action step in the series of five steps listed above. Before any sale can be closed, the buyer has to go through the first three steps. It is the salesperson's job to know which step the customer is on. Sales cannot be closed, for example, when the customer has yet to develop a high level of interest; the seller must alter the presentation accordingly.

frame of reference
past experiences used for comparison and evaluation in making purchasing decisions.

closing
the completion of a sale—when money is paid or an order is written.

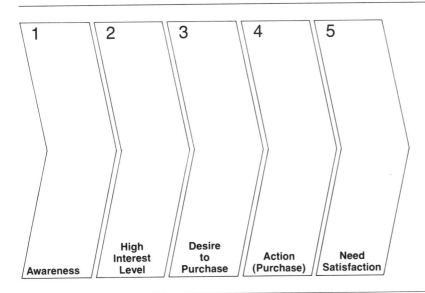

**Figure 4-1.
Stages of purchasing decision**

1. **Using the five steps in buying, identify selling jobs where the entire burden would fall to the salesperson. Is there any relation to the size and type of firm?**

2. **Find examples of advertising—retail, commercial, or industrial—designed to accomplish at least the first two steps to buying. Compare and contrast the approaches used.**

Adoption of innovations

The flow of new products to the market can only continue to increase as technology grows at a rapid pace. A major challenge facing salespeople is the introduction and successful selling of innovative products. People tend to continue their old and comfortable ways, resisting the unknown, and it is important to know how new ideas are diffused through a given market.

Product life cycle

Most products today have a relatively short life. Fad items often may last only a few months, while other items may continue without modification for several years. The **product life cycle**, in five stages, is usually illustrated on a graph reflecting sales in relation to time, as in Figure 4–2.

product life cycle
the stages every product passes through, though the duration of each stage varies from product to product. The stages are: innovation, growth, maturity, decline, and death.

There is good evidence that the average product lifetime is becoming shorter, which means the salesforce must distribute the product through a given market at a faster rate. Herein lies perhaps the most challenging situation in selling today: *many new products and short product life cycles.*

Researchers have been able to identify and categorize those who typically buy a product in a specific stage of its life cycle. These five categories may be called innovators, early adopters, early majority, late majority, and laggards. Each group tends to buy at a certain stage of a product's life as illustrated in Figure 4–2 and the table on the next page:

Product stage	Purchasers
Introduction	Innovators, early adopters
Growth	Early adopters, early majority
Maturity	Early majority, late majority
Decline	Late majority, laggards
Death	Laggards

This concept is based on the fact that different people will adopt a new idea at different times. Some will purchase the product as soon

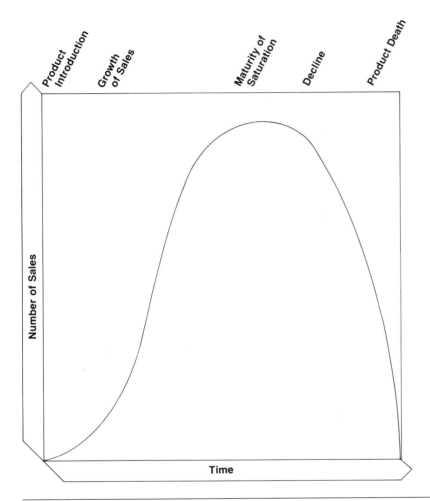

**Figure 4-2.
Product life cycle**

as it comes on the market while others will wait until those who first purchased it express their satisfaction. The introduction of television, dishwashers, and microwave ovens provides good examples of this diffusion process. The five classes of buyers are spread through the population as shown in Figure 4–3 on the next page.

Characteristics of the innovator
It should be obvious that for a salesperson to introduce a new product to a market successfully, the first efforts must be concentrated on the 2 to 3 percent of the total market classified as innovators. There is no magic formula for accomplishing this task, since those

**Figure 4-3.
Buyer identified with
product life cycle**

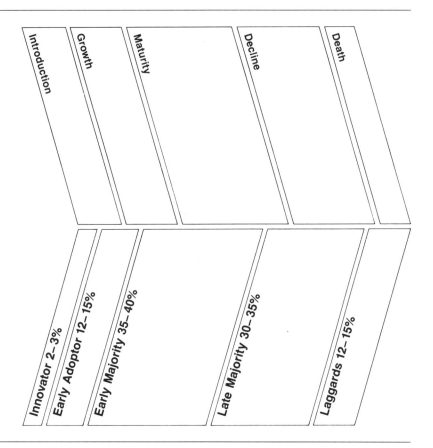

who are *innovators* in one product may be *early adopters* in another. Demographic generalizations may be helpful, however. Younger people will adopt new concepts more readily than older people. Those with college degrees are more receptive than those who have not finished high school. People with higher incomes can experiment with new products more than those who have limited finances. (In the business sector, however, the small firm frequently will adapt to changing conditions more readily than large corporations, whose internal inertia works to maintain the status quo.)

One interesting aspect of innovative buyers is their heavy reliance on advertising, trade journal and magazine articles, business and social contacts, and other learning activities to keep themselves informed of recent developments. With this in mind, serious thought should be given to developing the new product awareness stage by some method other than the sales call. While most consumer goods firms have long recognized this, commercial and industrial firms have been slow to provide their salesforce with promotional support aimed at this select group in order to speed up the adoption process.

Early adopters closely monitor the activities and purchases of the innovators. Adoption by these groups triggers purchasing by the next group. Those they reject will die, thus reflecting poor product planning and development.

Factors that speed adoption

Certain factors affect the speed of adoption of an innovative good or service. One such **adoption factor** is complexity. More complex products are generally adopted more slowly than simpler ones. Data processing equipment has only recently been adopted by small firms, even though price reductions have made it affordable for some time. The use of videotapes by film producers has faced a similar obstacle. Sale of new products will gain significantly only when these and similarly complex processes are simplified, or the potential buyer is educated.

Another factor is *advantage*. Advantages are relative to the user, of course, but in general the greater advantage the new product has over existing ones, the faster the adoption rate will be. Business goals are cutting costs, increasing productivity, and making greater profits. Computer-run machinery has greater accuracy, smaller tolerances, fewer rejects, and has been well received when significant advantages can be easily demonstrated. Consumers respond to items that save them time, make them more attractive, and provide more enjoyment. Many new products have been successful because they provide these advantages.

A third factor is *continuity* or *compatibility*. People tend not to change their habits drastically because there are too many psychological and social pressures for consistency. Many simple-to-use products with significant advantages to the user have failed to sell because they required the user to drastically change behavior. Since many, if not all, new products ask the buyer to change habits to some degree, it becomes the salesperson's responsibility to minimize these effects and to smooth the transition.

A fourth factor that can be used to speed adoption is the *sample* or *trial use*. Consumer goods such as groceries or drugs are mailed to homes or sampled in stores to promote a trial use. Drugs are given to doctors, lettering machines are loaned to graphic art studios, and ingredients are given to food processors for testing. Not only can the trial use overcome resistance to new ideas, but it can help develop new habits that will themselves become resistant to change and ensure continued repeat sales.

adoption factor
a product feature that speeds or retards the sale of innovative goods and services.

3. Find out what the newest innovative item is in the appliance market; include electronics. As a salesperson, how would you identify persons who would be considered either innovative or early adopter buyers? Be fairly specific.

4. Your firm has developed a truly innovative typewriter computer. Letters, memos, and so on, can be typed by voice input without a secretary. Multiple copies are easily made. How would you identify innovative firms for your first sales calls?

Motivations for buying

Factors that cause people to buy are divided into two areas: the rational and the emotional. In reality, rarely is one and only one motive involved in closing a sale. People are very complex; several motives are usually involved in a purchase decision. One person's motives for buying a product may be quite different from those of another person who purchases the same product. The salesperson's task is to determine the set or combination of motives for the **target group:** that is, the market segment the particular firm is concentrating on.

There is no wide agreement on a comprehensive list of buying motives. Some advertising textbooks have very long lists; other books have quite short lists. This is true with most books on professional selling. It could easily be argued that those presented here could be further divided and more precisely defined.

Rational motives

Rational motives are those based on facts as the buyer identifies them. They may be closely allied to the economic factors of supply, demand, and prices. They may also be associated with the buyer's needs for availability, quality, or service features. Or they may be allied to the time constraints of the buyer.

One important factor is *economy*. Most consumers live, in the short term at least, on relatively fixed incomes. If they reduce costs in one area they can expand in another. Heavy sales of compact cars in the early seventies reflected the desire for economizing transportation costs, and the popularity of do-it-yourself kits resulted from the need to achieve economies. Business firms always look for ways to accomplish tasks at a lower cost.

Price alone is not the only rational factor. We will increasingly find ourselves with excess and shortage. Where supply is limited, being able to get an item when it is needed will override price considerations to some degree. This factor is called *availability*.

target group
group market segment a particular seller is concentrating on.

rational motives
motives based on economics, availability, or some other practical consideration.

Other rational buying appeals are based on *quality, serviceability,* and *performance.* Some feel that many business purchasing decisions place too much emphasis on quality. It does not make rational sense, for example, to assemble an item that has one component with a life of ten years when the rest of the components will last only five years. As more of the items we use in home, office, and factory are mechanical and electronic, service will become increasingly important. Shutting down part or all of a factory can be very costly. In all areas we find emphasis on lower maintenance and longer life. Appliance manufacturers must now provide information about operating costs, maintenance costs, and expected life of their products.

Other rational appeals concern *time.* Most authorities recognize that time is money, especially in business. Products that require less time to install or to maintain, or that will produce more in a given amount of time are welcome. In business, air freight sales are up: at home, microwave ovens have been well received, especially by the time-pressed working woman. Time is part of everyone's life. Just as people try to get the most for their dollar, they try to get as much out of their time as possible.

Most writers refer to rational buying motives as those most closely associated with commercial and industrial buying, while emotional motives are primarily associated with consumers. But *buying is done by people.* All people will respond to rational buying motives when they are applied to their individual circumstances.

Emotional motives

Buying motives concerned primarily with feelings people have about themselves and other people are **emotional motives.** They are generally more subjective, or personal, than rational motives are. These motives extend to buying goods that reflect the buyer's status or role, to gifts bought to gain approval, to purchases that will make one feel more comfortable, to items that add adventure to one's life.

emotional motives motives based on sociological and psychological criteria.

Expressing *love* for another person is very emotional and subjective. Intimate relationships produce a great deal of buying that could be classified as extravagant. While some of this buying is for the partner, a great amount is for conformity to some role each is playing in the relationship. Cars, clothes, furniture, and entertainment are often purchased to generate and maintain these roles.

As the scope of love is expanded to friends and relatives, buying gifts is strongly influenced by the strength of relationships. The needs of Maslow's middle level, belongingness, (see Chapter 3) play a great role in emotional behavior. Groups exert strong social pressure to conform to its standards or norms. This pressure is evident in both consumer and business purchasing but is most obvious in fads. A firm whose buyer does not adopt recent ideas faces social pressures too, involving strong motivators like imitation, recognition, and companionship.

All people need *pride* or *esteem,* which both men and women may express by their appearance through the selection of clothing, hair styles, and cosmetics. People also take pride in their automobiles, homes, furniture, and other material possessions, as well as in their work, hobbies, and entertainment.

A skillful salesperson recognizes that purchases that will not produce these social and psychological rewards for the buyer will result in cognitive dissonance, as we saw in Chapter 3. Care must be taken in choosing which of these motivators will produce good sales: using the wrong **appeals**—reasons for buying—for a given situation is costly, and may result in returned goods or lost customers.

appeals
reasons for buying; product features turned into customer benefits.

Emotional appeals extend beyond those involving relationships with others. Some appeals are personal. These would include appeals for *comfort, pleasure,* and *adventure.*

Many goods and services are sold to help people satisfy emotional needs, such as skiing and piano lessons, craft kits, vacation packages, or college classes in selling.

Other emotional needs relate to *health, safety,* and *fear.* Health is not necessarily medical, although billions of dollars are spent on health care. Health includes developing and maintaining a sound body and mind. Many recreational goods and services appeal to this motive. Bicycles, jogging apparel, karate lessons, weight reduction pills, weightlifting equipment, and tennis lessons are examples.

Safety and fear are somewhat related, although fear may also include fear of loss of possessions or finances, and so may be a rational motive. Safety, Maslow's second level, was discussed earlier as a motivator in selling a variety of goods. Fear must be handled more delicately as a buyer motive, for if used too strongly it can have negative results. The greatest and most subtle use of fear is probably exemplified by the insurance industry. Fear has been used effectively to sell new furnaces, tires, roofing, and other home and car repairs. With proper use fear is a powerful motivator.

The last group of emotional appeals includes *convenience, variety* and *individuality.* There may be some overlap here between the rational and emotional, considering today's time pressures and the resultant demand for convenience. In any event, convenience is a motivator to purchase. It affects both where the buying occurs and what products or services are purchased. Recent success has been enjoyed by firms in appliances and furniture that sell items in the

Courtesy of Honeywell, Inc.

This photo from an advertisement illustrates the subtle use of fear and safety in selling.

factory carton. Without the customary wait for delivery, the buyer can take the product home the same day and enjoy it.

Despite strong pressures for conformity, there is still a strong desire for variety and individuality. Some would say this is a need for recognition, or a need to have some level of esteem. But these needs are not incompatible with the need to belong to groups. For instance, blue jeans have been a widely popular means of conformity, but teens especially have decorated them in many ways to provide variety or individuality.

Controlling the psychological environment

Recognition of emotional and rational motives for buying results in the seller choosing a strategy based on the motive and on the selling place. In most retail selling the buyer is in your environment, the store. Most firms are using store design, layout, fixturing, lighting, signing, and color to create an emotional setting. The purchases will be used either by the buyer or by a close friend or relative. This personal involvement signals emotional buying motives. Care should be taken, however, not to exclude the rational motives. A good presentation will include both. You must judge each customer to determine which one to use and with how much emphasis.

In the commercial and industrial sector most buying takes place in the buyer's office; the environment is not at your control. Since many of the purchases are to be used by someone else, the amount of emotional involvement tends to be less, but rarely is it lacking altogether. Stated another way, the more the buyer will actually be involved with the use of the good or service, the more the seller can use emotional appeals. For example, purchase of furniture by a newly-appointed company president for his or her office will have more emotional than rational motives.

In commercial and industrial selling, with its heavy emphasis on the rational factors of cost, productivity, and profits, one can lose sight of the fact that people do the buying. All people respond to emotional motives, even in business transactions. Just as in successful retail selling, a mixture of motives should be incorporated. The salesperson must analyze each buyer individually and create a unique blend to fit the situation. *Sales are made in the mind.*

5.   What was the most recent item you purchased that cost over $50? Can you identify rational or emotional factors involved in your decision? Was one type dominant?

6.   Make a list of both rational and emotional appeals just discussed. Which ones would be least productive in selling a person on a career in professional selling? Most productive? Why?

Motivating retail purchases

Much retail buying is outside a salesperson's control, but awareness of the competitive advantages and disadvantages of each store is absolutely necessary. Collectively known as retail patronage motives, they are the reasons a consumer shops at a few stores and does not shop at all the rest.

One main factor is *location.* Consumers place high emphasis on convenience and view some sites as more convenient than others. The success of neighborhood and regional malls over downtown districts is ample evidence. Malls offer easy access as they are located on heavily traveled traffic routes. Parking is seen as another advantage, even though many downtown areas have large lots behind the stores with access to rear entrances.

Shopping centers have another advantage called *cumulative attraction;* that is, all the stores together offer a huge variety of merchandise under one roof. The same principle applies to concentrations of stores of a particular kind on certain streets, such as "automobile row," "furniture row," or "fast-food row."

Merchandise assortment can be another advantage. It includes quality, quantity, and price lines, and is a dominant retail patronage motive. Another is the store's *image.* In retail selling today, image and merchandise are frequently more important to buyers than price.

A store's most visible projection of its image is through advertising. A store that depends solely on heavy price appeal advertising may develop problems for its salesforce. One store's use of *"bait-and-switch"* advertising in selling appliances, as discussed earlier, was halted by the Federal Trade Commission, and the firm has now restructured their pay for commissioned salespeople. Most of the retail customers who enter a store have responded to the advertising, and so it sets their mood when they shop. This in turn sets the stage for the salesperson's presentation. Although advertising is outside the salesperson's control, he or she should be sensitive to the appeals used in the advertising and they should be included in the opening of the conversation.

The last retail patronage motive of significance is *personnel.* We are all acutely aware of outright rudeness on the part of some retail personnel. But actions do speak louder than words. Gestures, facial expressions, and clothing are powerful communicators of unverbalized thoughts. A former student, for example, was selling furni-

Courtesy of The Taubman Co., Inc., developer. Photographer: Balthazar Korab.

Shopping malls use entertainment and other attractions to attract customers.

ture for Montgomery Ward. He wore cowboy boots, jeans, and a western shirt and hat in the belief that Ward's customers were strongly blue-collar workers and that this costume was appropriate. The major displays, however, were all very contemporary chrome, glass, and vinyl; the store was suburban, not rural. His employment was brief.

The professional retail salesperson should study the patronage motives of the clientele the store attracts. These motives should govern such things as the salesperson's dress, appeals used in selling, and service offered after the sale. Some store traffic will also consist of nonpotential buyers for whom the store's image and merchandise lines do not match their needs. Skillful salespeople can differentiate between the two types of shoppers. When the difference is small, some may be converted into regular customers. Where the difference is large, a professional salesperson should direct them to stores where they can find satisfaction. No store can be all things to all people.

7. Select two stores with relatively identical merchandise that serve roughly the same market and use full time commissioned salespeople. Compare and contrast their patronage motives. Which salespeople would appear to have the advantage?

8. Survey an automobile row, furniture row, or similar set of businesses located close to each other. Identify how each have differentiated themselves and in what way they are identical. Is the collective appeal broad or narrow?

Motivating commercial and industrial purchases

Commercial and industrial buying behavior differs from retail behavior in some but not all aspects. As noted in the last chapter, personal psychological motives must not be overlooked as an influence on buying behavior. People play roles just as much at work as they do elsewhere. Cutting against these images can only end in no-sale presentations and even hostile feelings.

Rational factors

Individuals need food, clothing, transportation, and shelter; businesses need buildings, office supplies and equipment, and legal, financial, and accounting services. The retail sector has basic needs for display fixtures, merchandise, and cash registers. In the manufacturing sector, the need is for design services, raw materials, and operating supplies. Some goods and services must be purchased by all firms.

Because purchasing in the commercial and industrial sector is based on economic need it is often equated with rational buying behavior, but this view is inadequate. It does not take into account the fact that people do the buying, and nonrational factors enter into decisions.

The first false assumption sellers make is that the buyer has complete knowledge of alternative products that will satisfy a given want or need. While in simpler days this may have been true, today we live in a rapidly changing technological society. Few buyers can stay current with all the new products that keep coming into market or even with improvements in the old ones. In fact, a major job of today's professional salesperson is that of *educator*—of teaching people new ways to solve both new and old problems. Consequently it is the salesperson, not the buyer, who has the advantage. Salespeople who have done their homework know much better than the buyers the economic advantages and disadvantages of not only their own products, but also the products of competitors.

There are good reasons why people fail to use economics only as a purchasing base. First, the economic advantage must be significant and immediate. The saving of relatively few pennies will not cause people to change their present purchases. Also, businesses are very sensitive to current profit-and-loss statements. Additional profits that will not occur until a perceived distant future tend to be less important than profits on the books in the near future.

A second reason relates to convenience. Commercial and industrial buyers usually prefer to limit the number of vendors they buy from. Although a product offered by one firm may be economically advantageous, the business may continue to buy from a firm that offers a complete line of related products. Economic advantage, therefore, must not be viewed too narrowly. In some cases the savings generated by a purchase may be eaten up by an increase in costs elsewhere, so that total costs actually increase. Inefficient firms lacking accurate cost controls are particularly vulnerable to these irrational purchases.

This observation suggests a third reason why firms do not make rational purchase decisions. Inadequacy of cost controls may not enable them to record the true cost of any given purchase. They may buy a more expensive component than the application requires. They may fail to take into account time as a cost factor. For example, to be out of stock on a particular item may be costly to a firm in terms of sales lost, but still they choose a lower-cost alternative component with a longer delivery date, and so cannot fill orders on time.

Obviously, decisions based on price alone are not necessarily the rational decisions for a business purchaser to make. Those who sell a product on this basis alone are only telling part of the product story.

Psychological factors

Many of the psychological factors discussed in the previous chapter apply to industrial and commercial buying behavior. Items that make a job more pleasant, less tiring, and, perhaps, more interesting will find buyers. As with the economic factors, one must look at the larger picture. Computer-controlled machinery purchased by industry has shown a decided economic advantage. However, workers over 40 years old generally have resisted strongly such a major change in their job habits, and many see the labor-saving computer as a job threat.

Often in business purchases one person does the buying for many users. Where this is true, the psychology of both the buyer and the user must be considered. In the case of computers the buyers may see themselves as progressive business people; they take great pride in their computer equipment. The workers, on the other hand, may see only job elimination and greatly increased mental workload without adequate pay increases.

Group purchasing

Another factor of increasing importance in the commercial and industrial buying area is group purchasing. While routine purchases will still be handled by one person, as the value of the purchase to the business goes up one finds committees or teams evaluating major purchases. Most teams are composed of people from different areas within the firm, such as finance, production, personnel, marketing, and legal services. Some new product evaluation forms have sections completed by five or more people. A positive decision could trigger purchase of land, buildings, equipment, supplies, raw materials and fabricated parts, or a host of other items.

Other areas where purchase decisions are made by groups are advertising, training systems, data processing equipment, land, buildings, machinery, management personnel, and remodeling, to name only a few. Salespeople faced with this selling situation must now approach the problem from multiple viewpoints. While there may be some common elements among the group, each person has a particular sphere of influence or area of knowledge. Although the focus often appears to be from a rational economic base, one cannot disregard both psychological and social influences.

Characteristics of group purchasing

Group purchasing has two characteristics of importance. One relates to leadership, the other to the time required to take a positive action.

In most groups one person is a leader and the rest are followers. Discovering who is the leader and defining his or her perceptions of the purchase may save valuable time. Concentrating on those whose voice will be weak or unheard is not productive. This is not to imply that those people should be ignored, merely that the dominant people need to be identified.

The second characteristic of any group is procrastination. Groups tend to make decisions slowly because they wait until each member's evaluation of the facts is completed. Some people simply work slowly while others may find current daily activities interfering with their progress. Meetings cancelled because of schedule conflict also delay decisions. Some people believe the length of time to make a decision is directly related to the importance of the decision, and they keep extending their search for "facts" to raise their personal importance.

Detail selling through consultants

A final note on commercial and industrial purchasing is the increasing reliance on consultants as advisors in major purchase decisions. Many businesses place great weight on their advice. This may complicate things for the salesperson, since the consultant may be inaccessible much of the time. These people are usually much more aware of alternative product choices and economic and psychological factors. They also may try to view the situation from a broader viewpoint. Building materials companies often call on architects, who specify products, in order to sell to the contractors who buy them. Pharmaceutical firms must reach doctors in order to sell to drugstores. This practice is known as **detail selling.** The commercial and industrial salesperson may need to examine the extent of buying behavior influenced by consultants in other areas, and do some detail selling to these people. The influence of consultants selling for you can magnify sales greatly.

detail selling
selling to a third party who specifies a good or service (doctors, architects, consultants).

9. After making a presentation to an individual in a firm, you are asked to come back in one week and make a presentation to a group. What information would you like from the individual about the group? What information would be valuable but unlikely to be given?

10. You are selling a product that will be purchased by one person and used by another. Because the purchase will require the user to significantly alter their work habits they may react very negatively. How will you handle this presentation?

Mini–case

Judy has been selling for a discount furniture store for over a year. While the customers are usually attracted by the store's strong price advertising, she feels a better selling environment is needed. The store is old and dingy. The floor is bare boards, the furniture tightly packed in rows with narrow aisles and the lighting is dim.

While she agrees that too plush an environment would be uncomfortable for most of her customers, she would like the store to be more attractive. She has asked the owner to repaint the dull grey walls in light yellow; to double the number of lighting fixtures; and to add department signs.

The owner does not want to make any improvements. He feels that to do so would alienate many of his repeat customers.
Question: Who do you think is right—and why?

Define these key concepts

early adopter	emotional appeals
group purchasing	frame of reference
innovator	impusle buying
product life cycle	P.O.P. materials
rational appeals	psychological environment
demand creation	retail patronage motives

5 Self-preparation

Key terms

company knowledge
product knowledge
cross-selling
pricing policy
credit sales
sales support
knowledge about
  competitors
external environment
ethics

Overview

Today a buyer wants to be able to rely on salespeople for information. At the very least, the salesperson should know everything about his or her own product. The successful salesperson, however, will also have researched the customer's company, the company's competitors, and those competitors' products, and product applications. In addition, the salesperson should be aware of legal and ethical considerations of the product. Today's salespeople are educators and as such they must be knowledgeable about the business world in general as well as about products and services to be sold.

Self-preparation

Although the marketing concept has the needs of the customer or potential customer at its center, salespeople are equally important. The relationship between the salesperson and customer must be mutually satisfying and profitable in order to continue.

Compatibility

Compatibility is the ability to get along with or work with another. The salesperson must discover what interests are shared with the customer. These compatible interests may include age, education, experiences, or similar backgrounds. Differences in one category may make a continuing relationship difficult. For example, a recent college graduate may sell insurance to the president of a major corporation who is in her sixties. Building a long-term friendly relationship leading to more and larger sales may be difficult because of the age difference. Discovering that the customer graduated from the same college may overcome the age difference.

Another area of compatibility is *social activities.* Having similar social and recreational interests is a base for building friendships. Some people claim they close many sales on the golf course, even though not all conversation is related to selling. Hobbies, sports, community, and other social activities of mutual interest are excellent openers to a presentation. They help create a positive environment leading to sales, and make both parties more comfortable.

Compatible interests may result in friendships that extend beyond the selling environment. Many people have found selling very rewarding for this very reason. By discovering which backgrounds and social and recreational interests one shares with others, you may develop quite a large circle of friends. It is often remarked that you had better sell to your friends, because your enemies won't buy from you.

There are many good reasons for the salesperson to become involved in community and professional groups. The more one knows about an individual customer—or potential customer—the greater the chance of completing a sale. Community and professional organizations are excellent places to communicate with others. Which organization(s) the salesperson joins may be determined by his or her customers.

Personal interest files

Many salespeople keep a personal interest file on each customer, including information such as birthday, wife's or husband's name, hobbies, children's names, club and organization memberships, politics and philosophy, and peculiar habits. The less frequently one calls on an account, or the larger the number of customers one serves, the more important such a file is. The file helps the salesperson maintain a friendly relationship. A personalized card on a customer's birthday is a powerful sales support. A newspaper clipping relevant to a customer's interest or hobby is an important kind of contact.

When preparing for a presentation, the file will provide clues to opening the conversation, reminders about "forbidden" subjects, and other aids for tailoring the presentation to the customer's perspective. Contents of the file depend on the kind of selling one is doing. The salesperson must determine what to include and what to leave out.

Grooming
A final point on self-preparation concerns the salesperson's personal habits—primarily dress and *grooming*. With a few exceptions, one's personal habits should be somewhat similar to those of the

Appropriate attire is essential to the success of a sales call.

customers. Many a salesperson selling to an older, conservative customer has lost sales by dressing in loud, flashy, or too-casual clothes. Remember that in most cases the customers have mental roles they expect the salesperson to play. Preparing to sell includes preparing one's appearance. A professional salesperson knows what dress and behavior are appropriate to each customer. An appendix to the book contains excerpts from a best-selling book on this subject.

1. **Prepare a personal profile detailing your interests and activities. Match this with a customer market to which you would feel comfortable selling.**

2. **Prepare a file card with space for listing the important information you would like to keep about your customers. Limit yourself to a 4" x 6" card.**

Gathering facts about the products and the company

The information most vital to customers is product data and applications. Since selling is usually done to a variety of customers, **company knowledge** —knowing all about a customer and how and where that customer might use the product or services you are selling— must be thorough. This knowledge can be acquired formally or informally, but the salesperson should always know where to get it when needed.

company knowledge
awareness of a firm's history, organizational structure, key personnel, facilities, and product lines.

Sources of information

Firms provide their salespeople with **product knowledge** —specification sheets, brochures, and other printed materials that contain technical details. Good materials will also present these features as buyer benefits. *People buy benefits—not features.*

product knowledge
knowledge of the history of a product and customer benefits.

Other sources of useful product knowledge are training sessions, plant and warehouse tours, and presentations by the research and development department. Market research people also have recently become involved with information on how people perceive the products. Their work often determines the basis for advertising and sales promotion support in the area of theme development and objectives.

As product life cycles grow shorter, the salesperson's job as educator takes on more importance. New products are coming into the market so rapidly the salesperson must spend more time developing product knowledge. This problem is compounded at the wholesale and retail levels, making it very difficult to be an educator to one's customers. The rapid expansion of sales of digital watches, calculators, and video games are fine examples. A recent survey of company sales training programs found almost *50 percent* of the time devoted to product knowledge.

History is a good starting point for becoming informed about products. Fashion merchandising schools require students to study the history of costume over the last 200 years. They also cover the development of woven fabrics, nonwoven fabrics, and synthetics. All fields have a history that the salesperson should know.

One should also learn the history of the firm's product development, especially the product line. Some firms are leaders—that is, they develop new products; others are followers—they offer products or services already made popular. Good things can be said for each strategy. At the retail level, for example, Sears has long been a leader in hardware and appliances; J. C. Penney has only recently added these lines (a follower). Penney, however, has taken the lead in adopting a Uniform Product Code and is now selling national brand merchandise rather than following Sear's heavy reliance on private labels. Most firms change their product strategy over time. It is important to know when the most significant changes took place and what effect this had on the company. For some firms this history may go back over one hundred years.

Information flow

A salesperson can build trust and confidence by displaying a sound knowledge of the firm. For those selling for small firms this is a minimal job. Many more people, however, sell for the giant corporations, and many of these firms not only have many divisions and subsidiaries but are international in scope. Maintaining current company knowledge about their operations is a continuing activity for salespeople. New firms are acquired; others are sold; divisions add or drop products; and personnel are transferred.

The most troublesome part of selling for large concerns is knowing about major changes before the customers do. It can be embarrassing to have customers tell the sales representative about the company's activities or future plans. At the same time the company's information pipeline is probably outside the control of the salesforce. If it is inadequate, it may be necessary to apply pressure for improvements.

Many firms that have several diverse divisions have formalized **cross-selling** systems. The salesforce is kept current on the activities of other divisions and in turn the salespeople provide a feedback of information about the needs of potential customers to product

cross-selling
providing prospects for other departments or divisions, or team selling by people from different departments or divisions.

development or market research. One salesperson may have customers who need another division's products and may in turn be able to use leads developed from another salesperson's sources.

At the retail level, salespeople from one department will refer customers to other departments. In some cases people from different departments will sell as a team the furniture, carpeting, and china needed to furnish a dining room. As we have noted, the trend in most areas of selling has been toward team selling. This has come about as each salesperson becomes more of a specialist. There is some limit to the range of selling skill an individual can effectively acquire. Some selling today is primarily the bringing together of experts from several sources to solve a given customer problem.

Pricing and financial policies

Since pricing decisions are usually outside the salesperson's control they will not be discussed here. But it is necessary for the salesforce to understand the company's pricing policy. The **pricing policy** includes the company's objectives and financial factors considered to set a product's price. An informed salesforce may ask for a price cut as a lever to increase volume, thereby lowering the profit percentages. Under most firms' profit structures, sales volume may have to be doubled or tripled to return to the previous profit rate—a difficult task at best.

pricing policy
a price setting decision based on financial factors and long term objectives of the company.

In their concentration on price, salespeople should not ignore the more general area of finance. Many sales transactions have multiple costs such as storage and transportation costs that must be calculated for an effective presentation. Those persons selling to astute retailers know that inventory turnover is a prime consideration because of its effect on a store's profits. To a point, the ability to provide rapid replenishment of stock in relatively small quantities may override cost considerations. Retailers know that out-of-stock means no sale—and no profit. The salesperson's presentation should concentrate on delivery—not price—in this situation.

The ability to deliver a guaranteed quantity over time to a production line may be to your advantage for the same reasons. Quality control reputation, service facilities and technicians, and many other factors often are of greater interest than price alone. Effective selling requires knowledge not only of product features and benefits but also of the firm's production, storage, delivery and service capabilities.

credit sales
sales made on the basis of the buyer's promise to pay at some future date.

In most instances the area of price that directly involves the salesforce is credit. A **credit sale** is the seller's acceptance of the buyer's promise to pay at a future date.

Because credit is widely used today, a salesperson must know his or her firm's *credit policies*. These policies generally fall into two areas: credit information and collections. The salesperson may be required to produce the required data for credit approval or rejection, even though the final decision is based on the company's criteria.

In many areas of selling one is required to monitor an account's *credit rating* or watch for signs of decaying conditions. A few wise firms give their salesforce definite guidelines that are indicators of when things are not going well for a client. Customers having difficulty try very hard to cover their problems and this makes discovery difficult. It is worse, however, for the salesperson to make sales for which payment is never received than to lose the sale in the first place.

This leads directly into the other area where most firms have policy and procedures: slow-paying accounts and bad debts. The smaller the firm the more likely it is the salesforce will communicate with the client about unpaid debts. In larger firms other departments will take over after the salesperson makes one or two contacts. In any event, at some point a decision must be made either to refuse further credit or to try to help the customer develop a payment schedule it can meet. To handle this, the salesperson must know company policy on handling bad-debt accounts.

Sales support activities

sales support
the work of engineers, artists, technicians, or other specialists who aid in the preparation of presentations, take part in presentations, or work in the home office to provide information and service to customers.

As more firms go to team selling they are expanding **sales support** activities beyond those discussed earlier in advertising and sales promotion. Many firms have added inside sales service or customer service personnel. The customer can phone these people directly to place orders or make inquiries about the status of an order. Their position in the company structure is illustrated by the organizational chart in Figure 5–1.

These people provide two valuable services. First, they give the customer better service because they can be reached any time during business hours, even though the salesperson may be out of the office. The salesforce can spend more time in face-to-face contact. There is a direct relationship between a firm's volume per salesperson and the time spent actually selling. In many firms the salespeople actually spend less than three hours a day in face-to-face selling.

In some areas of selling, support personnel such as engineers, technicians, and service specialists share the sales load. The wise salesperson knows who has what talents within the firm. This team selling is now frequently seen in such areas as accounting, banking,

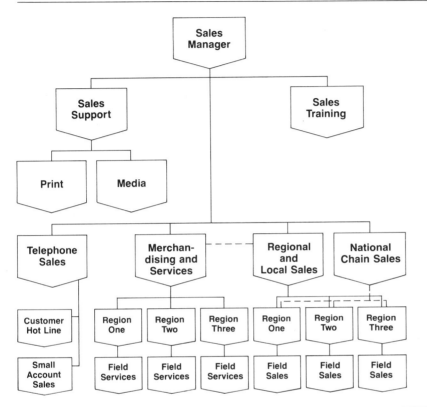

Figure 5-1.
Organization of sales and sales support to cover national, regional, local, and small accounts

advertising, insurance, sales training, and other service-based firms. Much construction involves subcontractors who are involved with the selling and bidding for a contract. The more complex the product sold, the more likely it is that the salesperson must act as coordinator of specialists acting in a consultant capacity. In some cases these people will also be from other firms.

3. Using sources available in your library, such as *Moody's, Standard and Poor's,* corporation annual reports, and others, prepare a statistical profile of a business from some sector where you have a career interest.

4. Interview an account executive with a major service firm. Describe the scope of his or her selling activities with respect to internal operations (sales support, customer service, etc.).

5. Interview a sales training manager or director about training of new salespeople. How much time and materials are devoted to company and product information? What is the total cost?

Gathering facts about competitors

**knowledge about
competitors**
*information about
competitors' products,
prices, sales promotions,
and distribution strategies.*

Knowing one's own products and company is only half of the learning job; **knowledge about competitors'** products and policies is also necessary. The salesperson must be able to compare one's company's products with competitors' products. No one product can be all things to all people. Advantages and disadvantages of competing products must be based on defined market segments. As a sales aid some firms provide product comparisons in chart or graph form. At the retail level, stores use comparison shoppers—people hired to list groups of similar items carried by a store—or require department managers to survey competing stores at regular intervals. Others require the salespeople to report on other stores' activities. Copies of those reports are circulated to all personnel.

Usually the easiest information to obtain about competing products concerns tangible features, such as quality of materials, construction, workmanship, and available accessories. As one moves into the intangible aspects, however, the assessment becomes more subjective. These areas would include company image, prestige of the salesforce, types and quality of services offered, and the nature of advertising and promotion support. The salesperson should analyze both tangible and intangible factors from two points of view: the customer's perspective of all available products and one's own perspective of significant differences between competing products.

Share of the market

Any given market can be assessed in terms of both potential and actual sales. Potential is the total volume that could be sold under ideal circumstances. Actual sales is the volume being sold. A good salesperson should know the current sales in a given market as well as the company's share of that market. In many cases this information will be collected by the firm. In real estate most firms closely monitor total sales for each month by categories and calculate how much of the business their firm accounted for. This kind of information is also gathered by most consumer goods manufacturers.

Markets are constantly changing, however, and change has two dimensions the salesperson must watch: the change in demand for a particular good or service and the change in the level of competition. A sudden drop in demand may see a corresponding drop in volume even with an accompanying aggressive competitive push. In an expanding market, however, the aggressor may easily double volume.

Financial and support policies

In order to present your product as superior to your competitors' products, the salesperson needs to know about competitors. A salesperson needs to know competitors' locations, the scope of their promotion program, geographical arrangements of sales territories, and expertise of their support personnel. Additional information would be their pricing policies and strategies, including the variety of discounts offered. Included here also are the credit policies and the degree to which competitors are involved in the financing of the sale by offering credit or time-payment plans. These aspects apply to almost all commercial and industrial selling as well as big ticket retail items. For instance, leasing is expanding into the retail market as a competitive tactic. Many expect the salesperson's need for an understanding of finance to expand in many areas of selling. In some areas it is crucial to making sales.

6. Make a comparison of competitive similarities and differences of three retail stores selling similar merchandise at roughly similar prices. Prepare a chart highlighting each.

7. From the Standard Rate and Data source book *(SRDS)* on trade publications, prepare a list of magazines available in a given market area. Rank order them in terms of usefulness as a source of information about your industry and your competition. Explain your criteria.

Gathering facts about the environment

After learning about one's own firm and its competition, one must consider **external environment** factors. Businesses do not operate in a vacuum: they operate in response to an ever-changing environment. The environment has been categorized in several ways but the mot useful breakdown for salespeople includes six categories: society and ethics; politics and law; the distribution structure; competition; technology; and market demand.

external environment
social, economic, and political factors that affect a company's method of selling, potential market, sales volume, and profits.

Society and ethics

In Chapter 4 social change was discussed. But **ethics**—a code of right and wrong—have been under close scrutiny in recent years, and are usually closely associated with selling. The numerous reports of bribes and kickbacks by major firms in international trade have made headlines and resulted in congressional inquiries. The weekly Federal Trade Commission (FTC) report regularly reports on

ethics
a code of right and wrong.

**Leasing is one alternative
for financing a sale.
It is a common practice
in the industrial sector
and is becoming more widespread in the retail sector.**

Money is no object.

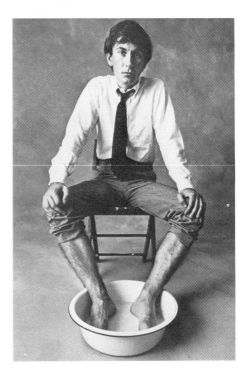

The object is sales.

No matter how sophisticated or technologically advanced your organization has grown to be, chances are you have yet to find a substitute for good old-fashioned pavement-pounding in the sales department.

In certain industries, though, especially when big-ticket capital equipment is involved, it takes more than shoe leather to make the sale. It takes an ability to see the whole process from the buyer's side as well – in effect to make the sale by facilitating the purchase. Since the best facilitators known are time, money and ideas about both, you should probably be acquainted with Trans Union Leasing Corporation.

We tend to be more interested in "how," than "if." Our decision-making process is shorter and involves fewer individuals than the larger banks and financial institutions. (Some firms have to go to their Boards of Directors for a decision on $500,000. We can let you know in 48 hours.)

Drop us a line at 111 W. Jackson in Chicago, attention W.W. Zwald, if you'd like to learn more about how our services may be of value to yours. More action on the dotted line should have the same effect on the bottom line.

Trans Union Leasing Corporation

cases involving questionable selling practices. While these are often flagrant violations, many are so-called grey areas involving ethics in professional selling. For instance, at what price does a Christmas gift to a customer become a bribe? Where do business transactions and personal friendships divide?

The code of ethics in Chapter 1 from the Sales and Marketing Executives International may be useful as a starting point. Ethics change over time, however, often in response to competitive pressures. Buyers looking for increased profits are frequently guilty of initiating a questionable transaction. A powerful firm may use its large buying capacity to obtain favorable pricing from small and financially weak sellers. Benefits are sometimes enjoyed by the firm, but often the price difference goes straight to the purchasing agent's pocket. The salesperson should know acceptable industry trade practices as well as legal restraints and conform to their guidelines.

Politics and law

The political and legal aspects of selling have changed significantly in recent times. Much legislation has been enacted regarding ethics. Truth-in-Lending laws now require salespeople to provide much more information. The Federal Trade Commission ordered one Chicago car dealer who sold to Spanish speaking customers to translate the contract information from English to Spanish. In-home selling has been influenced by the passage of many new laws.

Firms that falsely approach the prospective customer under the guise of contests, market surveys, or opinion sampling must now present a card stating they are there to sell. Encyclopedia companies were the first to be hit with this regulation. All states also require the cooling-off period discussed earlier for cancellation of in-home sales; the information must be in bold type on the order form.

Other firms have suffered from suits concerning illegal use of promotional allowances, especially with certain cooperative advertising payment schedules. Manufacturers' "purchase" of space in food stores and drugstores has been under investigation (see *rack jobbers*). Land sales for future residential use have seen many investigations and regulations, and large refunds have resulted in some cases.

Additional laws will continue to be passed that will further control sales activities. Some laws will have a negative effect on those firms now operating both ethically and within current laws, primarily because of bureaucratic paperwork and the resulting costs. Perhaps the greatest challenge facing selling is the conflict between what is legal and what is ethical in a competitive environment. As professionals many salespeople advocate sanctions against certain companies.

Distribution structure

A third area of change is in the distribution structure. In the past this was confined primarily to industrial and consumer goods, but the services sector has seen dramatic changes. In the industrial sector institutional foods are being increasingly concentrated in large wholesale distribution firms, thus changing traditional flows. At the retail level, business has seen more concentration in large corporate chains and franchise networks. The regional malls have captured billions of dollars from downtown units. Mass distribution, along with mass production and mass selling through self-service, is an integral part of our economy.

The service sector has seen great growth in multiunit firms. Real estate now has local sales offices tied to a nationwide parent corporation with telephone and electronic (EDP) connections. Banks, savings and loans, consumer finance, stock brokers, and insurance firms have all moved to either regional or national networks. General Electric maintains a nationwide repair service for their consumer and industrial goods that has replaced many small, inadequate repair shops.

Many of these changes in the distribution of goods and services have far-reaching implications for professional salespeople. As selling jobs are eliminated, others will be created. The new jobs will require much more expertise than the former ones. They will demand that the salesperson have the ability to serve larger accounts with more complex transactions and to be as much a consultant as a salesperson.

Competition, technology, and market demand

Some aspects of competition have been discussed, but one aspect of competition involves the broader area of technological competition. One application of new technology affects the product line. The other, more important aspect requires societal changes to keep up with drastically altered ways of achieving things.

In the new-product application, technology may make some products obsolete within a given line. For instance, some predict that wall-screen television will replace the traditional box the public has enjoyed for the past 30 years. This new television will also have the capacity to communicate with banks and retailers, provide family game entertainment, and be linked with local schools, colleges, and libraries.

Technological advances also will contribute to significant improvements in existing products. In addition, new products will replace old ones, as the hand calculator replaced the engineer's slide rule.

But one should always look to the much broader picture of changes in societal patterns. Will government-produced mass transit and increased laws governing personal automobiles cause a significant shift to mass transit in all metropolitan areas? Will predicted energy shortages force changing technologies to eliminate whole product groups and replace them with others? What will be the impact of developing nations on world trade as they mature and exercise more controls over raw materials? On an international level we can already see a return to barter (an exchange of goods for goods) often involving three or four countries. The swiftness of the oil embargo, sugar shortage, coffee controls, and other raw material supply crises should dramatize the fact that these problems are not necessarily far off. They will have an impact on a person's selling job. One should know how national and international events may affect one's firm, products, and therefore one's selling strategy.

8. Survey current business news magazines such as *Time, Newsweek, U.S. News and World Report, Forbes, Fortune, Dun's Review, Barrons.* What new products are making others obsolete? Are these products from existing companies in the market or newcomers? How will it alter the market and market shares?

9. Visit a major wholesale unit in your area. Discuss with the manager how their operation has changed over the past five years. How has this changed the role of their sales force? Report.

10. Visit a local office of a national real estate franchise network. What service does the franchisor (parent company) provide and how have those services altered the salesperson's job? What additional schooling have salespeople taken after joining the franchise that was not considered necessary before the firm joined the system? Report.

Your role as educator

In a rapidly changing world the salesperson's roles as communicator of information and educator will continue to increase in importance. It will be important to know the needs and wants of customers or potential customers better than they know themselves. Some realtors begin with a new customer by preparing an "audit" of their interests, activities, and finances before trying to find them a home. Increasingly, salespeople calling on retailers must know about store design, layout, lighting, color schemes, signing, accounting, advertising planning, traffic flow, and point-of-sale techniques. In some of these areas they may become more knowledgeable than the retail manager. The role of the salesperson then becomes that of an educator.

In preparing to sell, the salesperson must be viewed as a consultant. A consultant does not by any means have to be all-knowing. Our society is too complex for each salesperson to be a walking encyclopedia. The task is determining what information must be known and what information must be readily accessible. Rarely will a salesperson be able to answer every question every customer asks.

As a consultant one must know specialists who can be called upon to answer questions, usually people within the firm in staff capacity. At the manufacturing level these may be production supervisors, legal staff, advertising or promotion managers, warehouse supervisors, or credit managers. Service technicians and research and development personnel often are called upon to answer technical questions too.

In addition to the firm's own support people, supplier's salespeople may be called upon to provide answers at the retail and service levels. In real estate, bankers and lawyers are often used as independent appraisers. More and more frequently salespeople must bring in specialists to deal with very complex problems.

A professional salesperson builds and maintains his or her own files and library. Neither needs to be elaborate, but both must be somewhat comprehensive in the necessary topics covered. A library for a furniture salesperson, for instance, may contain three or four books on furniture construction, a half-dozen on consumer behavior and psychology, and a like number on professional selling. Add to these a couple of books on finance, retailing, and marketing and the whole collection probably would not number more than two dozen. One new book on professional selling should be purchased and read each year.

Files are often used for more technical data. For the furniture salesperson, information on new fabrics and finishes would be included. The file would contain catalogs from regular buying sources and from firms producing specialty items that could be special-ordered to meet particular customer's needs. Also included would be special notices from suppliers, trade journal articles of importance, and similar information useful in answering customers' questions or doing a better selling job.

Preparing to sell is a lot of work. It is being a student for life. The learning is a continuing activity that needs a given amount of time each week set aside for study. Sources of information are numerous and diverse. It requires an organized plan to see that these sources provide a steady flow of information necessary for professional selling.

11.   After selecting a selling area in which you are interested, prepare a list of books your personal library should contain. Discuss the list with a book store manager, select specific titles currently available, and compute how much an initial basic library would cost.

12.   Interview a sales manager for a medium to large firm. What is his or her perspective on knowledge required to sell? Using five categories—product, company, competition, customers, and environment—where is the greatest emphasis? Where is the least? Report.

13.   Information comes from many sources. Prepare a list of information sources for a selected selling position. After each source note whether you must acquire the information on your own initiative or it would normally be provided by your employer. Organize the list in the order of importance and estimate the time required each month for the top ten items. (Note: This item may be best used as a group discussion project.)

Ken, Judy, and Sandy are having coffee during a break at their quarterly regional sales meeting. Their sales manager has just asked them for suggestions for training new salespeople. The firm now has twelve, all with the firm three years or longer, and is planning to expand the force to eighteen during the next year. The new people will be placed in existing territories and the people there will be moved to open up new markets. The firm makes a variety of goods for the camping market. They sell to both retailers and manufacturers of recreational vehicles.

Mini-case

Ken feels anyone new should first spend a month in the research and development department, then work with the plant manager for a couple of months. He thinks a thorough knowledge of the products is essential.

Judy disagrees. She thinks the new people should be assigned to work with one of the firm's best salespeople for two months, then assigned to their new territories. They would work with the current salesperson there for two months before that person was reassigned.

Sandy doesn't like either suggestion. He thinks selling skills are of prime importance. He suggests sending the new people to a sales training seminar and then providing them with a self-study sales training package. Product knowledge can be learned from the many brochures, pamphlets, and other materials available.

Question: What solution do you propose that will get the new people productive at the least cost and in the shortest time.?

Define these key concepts

company knowledge
competition knowledge
cross selling
external environment
market share
product knowledge
self analysis

compatibility
credit policies
distribution structure
grooming
price policies
sales support

The selling process 3

6 Developing new customers and volume

Key terms

prospecting
prospect
cold canvas
referral
pyramid
secondary data
SIC
qualifying
tickler file

Overview

No business ever stands still; it is either growing or dying. For a firm to grow it must survey a changing market and attract new customers, generate more business from existing customers, or both. This chapter will examine the key role a salesperson plays in generating new business and see why it is vital. A variety of successful prospecting techniques initiated by the individual and the company will also be examined. We will determine which techniques have a high chance of selling successfully and which may waste time and money.

Market changes caused by customer turnover

If you were to invite a few close friends to a casual dinner party this
Saturday night, who would you include? How many were close
friends five years ago? Probably none.

We live in a society on the move. Relatively few people maintain
close relationships with others, either within or outside their family,
over long periods of time. Business isn't any different, and that fact is
important to personal selling today. The principle holds for the retail
sector and for the commercial and industrial sector.

Retail changes

People are born and they die. They move, get promotions, and are
fired; they get married, divorced, and separated. As they move
through different periods of their lives, needs change continually.
Teenagers need clothing, cars, entertainment, and items associated
with dating and getting married. After the age of fifty, needs center
on health care, vacations,and freedom from home maintenance.
Retail markets are constantly changing and even the best salesperson will sustain loss of customers—to competitors, to changes in
finances, to relocation, to death. Figure 6–1 on the next page illustrates these changes.

Retailing has also undergone a major revolution in the past twenty
years. The growth of regional shopping centers and, more recently,
the rapid proliferation of strip developments have altered the nature
of competition. Many decaying downtown areas and their federally
financed rebuilding are constant reminders of the struggle. The
major corporate and franchised chains are steadily increasing their
share of the total consumer dollar spent. With them comes the power
of advertising on a regional basis to attract and hold customers. But
with them also comes more pressure on the salesforce to use that
advertising as a base for finding new customers and holding them.

Commercial and industrial changes

The commercial sector faces many of the same problems. Business
mortality is significantly greater now than in recent years. Not only
may a customer be lost when a firm goes broke; if the account has
been managed poorly the seller may also be stuck with a bad debt.
Depending on company policy, part of that loss may come from the
salesperson's pocket. Businesses are as mobile as the general
population and have been moving to metropolitan suburbs and to
the warm southwestern states. These moves have significantly altered markets for items such as office supplies and equipment,

Figure 6-1.
The effect of changing
markets on market share

A change in the number of
competitive firms will cause
a change in demand and
market share; a change in
demand will cause a change
in competition and market
share.

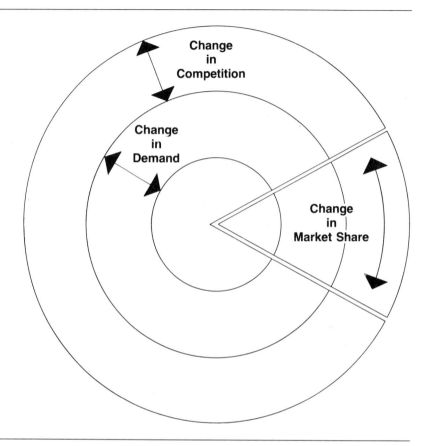

Change
in
Competition

Change
in
Demand

Change
in
Market Share

insurance, accounting, construction, real estate, and operating supplies. Recent statistics show that the major midwestern industrial states are losing population and businesses; rural areas are gaining both. Since the business sector will continue to grow on a national basis, commercial business will also grow. Some firms will be losers; others big winners.

The industrial sector is heavily influenced by consumer demand for goods, changing technology, and competition. As consumers become more affluent, goods that were once luxuries will become necessities. Other goods will become obsolete. Perhaps ultrasonic cleaning will replace dishwashers, clotheswashers and dryers, and dry cleaning. How long will it be before almost every home has a microwave oven? Will mass transit in metropolitan areas significantly reduce the demand for automobiles in 10 or 20 years?

The impact of technology is tremendous. Many manufacturers estimate that over half their existing products have been on the market less than five years. As a company's products are eliminated so are the sellers that supplied parts or ingredients for the products. But new opportunities constantly arise to supply materials for new products as well as new machinery involved in their production.

1.   What stores do you shop in for clothing where you are waited on by a salesperson? Are these different stores than you shopped at five years ago? Why?

2.   If you were considering the purchase of a new house, what clues would a salesperson have that you had become a prospect? Marriage, promotion, and job change or transfer are some examples.

Prospecting as a planned activity

To be successful in professional selling, one must devote some time to **prospecting,** or to finding new customers. Part of the prospecting effort must be devoted to qualifying **prospects** to determine whether or not they are actually within one's target market segment. One also must devote time to building volume for current accounts and be attuned to changes in needs, whether the buyers are retail consumers or commercial or industrial customers. But simply saying "I will" cannot alone ensure success for a salesperson. If you want to see results you must develop a plan.

prospecting
those activities involved in finding and qualifying prospects.

prospect
a person or firm within the market segment(s) to which a firm's products are directed.

The first step in the development of a plan is to select the method or methods that will most effectively reach those people that have a high potential. This assumes that you have used the principles from previous chapters to determine the characteristics of those customers most compatible with your product. The methods can be self-initiated or company sponsored. In most cases, both will be employed.

The second step in your plan is to set goals. Prospecting and account building are most successful when goals are set: many firms are beginning to set goals for their salesforce to meet. If your company does not set objectives, you must determine your own goals and these goals will vary significantly from one type of selling to another. They must, however, involve either an allocation of time per day or week or a specific number of new contacts to be made in a given time. Some selling, especially telephone solicitation for appointments, sets goals for the percentage of contacts that are converted into presentations.

Prospecting is frequently put off because most people would rather deal with existing customers and their problems than contact strangers. Daily problems often may interfere with immediate goals of developing new customers. For this reason you should keep a tally sheet of actual contacts compared to goals. If you consistently fall short of meeting goals, the goals should be reevaluated. Perhaps they were set too high. If not, you must learn to manage time more efficiently or your income will suffer.

3. Develop a weekly timetable for an automobile salesperson including prospecting, selling, servicing recent sales, paperwork, and other activities considered important. How does your timetable compare with others in the class?

Self-initiated prospecting methods

No matter how much support the company provides, to be successful at selling you must take the initiative yourself in several kinds of activities. In the next section we will discuss company-sponsored prospecting methods; in this section we will introduce those methods you alone must be responsible for: observation, the cold canvas, personal referral, "bird dogs" (people who do not sell but seek out prospects) and the use of secondary data.

Observation

One of the salesperson's most important prospecting tools is *observation*—keeping one's ears and eyes open to relevant information. Many salespeople, unfortunately, fail to understand that you have to be in the right place at the right time to see and hear the right things. You must be with people who have information that will be beneficial in order to hear what will help you. This may be at professional and fraternal meetings, church, school, and community board meetings; or wherever people meet, greet, and talk. Where will you have the greatest opportunity to develop prospect information? At private clubs, social organizations, community volunteer groups, and trade associations, to name a few places. The people need not be potential prospects themselves but they may have current data that will provide leads for you to follow. The daily newspaper provides clues. Newspapers are full of people's activities, such as news of promotions and notices of building permits, marriages, incorporation, births and deaths, and grand openings. In your everyday travels to and from work or around a territory you can see evidence of changes in buildings going up or coming down, for sale and for rent signs, or help-wanted signs for growing businesses. Moving vans and rented trucks as well as listings of real estate transactions also signal changes.

Cold canvas

Prospecting by the ***cold canvas*** method, that is, calling on a person or firm without any prior contacts, is normally not held in very high esteem. This method is most often associated with those selling brushes, magazine subscriptions, or encyclopedias door to door. The method has been further hampered by recent legislation in most states and by FTC rulings against specific firms. Certain communities require those calling on consumers in their homes to register with the city and obtain a permit. All states have laws regarding a cooling-off period, as we have already seen. Consumers in high-rise complexes are often protected by security guards who restrict entry into the building.

Nevertheless, the cold canvas may sometimes be a valid prospecting method. Some real estate firms have identified sections of a city where homes are bought and sold more often than in other areas. Salespeople are expected to spend time each day going door to door in these sections, to introduce themselves and leave a business card. They do not use a hard-sell approach, but usually inquire whether the homeowner or any other neighbors are considering selling or buying a home. This method is most prevalent in those franchised chains supported by heavy regional advertising. The salesperson's call adds to the promotional synergism to produce the maximum impact.

A similar approach can be used effectively in the wholesale and commercial area, and has been used successfully to sell fire extinguishers, first-aid packages, and similar one-time items. The primary consideration in the cold canvas is the kind of product or service one is selling and the number of potential customers in an area. Where potential customers are either universal or highly concentrated, cold canvas may be considered.

Referrals

If you are doing a very good job as a salesperson, many new customers will come to you through word-of-mouth advertising, ***referrals*** by others. You cannot rely entirely on satisfied customers, however, to spread the word. Ask satisfied customers for leads to follow; don't wait for them to give leads voluntarily. Suggest that they refer their friends to you.

One systematized referral plan widely used in consumer in-home selling is the ***pyramid.*** After closing the sale, the salesperson asks for five to ten names of friends and relatives. The optimal number is mathematically determined by past records of the number of leads required to close one sale. For safety the number requested is usually greater than needed. For instance, a person who normally

cold canvas
a sales call made without any prior contact.

referrals
names of people or firms in a market segment; provided by a customer, friend, or other contact.

pyramid
to accumulate referrals; one person gives you names of four prospective customers, those four people give you sixteen names, and so on.

closes one sale for every six leads would ask for eight to ten names to build an inventory. The name of the person who supplied the names is used to secure subsequent presentations, of course. This type of referral is also known as the *endless chain.*

In the commercial and industrial sector the use of the referral method is normally not as aggressive. Salespeople in this area prefer to get just one good name at a time, of people they do not know or people they know but have been unable to see. These leads can be handled in one of three ways. First, you can follow up the information in the same manner as you would when getting the information by observation. Second, you can actively involve the referring customer in the approach, either by letter of recommendation or personal telephone call. The letter is helpful when a secretary screens phone calls. The phone calls act as an introduction to prepare the prospect for a request for an appointment. The third method involves the referring customer in the initial interview. It could be a joint meeting for lunch or cocktails, a professional meeting where you can be personally introduced, or some other similar arrangement. This method has the added impact of building confidence in the new prospect in both the salesperson's ability and the product being sold. This lowers buying resistance and reduces selling time when the formal presentation is made.

Influence centers are another source of referrals. These people often are not customers but by the nature of their jobs they discover people who are very high potential prospects (see Figure 6–2). Bankers, lawyers, stockbrokers, real estate and insurance salespeople, and other salespeople covering the same territory with non-competing products are all potential influence centers. Each sees the market from a perspective different from yours. It is like having a second pair of ears and eyes to assist in observation. Regular planned meetings with these people, as opposed to chance meetings, should supply many leads. Also, as with satisfied customers, these people may be involved in your introduction.

"Bird dogs"

Bird dog is the term used to refer to people hired, full or part time, to seek out potential customers. They do no selling themselves, but are paid observers and researchers. For example, a tire company hires a high-school student, the "bird dog," to place sales brochures on automobiles with worn tires. Other companies have photographed license plates of customers, obtained addresses and phone numbers, and telephoned the people for presentation appointments. Other salespeople who cover wide markets may retain people to "bird dog" in selected areas to keep track of local activities. They read local newspapers and talk with influence centers on a regular

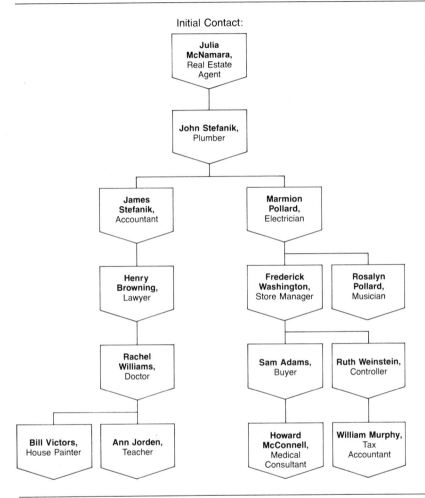

Initial Contact:

**Figure 6-2.
Prospecting by the
influence center referral
method**

basis. These people perform a dual function for the company by
regularly feeding back information on changes in their markets.

Secondary data
A valuable prospecting tool used by all areas of selling is the white
and Yellow Pages of the phone directory (in metropolitan areas, B
and C Yellow Pages). Further information sources are lists and
directories provided by trade associations, membership rosters of
all kinds of clubs and organizations, school faculty and student lists,
car registrations, real estate transfers, and so on. Talk to the reference librarian in your college resource center or your city libraries
for more sources of **secondary data**.

secondary data
*published information from
sources outside the firm;
directories and
membership rosters are
examples of secondary
data.*

Bird-dogging is one means of prospecting.

4.   Select a sales role that interests you, in retail, commercial, industrial, or services. Place the self-initiated methods just discussed in order of importance, viewed from both a time requirement and potential productivity. What obstacles might you face in implementing your top choice?

5.   Contrast the prospecting problems in selling automobile insurance to consumers and to commercial accounts.

Company-sponsored prospecting methods

In most large companies today it is the function of the marketing department or other sales support areas to prospect for new customers. Prospects are usually chosen from among the target market segment. Your company will have a variety of sources for names of prospects, including directories, computer sources, advertising and direct mail response, sales promotion activities, and trade shows, exhibitions, and display areas.

Directories

Lists of names of prospective customers are often prepared for salespeople by the marketing department personnel from professional directories or other printed lists. Each salesperson receives lists of names of individuals or companies to approach in his or her own territory. Salespeople are usually expected to feed follow-up reports back to the marketing department. This requirement has two functions: it ensures that the salesperson actually carries out the prospecting plans and it allows the company to evaluate the productivity of the lists.

Other good sources for customer lists are noncompeting firms serving similar markets. For example, chain or franchise organizations may make an agreement with a marketing organization to sell a series of lists. The company then provides a list of locations, names of owners or managers, and other valuable information. These lists are most valuable to firms new to a particular market that have few customers in that market.

Computer-generated lists

One major advantage of *computer-generated lists* is the ability to program the system in such a way that it selects only those individuals defined as potential buyers. For example, those who have already purchased by direct mail are more likely to make a purchase than those who have never responded to a direct mail advertisement.

In the retail sector the most widely used source is the firm's credit card holders. Selection of potential buyers of an item is based on information provided on the credit application (income, place of residence, occupation) that may include or exclude potential buyers. *Profile matching,* a further refinement of this method, allows recent credit purchases to be computer analyzed against application information in order to develop buying patterns and categories of customers. While everyone on such a list is not a true potential customer, the odds are increased greatly so that fewer contacts are required to make an equivalent number of sales as opposed to the cold-canvas method. Sales expense is thereby reduced.

Another use of profile matching is in the selection of merchandise to stock. A product that cannot be delivered is a sale lost and commissioned salespeople at retail stores may lose thousands of dollars if the merchandise wanted is out of stock or is not carried.

In commercial and industrial applications, computer generated information is of growing importance. Figure 6–3 is a sample of one form sold by Dun & Bradstreet, a credit reporting firm. Note that the form contains more than just a name and address. Besides the firm's credit standing and volume purchased, one finds the different goods and services the firm sells coded by **Standard Industrial Classification (SIC),** a system designed by the U.S. Department of Commerce to give each area of business a numerical classification. This is valuable in determining what product com-

Standard Industrial Classification
SIC—*a widely used method of categorizing businesses by numerical codes.*

Figure 6-3.

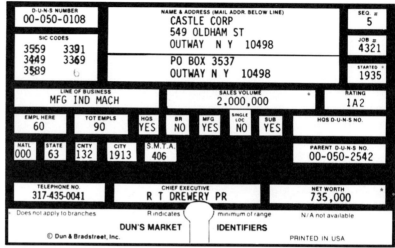

Marketing Services Division—A Division of Dun & Bradstreet.

panies may buy; the sales volume figure aids in determining how much they might buy.

Dun & Bradstreet, along with many other companies, sells a variety of prospecting aids for as little as a few hundred dollars; their other services can cost many thousands of dollars, where detailed market studies are done for use by both sales and marketing management. These are, of course, very valuable to the sales force in both prospecting and building their presentation around known customer needs.

The information is also sold in a variety of formats: some are simply print information; others sell data on either magnetic tape or punched cards. A company can load this prepared information into its computer, combine it with data already there, and generate new information. Computer address lists can be used to print labels directly on sales pieces. It is certain that the volume of data in computer storage will continue to increase. As this happens, innovative people will find different ways to use it both to prospect and to develop presentations.

Advertising response

Another company-sponsored prospecting aid, *advertising response,* is widely used at the retail level as well as by commercial and industrial firms. At the retail level, media and direct mail advertising is used primarily to attract store traffic. In these cases the prospect comes to the seller. In the most effective use of direct mail the mailing piece is targeted to specific groups; the salesforce is expected to follow up with a *warm canvas*—either a telephone call or a personal call.

Unfortunately, the design is not always followed. Ford Motor Company, for example, once sent a specially prepared piece to owners of two- and three-year-old station wagons whose names were obtained from a computer service list. These names, however, were not supplied to local salespeople for followup. Think of the synergistic impact this direct mail piece would have had if it had been followed by a letter from a local salesperson with a follow-up telephone call a few days later.

Commercial and industrial firms have long used advertising response to develop new prospects, especially where the company's products are used in a wide variety of applications by distinctly different firms. Trade magazines and direct mail are the primary vehicles.

Trade magazines provide three normal avenues for developing prospects. These are space advertising with some coupon or form to be returned: classified advertising inviting people to inquire for more information, and *bingo cards* in a variety of forms.

Several strategies are used in *space* and *classified advertising* approaches. Some firms simply try to get as many replies as possible; others seek information to screen out those replies that experience has shown are not real prospects. Others use glued or stapled inserts with perforated reply forms on heavier paper. A typical prospecting advertisement is illustrated in Figure 6–4.

Bingo cards are designed to increase response to advertising. The magazine numbers each advertisement and provides a return card with numbered boxes—hence the term "bingo." Subscribers return the card to either the publisher or a clearinghouse. At regular intervals the advertisers receive a list of respondents the publisher has already entered into computer data storage.

In response to most inquiries most firms simply send a packet of additional information about the good or service, but to be truly effective the respondent's name should be forwarded to sales personnel for followup.

Screening of potential prospects is a service performed more and more by magazines or marketing agencies. *Industrial and Engineering News,* for example, requires the person requesting information to provide fairly detailed information about his or her firm and position on the reply card similar to that provided by the Dun & Bradstreet illustration (Figure 6–3). With increasing costs, in both money and time, to make a presentation to a potential account, more prospecting will be combined with screening to reduce the waste in selling by eliminating those who are not truly prospects.

Figure 6-4.

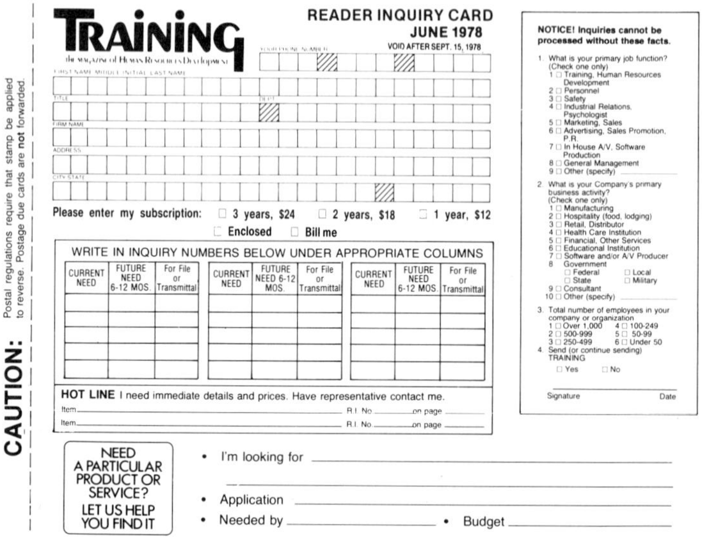
CAUTION: Postal regulations require that stamp be applied to reverse. Postage due cards are **not** forwarded.

TRAINING The Magazine of Human Resources Development

READER INQUIRY CARD
JUNE 1978
VOID AFTER SEPT. 15, 1978

Please enter my subscription: ☐ 3 years, $24 ☐ 2 years, $18 ☐ 1 year, $12
☐ Enclosed ☐ Bill me

WRITE IN INQUIRY NUMBERS BELOW UNDER APPROPRIATE COLUMNS

CURRENT NEED	FUTURE NEED 6-12 MOS.	For File or Transmittal	CURRENT NEED	FUTURE NEED 6-12 MOS.	For File or Transmittal	CURRENT NEED	FUTURE NEED 6-12 MOS.	For File or Transmittal

HOT LINE I need immediate details and prices. Have representative contact me.
Item ______ R.I. No ______ on page ______
Item ______ R.I. No ______ on page ______

NEED A PARTICULAR PRODUCT OR SERVICE? LET US HELP YOU FIND IT

- I'm looking for ______
- Application ______
- Needed by ______ • Budget ______

NOTICE! Inquiries cannot be processed without these facts.

1. What is your primary job function? (Check one only)
   1 ☐ Training, Human Resources Development
   2 ☐ Personnel
   3 ☐ Safety
   4 ☐ Industrial Relations, Psychologist
   5 ☐ Marketing, Sales
   6 ☐ Advertising, Sales Promotion, P.R.
   7 ☐ In House A/V, Software Production
   8 ☐ General Management
   9 ☐ Other (specify) ______
2. What is your Company's primary business activity? (Check one only)
   1 ☐ Manufacturing
   2 ☐ Hospitality (food, lodging)
   3 ☐ Retail, Distributor
   4 ☐ Health Care Institution
   5 ☐ Financial, Other Services
   6 ☐ Educational Institution
   7 ☐ Software and/or A/V Producer
   8 Government ☐ Federal ☐ Local ☐ State ☐ Military
   9 ☐ Consultant
   10 ☐ Other (specify) ______
3. Total number of employees in your company or organization
   1 ☐ Over 1,000 4 ☐ 100-249
   2 ☐ 500-999 5 ☐ 50-99
   3 ☐ 250-499 6 ☐ Under 50
4. Send (or continue sending) TRAINING
   ☐ Yes ☐ No

Signature Date

Training: The Magazine of Human Resource Development.

Direct mail response

Direct mail pieces are designed for many different purposes—to close a sale, generate interest, to qualify prospects, and to generate response. They are heavily used for prospecting, and their use in this area has proved overwhelmingly effective in direct consumer selling.

Commercial and industrial firms also make heavy use of direct mail. Greater selectivity in computer-generated lists is a major aid. Direct mail may be used more frequently as a screening device than as a prospecting aid. Even where good lists are available, they may contain too many names for the sales force to cover in the time available. Direct mail is used to identify those with a current interest. Those responding are called upon first; the remaining names are approached when time permits. Figure 6–5 is a sample from a package of reply postcards sent four times a year to people in education, training, consulting, hotel and motel, and other fields.

Sales promotion efforts

Activities used to generate new prospects at the retail level may be sales promotion events such as contests, demonstrations, and entertainment. Many shopping centers are using well-known performers to attract traffic. Shows put on in the afternoon and evenings draw crowds. Some salespeople complain because shoppers watch the shows and leave without making any purchases, but salespeople working for aggressive firms will always find rewards.

Retailers often use *in-store demonstrations* that are sponsored by the manufacturer. Some camera firms have their own salespeople sell direct to the public by means of special demonstrations in their retail outlets. Other firms hire full-time personnel to give fashion shows; make-up demonstrations; and craft, home repair, or decorating workshops; these people not only attract crowds but also sell to them. Retailers also run classes to build repeat customers and attract new ones. These have been especially effective in arts and crafts, sewing, home improvement, and photography.

Where the prizes are valuable, registration for a variety of *contests* can produce new traffic. Some contests are run in conjunction with promotions by radio stations and other stores. Sometimes stores

USE US!

We want to give you the opportunity to learn more about Kodak AV products. Use this card to tell us how we can be of service to you. Fill it out, fold, tape, and drop it in the mail. If you have specific comments about our products or programs, now's your chance to let us know. We've even prepaid the postage.

☐ **DEMONSTRATION**
Please arrange for a demonstration of the following Kodak AV products:
☐ 16mm   ☐ slide   ☐ super 8

☐ **TELEPHONE**
Please telephone me. I have questions that could be answered by phone. My number is listed below.

☐ **LITERATURE**
I'd like more literature on the following Kodak AV products:
☐ 16mm   ☐ slide   ☐ super 8

☐ **MAILING LIST**
Place me on your mailing list to keep me aware of the latest in Kodak AV products.

Check the appropriate symbol to tell us how we can serve your needs

COMMENTS:

NAME _____

COMPANY/SCHOOL _____

STREET _____

CITY _____ STATE _____ ZIP _____

PHONE NUMBER _____

V3-3   Printed in U.S.A.

Figure 6-5.

Eastman Kodak Company.

develop their own contests, offering cars, TV sets, vacations, and cash or gift certificates. To draw traffic for retail outlets manufacturers sometimes sponsor contests aimed at the ultimate consumer. (More frequently, however, these contests are directed at the retailer or wholesaler. In these cases the direction is not toward prospecting but account building.)

Trade shows, exhibitions, and display areas

For some salespeople the annual trade show is their only personal yearly contact with small accounts. It may be the only way to pick up business from new accounts that are too small to warrant a personal call. Many firms, however, who serve defined markets and already know all possible customers, have eliminated trade show participation, especially in the industrial area. The expense of the show plus the cost of removing the sales force from the field was greater than any benefits.

Retailers are now discovering the trade show, usually with heavy manufacturer support. Shows are widely used to introduce consumers to new automobiles, boats, snowmobiles, recreational equipment, and home improvements. The bridal show with sponsorship of several stores has been very productive. State and county fairs have experienced renewed interest by the consumer, and more firms will be seeking this traffic with booths and outdoor exhibits.

In recent years, many manufacturers and agents have established permanent offices and displays in trade marts. While not usually considered a prospecting tool, the location makes it very easy for new businesses to find resources or for old firms to find new sellers. These marts sponsor visitor weeks when firms send buyers to look over the offerings. In fashion and furniture particularly, these are accompanied by shows and seminars. The fashion mart in Dallas, one of six buildings and the world's largest complex, produces 15 fashion shows each year. Buyers come from around the world to the new Dallas World Trade Center, which opened in 1974.

6. **You are a salesperson for a furniture store that attracts customers with a good advertising program. Of the company-sponsored prospecting methods just discussed, which would you recommend they add as a way of reaching specific, small but lucrative markets? Why?**

7. **As a salesperson for a printing company that offers a wide variety of services including packaging, design a direct mail piece to be sent to a computer-generated list of manufacturing firms in your territory. How would you follow up the mailing?**

Courtesy of Dallas Market Center

The Dallas Trade Mart (shown here) was the original building in what is now a six building complex serving both national and international trade.

Criteria to qualify prospects

Time is valuable and "no-sale" presentations are discouraging and wasteful. In most cases the salesperson's income is directly or indirectly tied to the volume sold. It only makes sense to develop some means of **qualifying** prospects and concentrating energies on the prospects most likely to produce a sale and income. Sales presentations made to people who have no need for a product result in a staggering waste of time and money. The salesperson loses; the firm loses.

To overcome this problem some firms have developed prospect evaluation forms, on which the salesperson records information about a prospective account. This form achieves two functions: to help develop an effective presentation and to screen out low-potential customers.

qualifying
determining if a firm is within the defined market segment.

Level of need

One criteria you should use in evaluating a prospective customer is level of need. A person who has purchased a new car in the past year, for instance, has a lower level of need than a person whose car was purchased three years ago. One who is being transferred by his or her company has a higher need for new housing than someone who has recently purchased a home. Some needs are based on rational decisions; others are based on emotion. This is especially true with consumer goods.

In some selling areas the potential customer is not aware that a need exists. This is frequently true in the services sector in both the consumer and commercial markets. This situation calls for demand creation by the salesperson, which is often a more difficult kind of selling. Your evaluation is not how strong the need is, but what your ability is to create the need. More information must be secured to make this evaluation.

Authority to buy

In selling to businesses, especially larger ones where many decisions are made on a group basis, the level of need will be felt differently than among those who will influence the buying decision. This leads to another qualifying point, that of authority to buy. Many presentations are made to people who may have, or feel they have, a high level of need, but who do not have the authority to make the purchase. Frequently at the retail level major decisions to purchase are being made only after both husband and wife agree on the purchase. Thus if one partner dominates, a sale cannot be made unless that partner authorizes it.

Similarly, a secretary may feel a need for a new typewriter with the latest features, but most secretaries do not have authority to buy. In many firms major purchases can be made only if they are budgeted, and usually several people are involved in budget development and approval. Many sales are lost because the person who has the final authority decides to cut the item from the budget.

Accessibility

A similar prospecting factor, that of accessibility, affects the salesperson calling on clients. *Accessibility* refers to the ease with which a salesperson can reach a decision-maker. Those with authority to purchase may be inaccessible to the salesperson. In the area of in-home selling, for instance, a prospect may have been "turned off" by the selling tactics of others, and consequently will not grant any salesperson an opportunity to make a presentation. Some firms have generated a similar hostile climate by using similar tactics with

small commercial and industrial firms. From a prospecting viewpoint, the salesperson must make a judgment as to accessibility.
Where it may take considerable time and money to gain access to
prospects, the difficulty must be weighed against the sales potential.

Financial status
A final main qualifying point is the financial considerations. Sales
that result in no payment or prolonged collection procedures have
no profit. While the salesperson's short-term goal of a commission
may be realized, in the long term both the individual and the company will suffer, and not only in the consumer sector. Business bankruptcy and companies in financial difficulty have increased in
number. Appearances can be deceiving; those with an affluent look
may be using outward signs as camouflage.

Other factors
Besides these four main factors, a few firms add other qualifiers they
believe are important. One is *continuity* or long-term potential. They
are not as interested in generating an initial order as they are in
generating repeat orders. In fact, a small first order may be only a
stepping stone to selling other goods and services to other divisions
of the prospect.

Another factor is *service requirements.* In all sectors of selling
some customers demand a level of service far greater than can be
realistically provided. They may expect the salesperson or the support people to be at their beck and call. These accounts often prove
to be profitless.

Other firms look at *volume potential.* Many consumer goods manufacturers sell their products only through major chain retailers or
only in major metropolitan markets. Few potential customers offer
identical volume potential. Concentrating your efforts on those with
the greatest potential should be rewarding in the long term.

tickler file
*a portable file of current
customers and prospects.*

Keeping prospect records
While many firms have formalized their prospecting procedures with
forms and reports, the majority of salespeople must create their own
forms. Just as you must determine methods along with prospect
criteria, you most likely will need to develop your own personal record system.

In the simplest form, all that is needed is a recipe box, index

cards, and prospect cards. This can be divided into current customers and prospects, since similar information is needed about
both. This is often referred to as a **tickler file.** Instead of idly waiting
for prospects or sitting in the car watching the world go by, the
salesperson can tickle the file for people to see or call. Keeping and
using a file is part of the job of the successful salesperson.

8. **Select a selling position of your choice. Prepare a profile of a
high potential prospect using the qualifying factors discussed. At
what lower limit or other point would a person or company be
eliminated as a potential prospect?**

9. **Design a 4″ X 6″ card for recording prospecting data for your
selling choice above. Allow room to enter the data in your own
handwriting easily. Does it effectively screen prospects? Does it
provide information to build your presentation?**

Mini-case

After much deliberation Tony and Janice decided to start their own
janitorial service. Both had experience and they had saved enough
money to buy a used truck and the necessary equipment. Initially
they wanted to concentrate on offices and retail stores. After they
were established growth would come from manufacturing firms.

They are confident that they can keep accounts once they have
sold them, but initially business will have to be taken from existing
firms. The market is growing and future business can be gained
from new businesses expected to open in the area. They have
figured that they must sell the following accounts in their first two
months to stay in business:

6 offices @ $50.00/month	$300.00
3 offices or stores @ $100.00/month	300.00
1 office or store @ $200.00/month	200.00
10 accounts	$800.00

Question: **How should Tony and Janice develop a list of qualified
prospects to call on?**

**Define these
key concepts**

accessibility	endless chain	qualifying
advertising response	influence center	referral
authority to buy	observation	screening
bingo card	profile matching	secondary sources
cold canvas	prospecting records	S.I.C.

7 Building the presentation

Key terms

probing
custom tailor
financial information
trade publication
informal organization
benefit-centered
  presentation
objective
product demonstration
underling barrier

Overview

Using all the knowledge about products, competitors and their products, and the social, legal, economic, and political environment, you can build presentations centered on individual customer's wants and needs. Rarely will two presentations be identical. Attention must be given not only to individual customer differences but also to content, method of presentation, and available support materials. Only after this preparation has been completed are you ready to sell.

Tailoring the approach

Customer differences

In preparing presentations it is useful to differentiate between two kinds of customers—those you must go after and those who seek you out. Presentations will differ for the two groups.

A great number of people seek out salespeople in their search for goods and services to fill their needs. Preparing to sell to these people takes one kind of preparatory work.

These people have already recognized a need. Often they know precisely what they want and they expect the salesperson to provide it. You should not expect selling to be any easier, however, simply because they called you. In their search they may also have asked for presentations from others selling products similar to yours. Your presentation need not mention your competitors unless you are sure of certain superior factors of your product. Be aware, though, that your product and presentation will be compared to those of others.

A different kind of preparation is required before you can make the presentation to a potential customer you have contacted.

Probing

Asking questions to discover whether individuals or firms are potential customers and, if so, whether you can provide the products or services they need or want is known as **probing**. This activity, known as qualifying the prospect, is often confused with the presentation because both are face-to-face meetings. If you cannot provide what the customer wants, direct them to firms that can fill their needs. Don't expect your firm to be all things to all people.

The questions you ask to identify needs will vary from one kind of selling to another, but they should be well thought out in advance. Your actual presentation will be built on the answers you receive. Wrong questions and answers do not produce completed (closed) sales. At the in-store locations of Allstate Insurance, for example, the salesperson questions prospects thoroughly about their needs, financial situation, etc., and then asks them to shop for a while. The salesperson then has an opportunity to develop two things: an insurance plan to fit the customer's needs and a sound selling presentation. This procedure results in a high rate of closes.

Don't judge people by looks alone. Visual clues can be deceptive. A farmer couple was shopping in a fashionable furniture department. The farmer, in work clothes, had dried manure on his boots. The couple was ignored by interior designers and sales clerks alike.

probing
asking questions of a potential customer in order to obtain information about that person's needs and wants.

Finally a salesperson approached them, and within two hours had written a $15,000 order. The farmer had just sold a large herd of cattle and was eager to spend the profits. Less than a month later the same salesperson approached an eye surgeon and her husband, both dressed in cutoffs and sweatshirts. The order was only slightly smaller. These experiences gave the interior designers a new perspective.

Identifying needs

The ability to draw out information from potential customers will vary with the salesperson. Those that are very extraverted will give out much information, some of which may be valuable and some which may be distorted. It takes a keen salesperson to recognize the difference. Introverted customers present more of a challenge; a very supportive atmosphere must be developed to obtain the information necessary. While the process may be slow and agonizing, once these people are won as customers they are also slow to change suppliers. Repeat patronage is very high among this group and is worth the probing effort.

1.   **Select a sales role where most customers seek you out. Develop a list of questions aimed at qualifying them.**

The information probe

Before beginning this section it may be wise to look back at the qualifying factors discussed at the end of the previous chapter. Criteria used for prospecting are the basis on which presentations are built. Qualifying factors are general in nature and identify market segments that have a high potential for sales. Once an individual prospect has been identified, it is necessary to accumulate data, to

custom tailor
to adapt a presentation to meet a customer's unique requirements.

custom tailor the presentation to his or her specific needs.

Information for commercial and industrial accounts can be divided into three categories: company organization and financial information, product applications, and personal factors. This information-gathering process is illustrated in Figure 7–1. Similar criteria can be developed for consumer sales Figure 7–2.

financial information
a firm's or customer's ability to pay for purchases.

Much of the probing is for **financial information.** At the top of this list is credit rating. The status of Lockheed, W. T. Grant, Penn Central, and other companies should be evidence enough that size and credit are not necessarily related. Selling to a firm on shaky financial ground is risky for both the firm and the salesperson, for reasons we have already discussed.

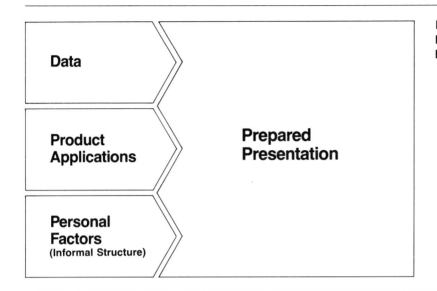

**Figure 7-1.
Business Presentation
Building Company**

Other valuable financial information can be obtained from annual reports and financial publications. A professional salesperson should be able to read and interpret both the income and balance sheet statements using standard ratios and percentages, such as current ratio and return on investment. Usually signs of poor financial health appear here before corrective action is taken, if it is taken at all. This is why the salesperson includes books on accounting and finance in his or her personal library.

More often, however, the information will come from regular reading in **trade publications**, that is, magazines or newspapers dealing with the industry. You can also pick up news through normal business activities and word of mouth. Moves, expansions, renovations, and new product entries all signal selling opportunities. The key is knowing about these events before they happen. Since more firms are setting up one- and five-year forecasts, this company information may be included in the annual report and therefore is available to you.

trade publication
a magazine or journal for professionals in a particular field.

Product applications

Most salespeople are somewhat concerned about product applications. Far too often, however, stereotyped presentations are made without proper research into individual firms' needs. Some data can be gathered before the initial sales call. Further, the purpose of an

**Figure 7-2.
Consumer Presentation
Building**

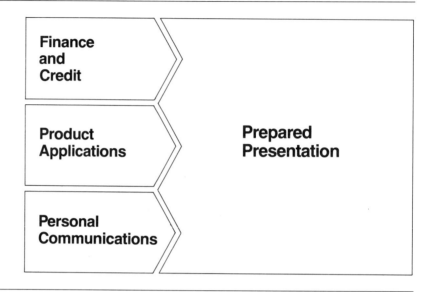

initial call may be research with no presentation attempted. It is primarily a time for listening and observing, not talking. If you have done your homework, you'll know what questions to ask. Even where problems and solutions are apparent, it may be prudent to wait until a second call to make a formal presentation supported with a written report for added professionalism.

As an expert on your products and their applications, you may find that the same use will fit the needs of many customers. Yet in your role of consultant you should approach each business as unique in some way. Seeking out product applications from this viewpoint will lead to better prepared presentations.

Personal considerations
This last area is tricky. All firms have two organizational structures: formal and informal. It is very possible that three people are involved in a mutually satisfactory sale: the person who authorized the purchase, the person who uses the product, and the person who evaluates its effectiveness. These may be the purchasing director, worker, and supervisor; or buyer, salesperson, and department manager. A fourth person may be involved as primary influencer or specifier. This person could be a consultant, designer, engineer, or forecaster.

Each organization is unique in its personnel and their relations to each other. Separate polls taken in 1974 and 1977 and reported in business magazines showed that a major problem for salespeople was the ability to determine the *primary decision maker*—the person who makes the final buying decision—for a given product. One reason for this is that communication channels in the **informal organization**—that which actually operates—are more powerful than the formal ones determined by title and rank. A company's organizational chart may be deceiving. In medium and large firms a preliminary call to develop a feel for the informal structure may be wise.

informal organization
a firm's "grapevine"; also relates to decision making—one must know who really makes the buying decision.

The last area relating to personnel concerns the habits and characteristics of the individual known to be the one primarily responsible for placing an order. Everyone has peculiarities, and attention to those details has a strong impact on closed sales. Knowing that a person dislikes smoking, for instance, may help make a sale. Your personal file can help you start a conversation on a topic of interest to the decision-maker. If done with sincerity, this move could get you the sale.

2. Collect some annual reports. Find out what standard ratios are normally used in their analysis. Make a comparison of the firms. What other information do they contain that is of value?

3. Prepare a listing of pet peeves or annoyances that would likely receive a negative reaction from a prospect.

The presentation plan

Although many presentations are extensions of the qualifying or probing activities, the presentation must be thought out in advance. A presentation *has content* and *uses techniques*. The content will be largely determined by the customer's priorities; it will be a **benefit-centered presentation**. Benefits are product advantages that are specific to the user. Those that are of medium and high interest should determine presentation content. Benefits that are of no interest to a specific prospect should be ignored. Thousands of sales have been lost when salespeople focus their presentation on benefits that are of no value to the prospect.

benefit-centered presentation
a presentation in which product features are translated into customer benefits—people do not want drill bits, they want holes.

Benefits should be presented in a specific order. Each presentation has unique qualities and no special formula will always be successful. The salesperson's perception of the value of the benefits may differ from the customer's perception. Any of the following three alternative models may be successful.

A successful sales presentation must be planned thoroughly. Attention must be given to the content of the presentation along with the psychological environment in which the presentation is delivered.

1. Start with the most beneficial and work down.
2. Start with the highest, go to ones of medium value, and conclude with high ones.
3. Begin with medium and work toward the highest.

All three of these models view the benefits from the customer's viewpoint, not the salesperson's.

Objectives

objective
a goal or stated result to be achieved; accompanied by means to achieve the goal.

The presentation plan must have an **objective,** that is, a goal to be reached. Often an individual presentation is part of a larger plan or sequence of objectives. The goal of one presentation may be to secure a trial order; of the next, to add a new product or seek a larger order. Salespeople often lose sight of objectives in dealing with established customers. An objective is necessary for *every* sales call.

The objective of each presentation will determine the content. Information that is not vital to attaining the goal should be discarded. Nonvital material only confuses and leads one away from the focus. With clear objectives, the salesperson can keep the discussion focused on the benefits.

Techniques

A presentation makes use of *techniques*. Bell Telephone presents some techniques in a brochure called "Phone Power" which lists particular words that sell. We've listed some of them in Table 7-1. The words used in a presentation are very important and deserve prior thought. Unfortunately, words are often chosen on the spot since each presentation is unique. How much more effective the delivery would be if at least half of a given presentation was carefully constructed of sentences designed to sell.

To analyze your techniques, try taping your presentation in a private practice session. Listen to yourself critically and write your comments.

Support materials

The presentation plan should also include drawing on available support materials and melding them into a smooth-flowing presentation. This takes advance planning, and for some it also takes practice in using the materials. More and more support tools are being developed to increase the efficiency of the salesforce. Salespeople tend to resist adopting these new tools. Keep in mind that not all items are practical or applicable. Good judgment is necessary in selecting the tools for a given presentation in order to increase productivity.

Chapters 9 and 10 deal with the final elements of the presentation: handling objections and closing sales. Both are vital ingredients of the presentation that deserve prior planning. Objections should be

scientific	safe	amusement	sociable	**Table 7-1.**
durable	popular	hospitality	stylish	**Power packed words**
clean	economical	youth	admired	
efficient	mother	hunting	in-the-swim	
time-saving	modern	status	royalty	
appetizing	health	enormous	beauty	
affectionate	quality	low-cost	personality	
value	elegance	genuine	independent	
fun	bargain	progress	successful	
ambition	sympathy	thinking	up-to-date	
love	necessary	excel	tested	
reputation	home	civic pride	expressive	
guaranteed	courtesy	patriotism	relief	
stimulating	growth	recommended	tasteful	

Source: Illinois Bell Telephone Co.

anticipated with prepared answers and closings should center on customer benefits.

The memorized presentation

Many have made light of the *"canned" presentation* — one that is thought out, written down, and memorized. The primary reason for the attitude is that the canned presentation has been used primarily by door-to-door salespeople whose training has been very poor. Almost all professional salespeople can make use of aspects of the canned presentation if it is viewed as flexible, not rigid. The key is the ability to pick those parts of a prepared presentation that relate to a given prospect and eliminate those that do not — and to change your presentation during delivery in response to customer comments. The total presentation, as prepared, covers all buyer benefits and uses more than one attempt to close.

By preparing a canned presentation you are forced to consciously think out all the components. You must select key words, evaluate selling support materials, and develop answers to objections. Memorize it with a thoroughness that permits you to select any given statement as it fits a situation and then deliver it smoothly. There should be no stuttering, stammering, or hesitation — leave your customers with the feeling that your words were thought out for them alone. For a more polished version of the canned presentation refer to the section on *sight sellers* in Chapter 14.

4.   Select a product and prepare a list of buyer benefits. Identify different types of buyers and list the benefits in order of importance for each group.

Planning support for your presentation

In this section we will discuss the incorporation of visual and other support tools of *sales aids* into your presentation plan. A graphic illustration of the steps you should complete is presented in Figure 7–3. Refer to the figure as you read this section.

Print

Almost every salesperson today uses print materials of some sort for support. At the retail level, for example, contracts, charge slips, and sales tax charts are nearly always used. Insurance salespeople have long used flip books; real estate uses legal forms. Others use brochures, catalogs, product sheets, and order forms. Developing a

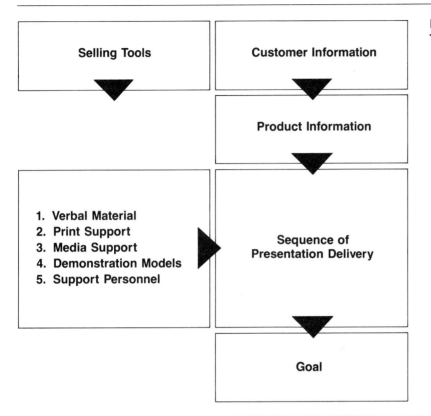

Figure 7–3.
The presentation plan

sound presentation requires becoming fully informed about the materials available so that appropriate items become a flowing part of any presentation. It also may mean developing a file of these materials for easy access. This file could include personal materials as well as case histories of satisfied customers.

The key to using print support materials in preparing a presentation is the proper selection of materials to do an efficient job. No salesperson would show up without an order book but many salespeople do try to sell without proper print support materials. Those who do have the materials probably have them all jumbled in a briefcase or tossed into the back seat or trunk, and they are not pre-sorted for a smooth presentation.

Just as key selling sentences are preplanned, so must be the use of print support materials. These materials are a primary part of the presentation, not an afterthought. The customer must not be kept waiting while you go to the car for files. The presentation should be focused on the customer. This takes preplanning.

Demonstrations

As more selling tools are developed and the range of sales activities expands, other presentation building activities must be rehearsed. Our society keeps on becoming more technical and the need for **product demonstrations** increases, for everything from computer terminals to electric wok cooking. Salespeople either make the demonstrations or train the demonstrators. It takes practice to produce a show that is flawless.

product demonstration
showing a product in use.

Media

The same is true of the wide and growing range of audiovisual sales support materials. Refer to Chapter 14 for more on hardware and current applications. While the most recent hardware emphasizes simplicity in operation, you'll still need to know about minor repairs and adjustments. Don't lose a sale just because the tape won't play. You'll also want to keep current on alternative *software*—that is, taped or filmed programs, that can be used.

There is always a danger that salespeople will rely too much on the media programs to sell for them and not spend enough time preparing their part of the presentation. But media selling has to be general in nature to be reproduced in quantity and sold at a reason-

Audiovisual equipment is becoming as common as the briefcase.

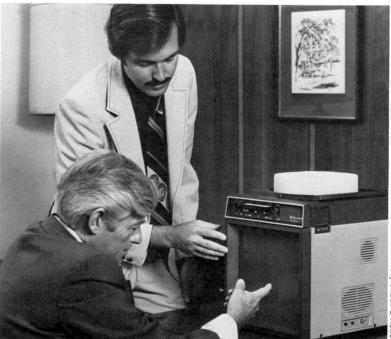

Courtesy of Bell & Howell

able cost. Your part of the presentation is specific and you must know what materials are available, how they can be adapted to given selling situations, and what their role is in personalizing the product to the needs of a specific customer.

Much of what has been said about media-based selling also applies to computer-based selling. Computer terminal devices, many portable which fit in a briefcase, have been expanding in numbers. Use of this equipment must also be practiced: it must be viewed as an integral part of the presentation. The danger here is that the remote terminal often is viewed as a futuristic toy instead of the selling support tool it is.

Your attention must always be focused on closing sales and servicing accounts. These items are the primary activities you will use to increase productivity and income.

5. Select either a consumer hard good or an industrial good. Prepare a list of materials you would like in your file as sales support. Note which you would expect your company to furnish and which you would obtain for yourself.

Obtaining the appointment

Getting an appointment with a busy customer may prove to be as tough a selling job as you will ever encounter. Obstacles that are placed in your path take the form of secretaries, full schedules, and resistance to change. You should master techniques to meet all types of obstacles that stand between you and your prospect.

Getting a foot in the door

With the exceptions of door-to-door cold canvas and in-store retail selling, salespeople make sales by appointment with customers who fall into three general categories: existing accounts, prior accounts that have been lost, and prospects. All of these account types must be called upon if the salesperson is to succeed, but the emphasis will differ significantly with the type of selling. Real estate, for instance, has a very high customer turnover; prospecting is of major importance. On the other hand, hardware wholesalers would be primarily concerned with existing accounts.

Selling to existing accounts is primarily a matter of knowing their habits and your requirements. The first consideration is time. From the standpoint of their habits, you should know what time of day and day of the week it is best to make a call, as well as how much time each account is willing to spend on each call. Your time requirement would include how often the account needs some personal attention. A frequent mistake is to allot too much time to very small accounts and too little time to major profit producers. With these determinations, a regular call pattern can be mutually agreed upon, the next appointment can be placed on the calendar regularly at the end of each sales call. This may require selling skill so your perception of how frequently the call should be made matches the prospect's.

Gaining appointments with old customers differs from calling on new prospects. One problem with new accounts is finding out who to make an appointment with, although with high turnover in some firms this may be equally true of old accounts. As shown in Chapter 6, this problem ranks high with salespeople. There are no simple solutions. Successful salespeople may make a preliminary data-gathering call; the purpose is to seek out the right person, the right time, and other information necessary to make a professional presentation later.

Other tools used to sell appointments are direct mail and telephone. Direct mail, especially useful for preliminary selling before a formal presentation is made, can accomplish much. Part of Chapter 12 is devoted to the use of this valuable tool. Direct mail can be used effectively with existing accounts by sending reminder cards a few days before the scheduled appointment.

Perhaps a more valuable tool in getting appointments is the telephone. The Bell System has a package of materials aimed at securing appointments by telephone. They also will offer a seminar on the topic if they feel the results will be mutually profitable. Chapter 12 of this book, which covers the use of the telephone as a sales tool, includes techniques for selling the appointment.

Overcoming obstacles

underling barrier
lower level personnel who can block access to the buying decision maker.

One major problem in seeking appointments with the right person is the existence of **underling barriers.** Most often these barriers are secretaries and receptionists who can block access to the actual buyer; first-level managers may also be barriers. Their job is to help their boss perform effectively and the salesperson who can convince these people that his or her products or services can achieve that end will have a helper—not a barrier. They will also be more helpful about letting you reach the boss by telephone.

It requires just as much selling skill to obtain the appointment as it does to make formal product presentations. Obviously the more friendly these people are with your competition, the more difficult this task will be. Inevitably you will find some who use their position to require gifts or favors before admitting the salesperson to make the presentation. Each of these situations has unique aspects. As with the sales presentation, preliminary planning is necessary.

6.   Assume you are selling fire extinguishers that can be used by all businesses and are cold-canvasing an industrial park. What techniques could you use to get to see a person with authority to buy?

7.   You have an appointment to see a prospective buyer but a receptionist claims he has instructions to admit no one this particular morning. How would you handle the situation?

Mini-case

Jenny recently took a selling job for a local free-circulation advertiser. She graduated last spring from the local community college, where she took a course in advertising. Her work in copywriting and layout received high marks.

In her new job she was given some accounts to service and told to develop new business. She quickly found that there was a lot of competition, especially from the Yellow Pages, four local weekly newspapers, four radio stations, a local TV program listing, and a daily newspaper. In addition, people were selling advertising specialities, space in both the college and high school newspapers, and time on the college radio station. Churches, clubs, and organizations also were after promotional dollars from these local firms.

To develop new accounts Jenny spent a great amount of time preparing a portfolio of statistics and support materials to show the cost effectiveness of using her publication. Her boss was impressed with its professional look.

However, in calling on new accounts she found very few had formal advertising budgets. Most bought only when they thought someone was offering a "good deal." Few were interested in going over her portfolio.

Question: Was preparing the portfolio a mistake? Why? What would you have done differently?

**Define these
key concepts**

benefit-centered presentation
formal organization
objective
presentation plan
product demonstration
sales aid
underling barrier

canned presentation
informal organization
power-packed words
presentation support
probing
trade publication

8 Delivering the presentation

Key terms

approach
buyer conditioning
listening
knowledge gap
feedback
nonverbal
  communication
personal space
spatial object
showmanship

Overview

The presentation may be considered your "moment of truth." The first few critical minutes may determine whether the sale will be closed or not. There are many variables to be controlled, including word selection, body language, environment, and the use of sales support materials. The skillful salesperson blends these variables into a unique presentation that will sell benefits to meet a customer's needs.

Opening the presentation

When a salesperson and a prospective customer first meet, several things happen before any words are exchanged. Prior to the meeting the salesperson who is calling on the customer has given some conscious thought to preparing the presentation. A customer who has called or agreed to meet the salesperson also has given some prior thought to what is desired of the product.

At the meeting, both the salesperson and the customer are aware of the environment, even though awareness may be subconscious. The salesperson observes a neat or messy desk, personal items on display, arrangement of furniture, and other factors, and sees these elements as clues to the person being visited. The salesperson also makes judgments concerning the appearance of the buyer: dress, manners, posture, hair styles, even body size and type will have an effect on attitudes.

As we saw in Chapter 6, if some of these clues are misleading they result in wrong judgments and wrong presentations. The first few minutes of any presentation should be viewed as an **approach** in which the tone of the presentation is set. One author refers to this period as one of **buyer conditioning**—making the buyer comfortable, building confidence in the salesperson, and getting the buyer ready to place an order.

approach
how a salesperson opens a sales presentation.

buyer conditioning
using the first minutes of a presentation to develop a friendly, comfortable relationship with the customer.

How a presentation is opened is determined in part by the salesperson's objective(s). Objectives for the call might be to increase order size, to secure a trial order, to collect part of a past-due bill, to reclaim a former account, to stop a delivery cancellation, or to settle a claim for defective merchandise. The buyer conditioning approach will be based on the objective. If, for instance, the object is to secure a trial order, the salesperson will want to convince the buyer of the quality of the product offered and, in addition, stress that the product can be returned if it does not meet the buyer's needs.

Common fallacies

There are several common fallacies (incorrect ideas) about the opening of a presentation at both the retail and industrial levels. At the retail level many clerks are insensitive to a potential customer's stage in the buying process. The standard "May I help you?" approach is acceptable for customers who exhibit interest in specific merchandise or are obviously seeking assistance. For customers who show neither interest nor desire, however, openings that create interest by providing information are more suitable. "Have you seen our sale items?" might create interest. A presentation cannot be

listening
a learned skill; being
aware of both the spoken
word and voice pattern.

made until a customer's needs are known. The opening must encourage the customer to talk. **Listening** becomes a key part of the salesperson's retail presentation.

Clerks at the retail level also usually operate without knowing the names of regular customers, but the ability to remember names is important because it makes the customer feel important. As our world grows more impersonal, especially in metropolitan areas, an opening that includes calling someone by name will maintain steady customers.

In the commercial and industrial sector most calls are made after some planning. The majority of calls are made on regular accounts in contrast to the high turnover in the retail and some service sectors. Surveys show that purchasing agents prefer salespeople to get down to business, with little time spent on pleasantries. Buyers know the person is there to sell and that time is valuable to both. A buyer who keeps an appointment is ready to give the salesperson full attention.

Successful openings

Begin the presentation with interest-generating remarks, preferably offering a *benefit*. For instance, the benefit may be lower costs, better profits, or both (they are not the same). Often profits can be increased by increasing costs if the resulting income increases faster. As with all selling, developing a friendly environment is crucial during the opening.

The successful opening of a sale requires that the customer *develop confidence* in the salesperson. Remember that customers' personalities will vary along the dominant-submissive scale. The salesperson should always control the content and direction of the presentation to fit the customer's dominant or submissive role. This control can be achieved even when you are in an apparently submissive role, as discussed in a previous chapter. Confidence can also be built by exhibiting a sound knowledge of the products, market trends, and customer needs. The first few minutes of the presentation are crucial. It is a time for gaining attention and generating interest.

1.　**Shop at several retail stores. Record each salesperson's actions that showed good and bad ways to open a presentation. Draw up a list of each.**

2.　**Interview two or three salespeople whose selling involves little repeat business. What procedures do they use in opening presentations with new prospects? Report.**

Communicating successfully

You can communicate successfully with your customers only if you work from their *frame of reference,* that is, their experience, interests, and knowledge. In dealing with a **knowledge gap,** where customers have no knowledge about what you are selling, serious problems are encountered. The less knowledge they have, the greater the communication problems will be. A significant amount of selling effort today is aimed toward discovering a customer's frame of reference.

knowledge gap
the difference between a salesperson's knowledge of a product and what the customer knows about the product.

Education

If a customer does not know about a good or service, the first part of the presentation will be primarily educational. For example, a life insurance salesperson calling on a young couple should explain differences in life insurance policies such as term, whole life, 20-pay life, and annuity. Many people purchase the wrong insurance for their needs because the salesperson has failed to take this step. Selling may take place, but it is not professional by our standards.

Take care not to provide this education in too large a dose. Too much information can simply overwhelm people and they will retreat. Many salespeople use a system of selling-by-objectives. They plan a series of sales calls leading to a buying decision. Each presentation is a *building block* leading toward a successful close.

Terminology

Another communication problem is presented by *terminology* — words used in a special way in some job field. Most well prepared salespeople are familiar with the terminology of their specific industry and each industry has its own language. Customers may not be familiar with such terminology and you can weaken your presentation if you do not explain unfamiliar words. If your conversation is way over their heads they feel uncomfortable and uncertain. The customer needs to feel important and believe that his or her buying decision is intelligent.

Choose words that are clear to the customer. This means you may need to select a different vocabulary for different customers. Selling points must be introduced in an ordered sequence with proper **feedback,** answers that ensure the customer understands each point. An effective technique often used is to ask the customer for agreement that each benefit is of value before proceeding to the next. For this reason many authorities now advocate the *"canned"* or *memorized* presentation or the use of flip charts or books. All require

feedback
information received from a customer that indicates how he or she has received your message.

careful word selection, with the message put on a level simple enough for any prospective buyer to understand. Good communication cannot take place unless the message has the same meaning for sender and receiver.

Choosing emotional or rational appeals

In delivering the presentation, some choice must be made as to whether to use more rational or emotional *appeals*. It is a very rare presentation that will not have both types. Practice and experience are the best teachers. It is important that your appeals are aimed at the customer's needs, keeping in mind that these needs change constantly. During the oil and gas shortage in the winter of 1976-77 great emphasis was put on the economy of a very well-insulated house. The public responded. A similar appeal, made earlier when the public believed oil and gas to be plentiful and inexpensive, fell on deaf ears. The affluence of the American people has made many emotional appeals, such as being the first on the block to have a certain product, are much more productive in selling than rational appeals such as economy.

Certain product lines or benefits also lend themselves to emotional appeals. The goal of having the latest computer, largest machine, latest fashion in clothing, or other outstanding possession is common to every type of selling. A given product benefit can often be sold with more than one appeal. For example, a product that produces economy for a firm can increase its profits, and increased profits are a source of pride for the managers involved. Success in one's profession is an emotional appeal.

The importance of feedback

Communication is a two-way street. The salesperson must constantly monitor the feedback to his or her words and actions. The skill of listening is often lacking in salespeople who go charging through their planned presentation. Two parts of the customer's response have to be monitored. One part is *verbal*—the words themselves and the meaning they are trying to convey. A more important part may be *nonverbal communication*—the qualities of voice, posture, and gestures that indicate emotions not being expressed in words.

nonverbal communication
sending a message by clues such as posture, gestures, and eyes, rather than by the spoken word.

Voice clues

A voice that is even and pleasant signifies a calm state. A voice that varies in loudness is often expressing fear or anger. The voice also

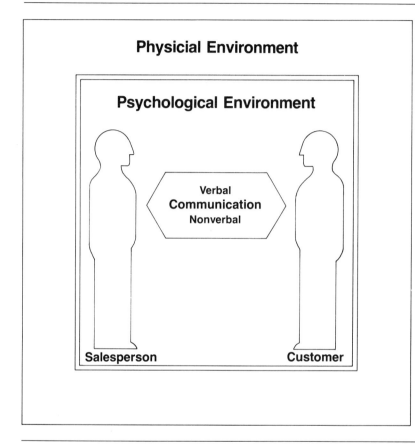

**Figure 8-1.
Dimensions of
communication**

varies in pitch or tone. No variation in pitch (a monotone) in the customer's voice may indicate that the customer is bored, disgusted, or perhaps fearful of the situation. These are bad signs that require an immediate change of direction in the presentation. The benefits being offered are not appealing to the customer's needs. Downward pitch can indicate boredom or sadness. Upward pitch at the end of a sentence is common when a person expresses fear or anger; it may also express surprise. In either case, the salesperson should respond to the clue as well as to the words spoken.

The last aspect of vocal feedback is the tempo or pace of the conversation. While this varies with personalities to some degree, a slow tempo probably indicates a methodical person. A rapid-fire presentation to these customers would be a very poor tactic because the sales message would conflict with the customer's manner. A fast tempo indicates interest and desire, something salespeople like to hear, but also may indicate anger. The salesperson must determine which clue is being given in order to respond correctly.

A salesperson can control a presentation to some degree by controlling the loudness, pitch, and tempo of the voice. By slowly building the tempo of the presentation towards the close, you can produce a psychological reaction and create excitement. By being sensitive to the voice patterns of the customer you will find clues about his or her current mental attitudes or "set." Often *what* is said is less important than *how* it is said. Notice the difference in voice patterns just before and just after you close your next sale. You'll get the message.

Body Language

The second part of nonverbal feedback in communication has been identified by psychologists as *body language*. Many books have been written on the subject, and at least one such book should be required reading for all professional salespeople. In this section we will cover only the highlights of one recent book on the subject, *Body Politics* by Nancy Henley (Prentice-Hall, 1977). Areas to watch include the eyes, facial expressions, gestures, posture, and the distance maintained between the participants. Refer to Figure 8–2 as you read this section.

Eyes are the most expressive part of the body and often reveal feelings not expressed in words. Yet one aspect of making a presentation that many salespeople find difficult is making and maintaining eye contact—"looking someone in the eye." The eyes may betray those who lack knowledge they should have, those who are trying to sell something they do not believe in, and those who just plain lack confidence in themselves and their abilities.

The eyes also reveal the customer's true feelings—feelings that can be positive, negative, or neutral. Positive feedback expresses approval or some level of intimacy. Applied to selling, agreement on given points can simply be shown with the eyes. *No* words are needed. Negative feelings are often expressed with hostile or angry eyes. A customer who looks everywhere but at you may disbelieve you, may not have authority to make a decision or may be bored. Whatever the reason, you must try to respond to this nonverbal communication.

Eye contact should not be maintained for very long periods, but rather with occasional glances. Prolonged eye contact makes most people uncomfortable in selling situations. Staring almost always produces a negative reaction. By avoiding prolonged eye contact one can make customers comfortable and more likely to buy.

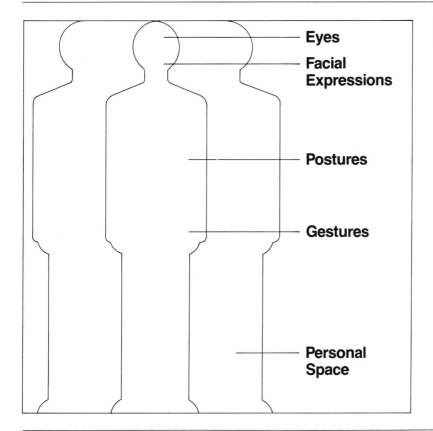

Figure 8-2.
Body language feedback

Facial expressions are almost as important as the eyes. Movement of the eyelid, eyebrow, and mouth are particularly important, as is the speed of the movement. Smiling is an obvious expression of pleasure, but the frown may indicate either displeasure or lack of understanding. These are valuable feedback signs in the communication process, although some people can exercise great control over their facial expressions to conceal their true feelings and hinder good feedback.

Gestures are also communicators but must be viewed within the context of the conversation. Most gestures support vocal communications to give emphasis to the intensity of feelings. Slapping a desk hard while saying no is quite final. Rubbing the palms together after a contract is signed would show pleasure. We all know people who would find it difficult to talk if their hands were tied behind their back.

Most gestures given without verbal communications serve to release tension. A shrug of the shoulder, turning palms up or down, and similar motions can be viewed as relaxers. Attention should be paid to the speed of the gesture as well. Usually there is a correlation between the speed and the intensity of the feeling being expressed. When someone becomes very excited the gestures are fairly rapid. As one approaches a close, these would be positive signs that the customer is ready to buy.

Posture also communicates both the salesperson's and the customer's feelings. Posture actions that normally would be positive in a selling situation are:

Leaning forward
Touching the arm or hand
Moving within eighteen inches
Facing another directly
Using a direct gaze.

On the other hand, depending on the context, these actions may be negative:

Leaning backward
Hands relaxed, arms hanging
Asymmetrical arm or leg positions
Not facing another directly.

Folded arms, for example, would indicate a closed mind; open arms with slow gestures, an open mind.

Posture also includes the *trunk* or torso, which conveys some important signs. An affected or artificial bearing usually indicates some inner conflict the customer may be unwilling to discuss. A drooping posture would indicate discouragement or helplessness—a posture often shown by people who have already shopped

Body position can indicate a person's attitude. In this photo, the woman has her arms folded indicating a closed mind. What other body language cues are given?

Personal space is a
culturally determined
concept. In this photo
proper personal space is
maintained. What other
clues are given?

at several stores without finding the item they seek. A salesperson who can help them will notice the postural change immediately. People with a very stiff, military-like bearing consider themselves or the activity they are doing important. Selling to these people obviously would take an approach different from the one used with the droopy person. "Reading" a customer's posture will give very important clues to word choice, one's own posture, and whether to take a dominant or submissive role in the exchange.

The *angle of communication* is another aspect of body language which also will affect results. Standing or sitting in a face-to-face position tends to lead to more confrontation than other angles. Most Americans prefer to put their bodies at a slight angle to the person they are talking to, and then they turn their heads to see each other. Moving to a side-by-side position is more intimate but makes many persons uncomfortable when the space is closer than eighteen inches.

Personal space, the last area of body language, concerns distance between people and how much space one needs to feel comfortable. A salesperson who moves too close to the customer can violate that person's personal space, provoking hostile feelings. Personal space in this country is defined as within touching distance, anywhere from eighteen inches to four feet. Closer than eighteen inches is considered *intimate space;* within this distance people frequently touch. If this makes the customer feel uncomfortable it will detract from the presentation.

Within the personal space distance of eighteen inches to four feet, selling is found to be effective. The participants experience closeness but not intimacy. From four feet out to seven feet—out of touching range—the conversation becomes more casual. Many

personal space
*the distance a person
wishes to keep between
self and another.*

The desk can be consciously used as a spatial barrier. If you are to communicate effectively, this barrier must be overcome.

spatial object
a desk, chair, counter, or other item used to control the distance between two people.

buyers, especially when the salesperson makes the call, use **spatial objects**—physical barriers—to keep the seller more than four feet away. A desk or counter is a dividing line between personal territories and can impede a presentation.

Tactics for closing the personal distance are available to every salesperson. Spatial objects, such as chairs, can be moved to the side of rather than in front of a desk. Similarly the retail salesperson can move around the counter to stand next to the customer. A salesperson should always be sensitive to this distance and should control it as much as the customer will permit.

In international trade, millions of dollars of lost sales have resulted from lack of understanding of cultural attitudes toward personal space. Italians, who like to conduct business at an intimate closeness, become annoyed at Americans who keep backing away to keep their own acceptable distance. The resulting feeling of rejection has doomed what otherwise could have been very attractive deals for both. If you are not sensitive to other people's personal space, it will cost you sales, too.

3. Prepare two "scripts" for selling a relatively new product. Word them carefully. Prepare one for prospects familiar with your technical language. Do another using simple language for those with little knowledge in the field. Will both sell?

4. Closely observe the body language of both men and women talking to friends of the same and opposite sex. How is personal and intimate space different in each situation? Is there any difference in the amount of touching?

Maintaining interest and desire

Building interest in the product in the first few minutes is a key factor of your presentation. Interest can be developed by **showmanship,** or adding drama to a presentation. The jeweler does not toss a watch or a ring on the counter carelessly. Props such as a piece of black velvet and gestures that are slow, even caressing, can build both interest and value. These devices focus attention on the hands and on the object. All of this is showmanship.

showmanship
adding drama or flair to a presentation.

People will develop an interest when the salesperson shows interest. Like a genuine smile, it is contagious. When the product line changes regularly, as in women's fashions, enthusiasm is not that difficult to generate. For the majority of salespeople, however, exciting new items do not come along very often, and this can make selling a drudgery.

Many men have made a fortune by learning how to generate and maintain interest. W. Clement Stone and his "Positive Mental Attitude (PMA)," Norman Vincent Peale's *The Power of Positive Thinking,* and Dale Carnegie's many courses are well-known examples.

Other authors of books and movies offer advice on building and maintaining motivation. The Dartnell Corporation (Chicago) has a movie called *Take Command.* Dr. Eden Ryl, a psychologist, produced and starred in a movie called *Pack Your Own Chute.* Robert Ringer, a successful real estate salesman, shares his secrets in a book called *Looking Out For #1* (Funk and Wagnalls, 1977). Workshops and seminars abound both on and off campuses for assertiveness training, transactional analysis, the art of negotiating successfully, and encounter groups. No matter how you title it, the generation of interest in your product, in your company, in you as a person must come from within.

Asking the right questions

One simple way to generate interest is questioning—asking questions that make communication two-way (See Figure 8–3). Direct questions asking for specific information are vital: "How many cartons do you use each month?" To encourage the customer to give more than brief, simple answers, questions of this sort can be more *open-ended,* that is, requiring an explanation or longer than a sim-

**Figure 8-3.
Generating verbal
feedback**

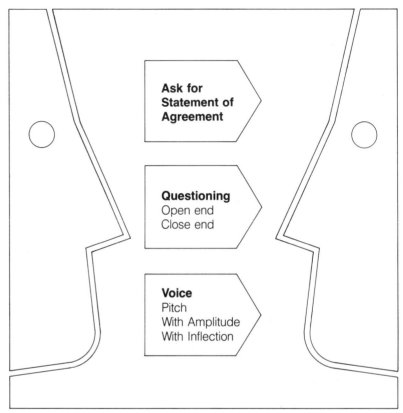

Ask for
Statement of
Agreement

Questioning
Open end
Close end

Voice
Pitch
With Amplitude
With Inflection

Listening is a skill to be developed with practice.

ple one- or two-word reply. "Would you tell me how many boxes you are using a month now and how you think your needs will change over the next year?" is an example of an open-ended question.

Questions may deal with attitude and opinion to generate interest. They function primarily to develop clues to appropriate appeals. Since people hold opinions and attitudes at different levels of intensity, the sales person must make sure they relate to the presentation. Certain social and political issues, for example, can take away valuable selling time and also generate conflict.

A customer's level of interest can be gauged by asking questions that will confirm their agreement with the stated benefits. Noncommittal or negative answers are good indications that things are not going well. Other questions may actually be feedback to the customer, showing that you do understand the benefits a customer seeks. A real estate salesperson may ask "Am I right that the land must be large enough for later expansion of the plant?" to show understanding of the customer's needs.

A widely used questioning technique that will maintain customer interest is the *forced choice* or paired choice question. The question contains two, and only two, alternatives requiring the customer to choose one: "Do you prefer the red or the green pattern?" Such questions require the customer to think positively about buying. A similar challenge, tactfully used, can identify and remove a barrier to buying. A statement as, "Can you pay all at once or do you prefer monthly payments?" will cause many customers to reach for a pen to sign the order blank in answer.

Silence is uncomfortable. A simple "Yes?" with an inquiring facial expression normally will cause the customer to respond. People also can be stimulated to respond by stating a benefit in the form of a question. "These products carry a 45 percent markup. Is that in line with your pricing policy?"

Support for your claims

During a presentation, claims of the benefits must be supported. This is most effective if they can be dramatized in some way. Holding a match to a fabric treated with flame retardant is effective. Retailers use a patch of carpet and powder to show that a vacuum cleaner will pick up dirt. Models, cutaways, clear plastic panels, and other devices are often employed to show benefits to the customer.

Claims of benefits to be received are more believable when they are seen than when heard. For this reason some form of sales aid should be incorporated into presentations whenever possible. Intangible benefits can be put into print as testimonial letters, for example. In making any inventory of the benefits customers will receive from a given product, serious thought should be given to how that claim will be presented in a presentation. Make it visual as well as oral.

Words that create desire

There are several ways to create a desire to purchase. The best way is to use power words. Certain words are more powerful than others. These words fall into two categories. The first—words that create mental pictures—are primarily adjectives, mild and gentle to describe a soap product, bold and daring to describe a men's cologne. They provide a frame of reference that enables the customer either to picture an object or to put himself or herself into a scene.

The second category of words used to create desire are more dramatic; they are carefully chosen verbs. *Chopping* is a much stronger word than *cutting* because it implies a hard and fast stroke.

For example, "Buy today and I'll chop off 5 percent; this is the last day of the sale!" Use of such action words stimulates the desire to purchase (See Figure 7–4).

Controlling distraction

The environment of the presentation should be controlled. Your primary aim will be to control distractions. Often in the selling of cars, real estate, loans and furniture the last part of the presentation takes place in what is commonly called a *closing room*. Even though they may have large windows to make them look airy, customers are seated so that their backs are to the window. This forces their attention on the presentation.

Many salespeople take their customers to coffee, lunch, or the golf course. In retail stores a quiet corner away from the main traffic flow can serve the same function. Where customers have a wide range of merchandise to select from, the choice should be narrowed quickly. Those not chosen should be hidden from view if possible. Salespeople calling on company buyers or purchasing agents find that co-workers interrupt frequently. Asking the buyer to move to a lunch or conference room is one way to control the distractions. Some of this control is the responsibility of the salesperson.

5.   Using the aid of a reference librarian, compile a list of power words that can be used in developing a presentation.

6.   Within the selling area you have chosen, develop a series of tactics designed to keep the customer involved with the presentation. Include items that require both oral and physical responses.

Mini-case

Jim has been selling for only two months. His firm has long sold a variety of physical education and recreation equipment to schools, colleges, park districts, day care centers, and health spas. Jim was hired to sell a relatively new concept—conditioning rooms for top business executives.

Evidence shows that regular exercise reduces heart attacks and improves work performance. Many firms face serious trouble each year when a top executive is lost to a heart attack. Often the executive is a key management member and replacement of the individual is costly. Also, during the time it takes to find a replacement daily activities may suffer.

Jim feels his best prospects are those who have high blood pressure. He carries a unit to test the blood pressure but finds that many of the people he calls on decline the offer of a free test for the key executives.

Question: Develop some dynamic phrases or sentences for Jim
designed to get prospective buyers to agree to the test.
   Would Jim be better off using a "fun" appeal rather than a "fear"
appeal? Why?

**Define these
key concepts**

approach
body language
buyer conditioning
feedback
forced-choice questions
knowledge gap
listening
nonverbal communication

open-end questions
personal space
power words
showmanship
spatial object
terminology
voice clues

9 Handling objections

Key terms

objections
win-win
distribution
cooperative advertising
direct denial
nonverbal objection
valid objection

Overview

Handling objections is an integral part of the selling process. Objections should be expected and even welcomed, since they provide clues to customer's needs. You will encounter many different kinds of objections to buying. Through advance preparation you can anticipate them and find ways of dealing with each one. Some objections that are expressed by customers may seem somewhat easier to deal with than their real objections, which they may conceal. Objections that are valid reasons for not buying require a different approach.

Meeting resistance

While all people have a need for new experiences and adventures, resistance to change is natural. Change must be slow. There is a strong need for continuity in people's lives, and radical changes make them uncomfortable. Some people are upset if their routine activities are changed for only one day, and they grumble about it for many days afterward.

Since technology creates products that require people to make some changes, **objections** to buying new products will surely be raised. People prefer to cling to the familiar and comfortable rather than chance the unknown. Old products that have been used with satisfaction are like Linus's security blanket. Very powerful motivators are needed to replace the blanket, and even then it may be only stored—not thrown away.

Objections are reasons given for not making a purchase. Some objections center on negative feelings people have about sales-people. Rude, inept, pushy, and callous salespeople do make a lasting impression, and many articles in trade publications cry for the profession to improve its image. Surveys continue to show that the selling profession is held in low esteem. This in itself will create objections to buying that only you can overcome by displaying pro-fessional selling skills.

A key factor in dealing with objections is the salesperson's at-titude. It takes skill to disagree without being disagreeable. Friction must be minimized and confrontation avoided. Sales cannot be closed in a hostile environment. The magnitude of any one objection can be reduced simply by maintaining a friendly atmosphere. The attitude of the salesperson sets this tone but the voice and body language discussed in Chapter 8 are important factors in conveying a friendly attitude to the customer.

Converting the objectioner to a customer

A successful sale is a **win-win** situation—one in which neither the buyer nor the seller loses. Objections are indicators that a win-win position has not been attained. Yet successful selling requires the customer to agree with the salesperson's point of view, not vice versa. Where the customer's objections are strong, it takes diplo-macy to get him or her to agree to another point of view and save face at the same time. Agreeing with the customer's objections where they have some merit will help develop common ground and good two-way communication. Many objections arise from misun-derstanding a viewpoint where actually there is agreement. Merely

objections
a buyer's reasons for not making a purchase.

win-win
a situation in which both the buyer and seller receive satisfaction from a completed transaction.

"I don't know who you are.
I don't know your company.
I don't know your company's product.
I don't know what your company stands for.
I don't know your company's customers.
I don't know your company's record.
I don't know your company's reputation.
Now—what was it you wanted to sell me?"

MORAL: Sales start **before** your salesman calls—with business publication advertising.

McGRAW-HILL MAGAZINES
BUSINESS • PROFESSIONAL • TECHNICAL

rewording the objection in a positive manner to illustrate the agreement is part of the development of a win-win sale. "You don't like green? What color do you prefer?" is an example of this approach.

1. Make a list of visual and verbal mannerisms by salespeople that you have found objectionable. Opposite each item list an action you can make to project a positive attitude.

2. What long-standing habits do you have? How do they provide barriers to your decision to make a purchase?

Two sources of objections

The most familiar source of objections to a purchase is, obviously, the customer. The customer lines up a number of reasons, which may or may not be valid, for not making the purchase. We shall review some of these reasons in the next section. Before doing that, however, let's take a look at an unexpected source of objections— the salesperson.

Objections created by salespeople

Of the objections created by salespeople themselves, a major one involves your control of the environment, which we've discussed in another chapter. It is easy to create a hostile environment unknowingly. For example, an aggressive presentation is threatening to a shy and quiet person. As a means of escape, the shy person will grab at any objection, whether real and valid or not, to cut the presentation short. In this situation objections are difficult if not impossible to overcome, since the customer now is deaf to your rational arguments.

Another common salesperson-created objection occurs when the customer has no real need for the product. This condition reflects inadequate prospecting and poor qualifying activities. It can happen even when the customer with known needs seeks out the salesperson but your company cannot meet those needs. These objections may very well be valid ones for not buying. Parting as friends without making a sale also involves good selling tactics.

Salespeople also create objections by failing to identify the real needs. They wrongly assume that a product will fill a need even though another good or service they are also selling would be more suitable. Despite customer objections, the salesperson continues to try to sell the wrong product. This situation, all too common in selling, is very frustrating for the potential buyer.

Objections created by customers

There is a natural frustration on the part of all people with almost unlimited wants and needs but with limited buying power. In order to buy any item sold by professional salespeople, the buyer must forgo countless other—perhaps equally attractive—purchases. Objections are often raised to delay the choice.

Lack of information is another source of objections. Most customers are less informed about a given good or service than the salesperson is. As we have mentioned, a significant part of selling is educational, yet people do not like to appear ignorant. They prevent this possibility by raising objections even before they listen to a presentation. This applies as much to the know-it-all as it does those who are quite insecure.

Some people are stubborn and reluctant to agree to anything. They have developed the habit of playing the "devil's advocate" when dealing with a salesperson. Believing they are cunning, they focus on trying to find any possible rebuttal, however farfetched. They pursue an offensive position and try to keep the salesperson in a defensive posture at all times. Even where factual data is presented they will try to discredit the source or raise other objections to accepting the information.

Customers will also create objections as a test of knowledge to see if salespeople really know what they are talking about. Objections such as these are commonly used by professional buyers when dealing with a salesperson for the first time. Often their technical sophistication is equal or superior to that of the salesperson. They want to buy from people who have done their homework. These objections usually have nothing to do with the product or the company but serve to reveal more about the person from whom they may be buying.

Customer objections more difficult to deal with include prejudice, which goes beyond sex and race.

Hair styles, manner of dressing, and personal mannerisms all affect people's feelings about other people. Many of these objections will not be voiced directly but other objections will be created to cover the real feelings.

Customers, like all people, have fears. They fear the product will not perform to their expectations; this will indicate a bad decision on their part. Remember the discussion about cognitive dissonance? The larger the value or the greater the social significance of the purchase, the greater will be the objection to purchasing.

Objections are excellent clues as to which product benefits are really important. They are beneficial to the salesperson in guiding the direction of the presentation. *Welcome them.*

3. Prepare a plan for dealing with objections you would expect from a know-it-all type of customer. How would you convert that person to a loyal customer?

Six types of objections

Although different methods have been used to classify objections, most will be concerned with only six areas. They may be objections to the *product*, to the *company*, to the *distribution*, or to the *promotion*. They may be *financial* or they may be *personal* objections.

Product objections

Objections to the product itself may be both rational and emotional. Rational factors are concerned with the quality of the product, functional design, color, packaging, and ease of maintenance or the suitability and reliability of a service. One survey showed that almost one-third of all new consumer products are rejected by retailers because their packaging does not fit existing display fixtures, and the seller did not provide alternative ways to display the products.

The key question is whether the product or service will perform as presented. Will the advertising campaign double the number of people asking for the product, as claimed? Will the insurance company pay claims fast and for the full amount without legal problems? Will a two-day consultant's workshop on closing sales actually achieve any substantial change? Objections to the product should be anticipated.

Company objections

Objections to the company may include images or policies and procedures. Let's look at the firm's image with customers. Salespeople will face resistance if their firm is unknown to the buyer, or if it has no image. Firms from time to time may be reviewed critically in local papers, on television and radio, as well as in trade publications. A government investigation into a firm's sales practices, even when the firm is cleared of all charges, will provide an opportunity for buyers to raise objections based on image.

Given a choice, people prefer to associate with or buy from winners, not losers. They are impressed by size, longevity, and performance record. Relatively few salespeople work for firms with an AAA credit rating and long records of outstanding performance, and who regularly receive trade publication recognition for innovations. Therefore attention should be given to a firm's weak spots. New businesses in particular will face serious objections based on image. Extra effort on the salesperson's part to build confidence can overcome image problems.

Other objections concern the company's policies and procedures. Some examples might be a minimum-order level in commercial and industrial selling or a minimum purchase amount for charge accounts in retailing. Some commercial firms refuse to sell to the general public and some retail firms refuse to give discounts to other retailers, commercial, and industrial firms. Policies of added charges by many retailers as a response to increasing numbers of bad checks have been greeted negatively by the general public.

Most firms have some credit policies that elicit objections from some customers. Salespeople new to a firm should be told the basis of these policies during their orientation although relatively few firms do this. Where there is a logical and rational explanation for the policy the objection can be overcome easily. It would be wrong to assume, however, that all company policies are logical and rational. Management makes mistakes, too.

Distribution objections

A firm's distribution of products is another area where objections are raised. **Distribution** includes all of a firm's methods of selling and delivering physical goods as well as services. These objections apply as much to services as they do to goods, and may include length of delivery time, number of selling outlets, or similar policies.

distribution includes transportation, storage, materials, handling, and inventory control of physical goods.

The number of locations operated by a savings and loan, bank, or small loan company, for example, will affect their ability to serve the public. Customers who feel competing firms offer more convenience will raise valid objections.

The number and location of distribution centers operated by manufacturers and wholesalers have a bearing on their sales as well. A firm without its own fleet of trucks must rely on private or common carriers, whose level of service may not meet a customer's expectations or requirements.

Most firms dealing with goods know the importance of inventory controls to distribution. An inadequate stock level, an unrealistic reorder point, slow order processing and delivery time, high storage and handling costs, and other factors can develop into objections to buying. It is true that many firms have become successful not because of the "right" product, but because they offer their product at the right time, at the right place, and in the right quantity.

Sales promotion objections

A firm's promotional activities—advertising and sales promotion—can also produce objections. At the retail level where we have seen many cases of false and misleading advertising, the sales force has to take the brunt of this heat. Fraudulent bait-and-switch advertising, using obviously inferior products or even items not in stock, is a commonly used tactic.

Other problems develop through error. Perhaps the customer has not read the advertisement carefully or merchandise not in stock has been advertised. Typesetters sometimes make mistakes with prices; artists with illustrations. In recent years most firms have adopted fairly liberal policies regarding these mistakes in order to ease the salespeople's burden and to win and maintain steady customers.

Wholesalers and retailers may resist buying a product for resale if they do not feel a manufacturer plans enough advertising support.

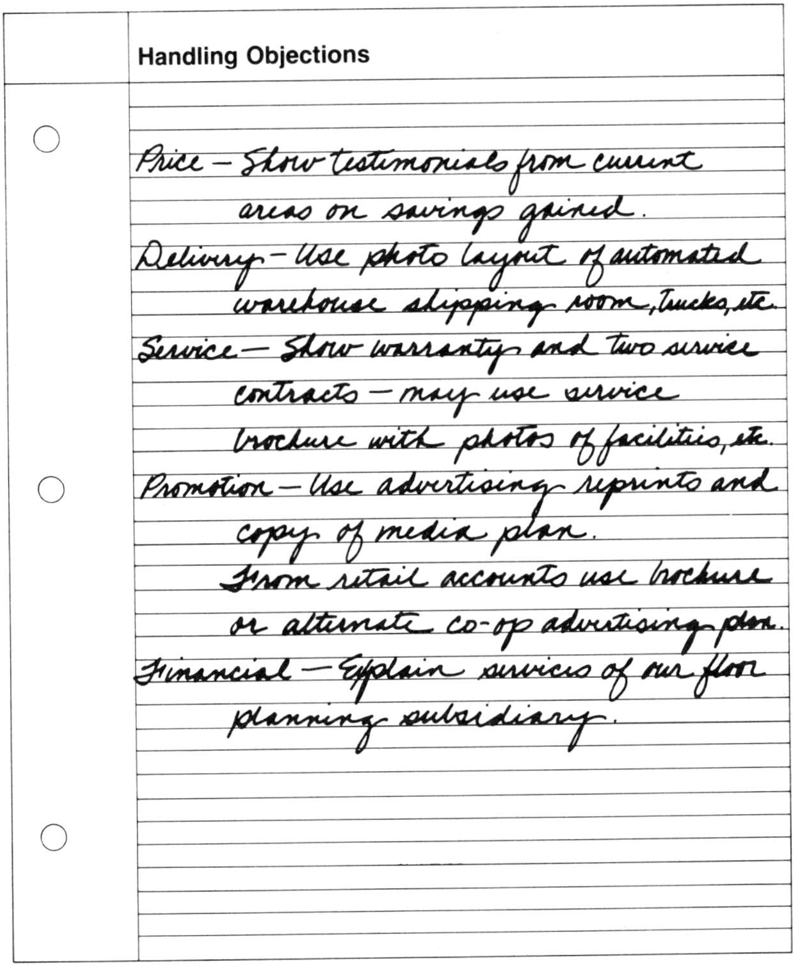

Handling Objections

Price — Show testimonials from current areas on savings gained.

Delivery — Use photo layout of automated warehouse shipping room, trucks, etc.

Service — Show warranty and two service contracts — may use service brochure with photos of facilities, etc.

Promotion — Use advertising reprints and copy of media plan.

From retail accounts use brochure or alternate co-op advertising plan.

Financial — Explain services of our floor planning subsidiary.

Figure 9-1.
Handling objections

Understandably, they are more willing to stock items that have a heavy advertising budget. Retailers are also sensitive to the amount a manufacturer budgets for **cooperative advertising**, in which the cost is shared by the retail outlet and the manufacturer. Many retailers will reject merchandise from firms not providing this essential support.

Cooperative support also includes sales promotion. Local shows promoting boats, cars, recreational vehicles, and other goods depend on the financial support of suppliers. Consumer contests, coupons, demonstrations, exhibits, point-of-sale materials, and other support is increasingly sought. Many businesses, in fact,

cooperative advertising
advertising activities whose cost is shared by the manufacturer and the wholesaler or retail outlet.

place more value on these services than on small price conces-
sions. Customers who view any of these activities as necessary to
maximize their sales or profits will raise objections if they are lacking.

Financial objections

Although many believe that financial considerations are crucial to
closing a sale, repeated surveys have put price not first but third or
fourth on the list of common objections. In reality most firms' prices
for their products are in line with their competition. They reflect both
the cost of doing business and the current level of demand. In
big-ticket sales the majority of retail customers are more interested
in what the monthly payment will be than in the purchase price. Few
customers remember the interest charges or know the total true
purchase price.

Other financial objections involve trade-ins, as with automobiles
and machinery. In real estate the purchase of one piece of property
may be contingent on the sale of another.

Perhaps of more importance today is the policy of pricing a base
unit, with all its options and accessories as extras. With automobiles
these extras may equal one-third of the car's base price, increasing
the purchase price by 25 percent. Similar tactics are employed in
tools and machinery. Objections will be raised when an anticipated
purchase price differs significantly from the real one. More astute
firms offer packaged deals and advertise the total price. When offering a packaged deal it is easier to remove an option and lower the
price, especially where the options constitute a significant part of
the total selling price.

Personal objections

Buyers may also react negatively to a salesperson's personal habits
such as smoking, eating, or chewing gum during a presentation.
Customers are put off by retail clerks who ignore customers while
standing in a corner chatting. Most people tend to make snap
judgments about others just from their initial observation of appearance. Salespeople must develop a sensitivity to these customer's
feelings. It usually is necessary to sell yourself before beginning to
sell your products.

Other personal objections deal with personality. Your customers
may be rude, belligerent, and obnoxious. They may be very
opinionated about religion, politics, or sports. These and other factors can develop into personality conflicts that reduce the amount of
good two-way communication. It is difficult to sell while a customer is
rambling on about who will be selected for the All-Star Game, and

even more difficult to deal with the person who tries to sell his or her religion while you are trying to sell a good or service.

In areas of high customer turnover such as sales of retail goods, real estate, and insurance, the personality problem is less important to salespeople than it is to salespeople who are trying to build a territory and a reputation. Here, many long-term relationships must be established for the salesperson to be successful. If personality is a barrier to selling, the salesperson must overcome the objections. Business friendships must be developed, since long-term relationships cannot be built until personality differences are minimized.

4. Identify a person with whom you have had a big difference of opinion. Feelings could be considered hostile. Prepare a plan by which you could return at least to speaking terms, if not friendship. Report.

5. You are employed to sell for a firm that has just opened. You are convinced its products are better than the competition. What company factors may need to be sold before you can sell the product? List them in order of importance. Report.

Price as an objection

Price is not as great a barrier to selling as most people think. When a sale is not made, price may be a convenient excuse to cover up for a poor presentation. The salesperson must develop a realistic attitude toward price and must learn to sell products on the basis of benefits rather than price.

Focus on benefits

One special problem with price is the salespeople's attitude toward their firms' prices. For many seller's this attitude is their worst enemy. Not understanding price structure and policies, they fear that no matter what the asking price it is too high. They are "horse traders" who view any given price as a starting point for haggling. In short, their selling approach revolves around a product's price, rather than its value or benefits to customers.

Too many salespeople fail to understand the relationship between price and profit. Profit for the majority of firms is a small percentage of the selling price; any reduction in price comes directly off the profit. If profit is 5 percent of sales and a customer is granted a 5 percent price reduction, the sale is profitless. Salespeople must readjust their thinking and become producers of *profits*, not of volume.

Many firms today emphasize nonprice competition as a marketing strategy; they attempt to influence demand by changing the product, the distribution, or the promotion. The sales presentation must focus on product benefits that no other competitor offers. Faster delivery, heavier advertising support, and consulting services often tip the scales in favor of one firm over another where the physical product has few if any differences.

High price is rarely an objection where shortages exist, and recent years have seen many shortages. A firm that can't deliver cannot make a sale at any price. This applies especially to repair parts and other areas where there is a monopoly. High price may in fact be an advantage for some products. In some areas customers take pride in buying the highest-priced item available.

When the price is too low
For the same reason low price may be a disadvantage. Price is used in our impersonal society as an indicator of quality. Most people have some idea of an appropriate price range for any given item. On the basis of this estimate they may reject as inferior goods or services at the low end of this range. Those below the price range are definitely rejected.

A filmstrip producer faced this problem when he developed a new way to produce the product. Although the going rate for filmstrips ranged from thirty-five to one hundred dollars, he charged only fifteen. Until the firm could provide testimonials that the products were actually better than most competing goods, they encountered great resistance. Here the seller saw price as a very strong selling point, but to the buyer it implied inferior quality.

No two firms are alike. Even firms producing products that appear to be identical must recognize that buying occurs in the mind. Price is only one factor in a purchasing decision. It usually ranks lower than quality, services offered, and company image. Focusing the presentation on customer benefits will minimize price objections.

6.   Without looking in the newspapers or other advertising, select four items you would consider a "luxury" and guess the current range in prices. Shop stores and advertising for actual prices. How do you compare?

Understanding the real objections

Objections cannot be overcome unless they are understood. If objections are raised that you feel are invalid or may be caused by lack of understanding, two approaches are available to you. One method is to restate the objection in a different way and ask the customer if that is what he or she meant. In the other approach you simply ask why the customer feels that way. The burden of proving the objection to be valid now rests on the customer. Both of these methods clarify the issues and provide opportunities to sell.

Often objections can be turned quite naturally into selling points or benefits. Objections to price may be met with illustrations of actual savings to be gained. Objection to delivery policies may be handled simply by agreeing to meet the schedule required. Never assume that most objections are valid. The truth is that most objections only provide an opportunity to turn them into benefits, or reasons to buy.

If the objection is obviously false and you know the customer is not well informed about a given product you can deal with this situation by **direct denial**. Some tact is necessary, however; contradicting a customer too boldly can produce negative—even hostile—feelings that can ruin any communication that has been built. A soft voice, a relaxed body posture and statements containing facts are required. Use supplemental materials to show customers exactly why they are wrong. Admittedly, wrong attitudes are much more difficult to deal with than mistaken facts.

Nevertheless some objections are valid. A method for handling these objections is to agree with the customer that the objection has merit. A firm that has a policy of pricing higher than competition, for example, would have to agree that its prices are high, but this provides the salesperson with two opportunities. First, it puts the buyer and seller together so win-lose or lose-lose situations are avoided. Second, it provides an opportunity to justify the higher price—by citing extra services, more credit, faster delivery, or more personal attention that may have value to the customer.

During a prepared presentation objections may be raised before the salesperson has planned to cover them. Answering some objections may be part of the close, for instance, rather than the opening. These objections can be *delayed* by saying, "I'll answer that in a minute, but first . . ." You will maintain control and keep the presentation progressing as planned. Take care to remember the objection and to see that it is answered. Many planned presentations have several points within them where attempted closes are made. There is some danger of attempting to close before you answer the objection. People dislike promises not kept.

Some objections can be *ignored*. Some remarks are not intended to be taken seriously; no response is anticipated. In other cases the objection is made only half-heartedly without any real conviction by

direct denial
the seller states that a buyer's objection is false by directly challenging the assumed facts.

Figure 9-2.
Six forms of evidence

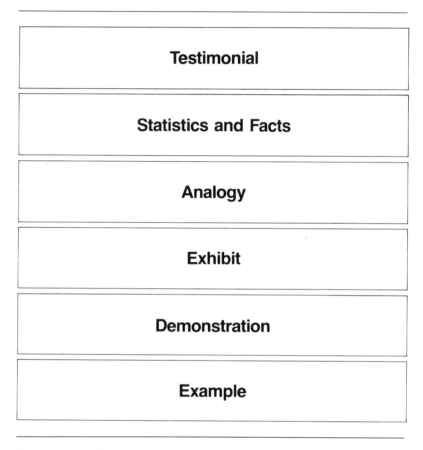

Testimonial
Statistics and Facts
Analogy
Exhibit
Demonstration
Example

the customer. Rather than pursue the point it may be best simply to ignore the objection.

Inject some *humor* into the presentation. Objections produce tension and humor can also be used to relax this tension. A common mistake salespeople make is to overreact to objections. By using humor to keep the conversation light and lively you help minimize customer's objections. Humor also smooths the way to closing the sale.

Body language clues
Those objections easiest to deal with are those that are expressed verbally. Much of this chapter has dealt with verbal objections to buying. But **nonverbal objections** can also be delivered with visual clues. A negative shake of the head, thumbs turned down, or palms turned out are objections. A posture with arms folded and leaning back in the chair indicate a closed mind—an objection. Visual and

nonverbal objection
those objections that are communicated by body language rather than by words.

verbal clues must be put together in a given context to judge the seriousness of an objection.

Body language can be a clue to those many objections that people do not freely verbalize—the suppressed objections. Suppressed objections may stem from a source of embarrassment to the customer. A desired purchase may be beyond the customer's financial ability. Admitting their financial situation would be painful, so they raise other excuses to buying to cover the real objection.

This principle applies to products of a personal nature as when a man buys lingerie for a special woman, for instance; people usually do not like to exhibit facts about their sex life in public. Most people have idiosyncrasies, or habits they will go to great lengths to conceal. Yet sometimes these objections to buying must be overcome if a sale is to be made.

Learn to use these nonverbal clues to discover the true nature of objections. You must constantly use your eyes *and* ears to be effective. Objections, whether expressed or suppressed, are barriers to closed sales.

What to do when the objection is final
Objections expressed by customers often are believed to be true and valid. Some will be, and a wise salesperson will admit it. Never lose sight of the fact that a successful sale is the mutual exchange of something of value by both sides. The seller has already decided what they want to sell and under what terms. The buyer must be convinced of his or her need for the item or service and of the correctness of the terms.

Not all presentations will yield a successful sale because of some *valid objections*. When it is apparent the objections are valid and not just another minor point, directing the customer to another firm is good business. Your cooperation may mean the customer will call you later for a product you do supply. To use a hard sell on such a customer would be questionable ethics.

valid objection
a true or valid reason for not purchasing an item.

7. How would you handle objections expressed by someone who is obviously using them to conceal other feelings? Would you use a blunt or round-about strategy?

8. How would you handle a customer who voices a few strong but invalid objections and then goes silent after you show how each is untrue?

Mini-case

For more than seven years Don has been selling stocks, bonds, and other investments with a firm well known locally. Due to several changes in the market he now handles a wide variety of investments and serves more as a financial advisor than a stock broker. After the bad winters of 1976–78, many of his more profitable accounts moved south and southwest for a warmer climate. He then found himself in the position of having to solicit new accounts aggressively.

Through various methods Don was able to accumulate a list of eighty-three people who were in the 50 percent and up tax bracket. When calling to set up an appointment to discuss his services he found that most had their money in savings and loan accounts. Their tax bracket, coupled with the current rate of inflation, was yielding a net loss of 2 to 4 percent a year. He knew he could offer several very conservative investments to these people that would yield at least 5 percent net, an increase of 7 to 9 percent.

He encountered great resistance. His image was still that of a stock broker and that market was currently very depressed. He tried to point out that the appointment was only to discuss their financial plans, not to sell stocks. Most declined the offer.
Question: How can Don deal effectively with the objections being raised?

Define these key concepts

cooperative advertising
delayed response
direct denial
distribution
invalid objections
nonverbal objection

objections
price objection
suppressed objections
valid objection
win-win

10 Closing the sale

Key terms

assumptive close
positive affirmation
financial close
emotional close
added incentive
SRO
minor-point close
paired-choice close
trial close

Overview

Closing the sale is a natural end to a well-planned and well-delivered presentation. Good professional salespeople develop a sense about timing the close. They pay close attention to both visual and oral clues. There are many reasons for failing to close, but the main one is that salespeople forget to ask for the order! All details need careful attention. Different types of closes must be studied. Distractions must be controlled. Not all closing attempts will be successful, however. No-sale presentations can make friends, too.

Failures to close

Sales may be lost for many reasons. Company policies or procedures may be unacceptable to the customer. Or the customer's credit status may not be acceptable to the company. At times, however, the salesperson's personality or presentation loses the sale, and this situation must be identified and corrected. In this section we will discuss several of these alternatives.

Company policies and support personnel lose sales

When sales are lost because of company credit policies the situation can be a great source of frustration, because it is largely beyond your control. If the customer's credit standing falls somewhere between good and bad, the judgment may be arbitrary. Two different credit managers may give opposite opinions even when working from identical information and the same credit policies. Our society is heavily credit-based and these decisions will often nullify an otherwise closed sale.

Without operating procedures, there would be chaos, and most procedures do not hinder selling. Nevertheless from time to time customers have special needs that do not fit within normal procedures. Some managers see these rules as ironclad; they would rather lose a sale than deviate from the procedures manual, and often do.

It is up to you to be knowledgeable about your firm's policies. Salespeople not familiar with their firm's procedures have made promises they cannot deliver. It is a two-way street. Management must be able to bend in unusual situations and salespeople must know what their firm can and cannot deliver. Helping present your customer's case to the company credit manager is part of making a close—it can mean the difference between a no-sale and a long-term account.

Today, your company's personnel may be a threat to your closes as more and more selling is a team effort. Consultants, technicians, service and maintenance people, delivery people, and others are involved in completing a transaction. In some sales areas, such as services, capital equipment, and research, support personnel are also involved in the presentation and in the development of bids. While most are technically competent, one incompetent person can wreck a well-laid plan.

Personality is the greatest factor. Furniture and appliance delivery people have developed a "bull-in-the-china-shop" reputation that has been reenacted often in many situation-comedy skits. Advertising agency accounts are often lost not because of the quality of work but over personality conflicts. This is frequently a key factor in an agency winning a new account. Others within an organization may have nothing to win or lose (at least personally and in the short run) with an individual sale. Meeting any unusual customer demands may be accompanied with rudeness or bungling. Secretaries, like delivery personnel, may be curt with customers. Millions of dollars of sales annually go up in smoke from the fires these people start.

Salespeople lose sales

Not all sales are lost because of company problems. Salespeople lose plenty of closes themselves. A major barrier to closing, especially with trainees, is attitude. A positive attitude is a state of mind that can be read clearly by customers. It's reflected not only in words, but in body language as well. People prefer to associate with those who exhibit a positive attitude. They react negatively to those who are constantly apologetic, make feeble attempts to answer objections, or who do not ask for an order.

The close should be made in a warm and friendly atmosphere. Some salespeople, in an attempt to be positive, come on so strong they create a climate that seems hostile to the customer. As the promise of a close approaches some salespeople become excited and lose the sale by actually scaring the customer away. While closing a sale is the emotional part of selling, you must keep a businesslike attitude.

Salespeople also lose sales by not being aware of their customers' changes in attitude. Many verbal responses by buyers are actually indications that they are ready to buy. Questions about factors other than the product, such as delivery, financing, service, and warranty, as well as requests for a trial use, may be taken as indicators that the product meets their needs and they are thinking about buying it. It is time to try for a close.

Other messages can be equally revealing. A person who has been listening rather nonchalantly begins asking serious questions or begins listening intently, for instance. Positive nods of the head, a warm smile, or eye contact often signal that a close should be made. Salespeople who do not correctly interpret these signals let opportunity slip by.

Ask for the order!

Several surveys taken among professional buyers reveal common reasons why salespeople fail to close sales. Consistently the number one reason is *they simply don't ask for the order!* Doesn't it seem strange that professional salespeople who make their living from closing sales neglect to ask for the order? It is strange, but true. After making a well-planned presentation they evidently expect the customer to ask to buy. They do not know the techniques of closing. They simply close up their briefcases and leave. Asking for the order does not occur to them. Don't make that mistake.

1. Using the good or service you are interested in selling, prepare a list of questions that would indicate a customer is ready to buy.

2. Given the environment you are likely to be in when selling, what visual clues would a customer make that would indicate a willingness to close?

Common closing techniques

The closing techniques you will use depend on the type of selling and the individual situation. As we have pointed out, a close is usually not attempted until a positive signal is given by the customer. This moment can occur at any time during a presentation; you may attempt to close before completing a prepared presentation if you sense that the customer is ready to buy.

Closing techniques also vary with different types of selling: retail, commercial, services, and industrial. If the purchase is a major item with a relatively long life, such as factory buildings, road construction machinery, or computers, more than one person may be responsible for the purchase. The salesperson coordinating the selling process may use a different approach to closing for each member of the buying team or committee.

The direct approach

We will discuss three types of positive-attitude approaches: the direct, the assumptive, and the positive affirmation approaches. The *direct approach,* the simplest, is often the most productive. While on the surface this approach may appear somewhat blunt or rude, within the context of a good presentation it should be natural. If the customer, by word or action, signals a readiness to buy it may be a mistake not to ask for the order. Continuation of the presentation may cause the customer ultimately to decide not to buy.

A direct question—"May I write up the order?" may really serve two objectives at once. An affirmative answer would close the sale. A negative answer can be equally productive because it often uncovers an objection to buying that once out in the open, can be handled. Without such a direct approach many customers will conceal their real objections, permitting the salesperson to cover points the customer considers unimportant.

Most customers actually expect salespeople to ask for an order directly. It is, after all, their job to sell and close. When this is done in a natural manner without nervousness, it's effective. Just remember to watch for the verbal and nonverbal clues first.

The assumptive approach

assumptive close
sale is closed nonverbally as the salesperson begins the mechanics of paperwork, wrapping, order writing, and so on.

The **assumptive close** is quite similar to the direct close but more subtle. The only major difference is that the customers are not asked if they are ready to buy. The salesperson simply assumes that they are and begins the physical procedures. At the retail level the salesperson either takes the merchandise to a cash register or begins writing up the charge slip. An insurance agent would begin filling out the necessary forms; others would start writing up the sale in the order book.

In some instances it is not even necessary to ask for the order. A retail customer, for instance, who selects an item and hands it to a salesperson, may be offended if asked if he or she wants to buy it. Many other visual clues, often more subtle, may communicate that the sale has indeed been closed. All that remains is to complete the mechanics of closing.

Positive affirmation

positive affirmation
use of a planned series of questions designed to elicit "yes" answers.

The **positive affirmation** close is an extension of the presentation; its use therefore requires forethought. For example, if you are relatively certain the customer does not like a given product, you would not ask if he or she likes it, because that would yield a negative reply. Instead the question is restructured as, "Am I right that this model does not interest you?" Note that the question itself is positive: "Am I right . . . ?" Throughout the presentation all questions are constructed to produce a positive response.

The principle behind using any of these three positive approaches is the development of a positive attitude within the customer. When it comes time to close the answer will still be yes. When selling to a group, salespeople will summarize all points of agreement immediately before asking for the order. This summary, phrased as questions, generate a steady stream of yes answers. This method is also recommended where the selling process has occurred over a period of time rather than in one presentation. Major benefits are restated: the objections are minimized: the sale is closed.

The financial close

In many selling situations the customer obviously likes the good or service but the barrier to closing is money. It's time to use the **financial close.** Many firms have responded to the customer's money problems by setting up leasing subsidiaries, developing their own credit department, and adjusting payment plans. With automobiles, for example, banks and finance companies now offer 48-month loans, and most dealerships have instituted leasing programs.

In closing these sales the focus is on the monthly payment, not on the total amount. During the presentation the alert salesperson has been able to determine the customer's financial situation. If he or she can present a monthly price within the customer's budget, normally they can close.

These closings have a psychological advantage for the salesperson. Because each payment is reduced to a small fraction of the total price, the size of the purchase becomes less overwhelming. Using a real estate example, a $45,000 house is redefined as a $450-a-month house. A car, after allowing for a trade-in, may be sold by quoting a monthly price of $136.25. The key to closing is knowing that when you ask, "Will $136.25 a month be within your budget?" the answer will be yes.

financial close
used where focus is on . size and frequency of payments rather than on product benefits.

The emotional close

We pointed out earlier that both emotional and rational factors are involved in selling. While one or the other will dominate the presentation, both are always present. It would be wrong to assume that all closes must use rational appeals.

Any of the appeals discussed in Chapter 3 can be used in an **emotional** close. "Since I know you would not want your wife and child left in poverty should you die, sign this form. This policy will provide for their needs." This is an obvious use of the fear appeal in closing, but the approach need not involve fear. Being the first to own the biggest, brightest, or fastest, for example, has sold millions of dollars worth of goods. The reverse of these appeals is to suggest that not buying will make the customer appear backward or old fashioned.

emotional close
use of fear, love, vani *and other emotional appeals in closing statements.*

The emotional close is readily adaptable to those goods and services that are highly visible and have social significance. Clothing, automobiles, housing, furniture and appliances, motorcycles, snowmobiles, riding mowers and landscaping all involve emotional buying. Consider too, the emotion involved in buying a wedding ring set, a Christmas present for a loved one, or the catering for a wedding reception. Wherever the emotional involvement in a purchase is high there is great opportunity to make an emotional close: "Drive this car down Main Street and watch the heads turn. Shall we sign the papers?"

Added incentives

Customers sometimes appear on the verge of buying but still express some hesitance. This is the time for an **added incentive** close. This is not possible with all types of selling because normally management must have previously approved the "bonus" for the customer. "Sign this order and I'll throw in an extra case of widgets." It will in some cases depend on the salesperson's willingness to have part or all of the cost of the bonus deducted from the salary or commission.

added incentive
some form of bonus offered to buy now rather than later.

The additional incentive close is most appropriate when the salesperson is trying to secure a new account that will have long-run profit potential. He or she is willing to forgo profit on the first sale because the primary goal is to get the customer to try the product. On that trial order a long-term relationship can be built.

The principle applies to sales of new products where the value of the subsequent purchases is great. Instant cameras, for example, can be sold cheaply because the profits are in the film and processing. Giving away a roll or two of film in order to close a camera purchase will lead to sales of additional film in the future. Even though the price of the give-away film is insignificant in relation to the price of the camera, it can close the sale.

Standing room only

The **SRO (standing room only)** close can be used by firms when the customer believes there is more demand than the seller can supply, even though this may or may not be true. The essence of this close is that the customer is made to believe, sometimes falsely, that there are plenty of others waiting to buy; that the salesperson is a very busy person and the customer may be taking too much of their time; and that the customer will lose if he or she doesn't buy immediately. To some degree it is an emotional approach to closing.

SRO (standing room only)
strategy used when product is unique or demand is greater than supply. Salesperson implies this is a one-time-only opportunity.

This approach is also used by people selling one-of-a-kind items. Real estate offers excellent examples of this close in residential and investment property. Since much property is offered by a multiple listing service, the salesperson frequently does not know if the property has been shown to others or not. Therefore a "better buy today: this property may be gone tomorrow" approach to closing is frequently used. By addition of a financial close—"$200 down will hold it"—the sale is made.

The SRO approach works well for customized vans, designer fashions, antiques, and other unique products. Not buying is presented as an opportunity missed. People do not like to miss opportunities that can add to their prestige, income, or personal pleasure.

This close puts them in the position of asking to be permitted to buy. It creates a high level of anxiety which the purchase releases.

The minor point close

Another method widely used is closing on a *minor point.* For many people the final buying decision is difficult. With so many alternative ways to spend limited money to satisfy unlimited needs, major decisions create internal conflict. Not buying is one way to reduce the conflict, even though the conflict may not be eliminated. The astute salesperson learns to focus the close on minor aspects of the sale. Although the salesperson assumes the prospect will buy, either the direct approach or the assumptive close may be threatening. Minor points can relate to the product's features or some aspect of the delivery.

When selling on the basis of product features the close may be made with the question, "Do you want it in maroon?" or "Shall we install the trailering package?" Delivery questions would include, "May we deliver it tomorrow morning?" or "Do you want it shipped by UPS?" In retail situations another minor point would include questions concerning cash, charge, layaway, delivery, or gift-wrapping. Service contracts, financing, and other minor points all provide excellent ways to close sales.

minor-point close
closing, when assumption of a sale has been made and focus is on color, delivery, options, or other minor decision.

Paired choice

The *paired choice close* has long been used by salespeople who realize that most people have difficulty choosing from among many alternatives. At the retail level salespeople narrow the choices to three as rapidly as possible. Many stores stock only three price lines in one given area. The three choices are quickly narrowed to two and the presentation is centered on the merits of each. A person can more easily decide, for instance, between two colors when interest in the item has been determined. It makes buying (and selling) easier.

The paired choice can also be used when the customer does not know the alternatives, especially when you are making telephone appointments and routing a territory at the same time. Instead of letting the customer name the day and time, the salesperson would ask, "May I call tomorrow at 11:00 or Wednesday at 3:00?" It simplifies the customer's decision making, while allowing the salesperson to control his or her own working time.

Paired choice questions should be incorporated throughout the presentation, not only in the close. The narrowing process continues to involve the customer in much the same way the positive affirma-

paired choice close
narrowing choices to the most attractive offerings. Related to the assumptive close; the salesperson asks which item the customer would like rather than asking if the customer would like either of the choices.

**Figure 10-1
Nine closing techniques**

1 Direct	"May I write up your order?"
2 Assumptive	Nonverbal assent given
3 Positive affirmation	Use short series of questions that will produce "yes" answers.
4 Financial	"That's $177 a month. If that is within your budget, we have a deal."
5 Emotional	"The coat fits perfectly and looks so elegant. Are you going to wear it home?"
6 Standing room only	"This is a one-day sale. Tomorrow it will cost you $50.00 more.
7 Paired choice	"Shall I order it in saddle tan or in burnt orange?"
8 Minor Point	"Can we deliver this on Thursday?"
9 Combination	Often more than one technique is used in closing a sale.

Closing phrases and sentences should be carefully worded and memorized. Consider them a "mental storage bank" to be used as they fit a given situation.

tion close does. Yet the customer must do more than agree with the salesperson's statements. One must make positive choices that draw one closer to commitment. It's the last question that gets the order.

Combinations of approaches

All the above closing methods, which are summarized in a chart in Figure 10–1, may be used in combination. For example, a minor point close will use a direct question, or a positive affirmation will end on a minor point. The important thing is that as a professional you should know all the approaches to closing. Serious thought should be given during the presentation, and even earlier in some selling, to the closing approach that will be used. Consideration should be given to the type of customer being sold, the kind of good or service you are selling, and the environment where the presentation is being made, both physical and psychological.

3. In the library find two other books on professional selling. Compare and contrast the techniques for closing presented in the two books with this text. Report.

4. Given the good or service you have decided to sell, prepare two statements (questions) to be used with each of the above closing methods. Type neatly and put in wallet or purse.

The element of timing

There is no great psychological moment when the close should be made. Sales presentations have no absolute beginning, middle, or end. Each selling situation is unique and should be handled that way. The real danger is approaching a sale as though it is a written play to be reenacted in its entirety, especially when you are using a prepared presentation.

Learn to read your customer's reactions. Many times the signals indicating the customer is ready to buy are quite overt. But many people, viewing buying as a game, will go to some length to conceal their real feelings in order to feed their own egos.

All of these situations can be handled by making a ***trial close*** — attempting to close using a variety of the approaches discussed in this chapter. The trial close can determine how near the customer is to buying; it can uncover objections to be answered; under the right conditions a trial close will close the sale. Caution is in order, however. Trial closes must not be attempted if it is obvious that the customer still has unanswered questions. Aim for the *win-win situation* discussed earlier. An attempt to close when the customer needs more information may lead to an unwanted confrontation.

trial close
an attempt to close a sale prior to completing a planned presentation.

Avoid being overaggressive or pushy when closing. It is the professional's job to help the customer buy. Although high pressure will work in some areas of selling with certain customer types, in most cases it will turn customers off. The more sophisticated the customer the friendlier the atmosphere should be: always provide a chance to close.

The controlled environment

Distractions are a major barrier to closing sales. As much as possible, these distractions must be controlled. They can be controlled by isolating buyer and seller in a closing room, by showing the product in a special showroom, and by other subtle methods. Selling has a psychological and sociological base. Distractions and the psychological effect of the environment do influence the closing process. This control is not manipulative, as some would suggest, but serves to make it easier for the salesperson to sell and the customer to buy. The transaction should always be mutually beneficial.

What to do about "no sale"

Many presentations made during the life of a professional sales-person will result in a "no-sale." In some areas of selling closing one sale out of five attempts is considered very good work. Often, how-ever, not closing has a negative psychological effect on the sales-person. That attitude must be changed.

Attitude

A no-sale customer is an opportunity. It is an opportunity to part friends, leaving goodwill towards both you and your firm's products. It is an opportunity to do some prospecting for other new customers. It is also an opportunity to set the stage for a return presentation later. If you are convinced the customer can use your product, but you somehow were unable to remove the objections, keep trying.

Building goodwill is the most important of these opportunities. Word-of-mouth information can travel very fast in an industry. For most people the salesperson is the company. If you make enemies in one firm you will find yourself with fewer leads, fewer open doors, and more difficult sales. It can also reflect on your co-workers as well as on other company personnel who have customer contact.

Analysis

Some time should be devoted every day to the analysis of those presentations that did not yield a sale. Just as closed sales offer clues to success, presentations which did not work offer clues to making better or faster closes in the future. Perhaps the best place to start is the question, "Was this a good prospect or not?" It may be the prospecting system that is at fault, or the method of qualifying may need refining.

Many presentations are made and many closes attempted with people who are just not good prospective buyers. Their reasons for not buying are quite valid, and perhaps the call should not have been made. On the other hand, a prospecting and qualifying sys-tem that yields a very high percentage of potential buyers may be unduly time-consuming and expensive. Balance must be main-tained.

You should also question your handling of objections: "What was the *real* objection to buying?" Handling objections takes tact and skill. Concentrating on features rather than benefits, or using rational appeals with an emotional product are not very productive ap-proaches. What was said or done that got negative reactions? Did interruptions or distractions produce the no-sale? And of course the key question: "What could I have done differently to close the sale?"

5. In your recent experience, what have the salespeople you have had contact with done to lose a close? What effect has their attitude had on you personally? Cite examples and report on alternate strategies.

6. You have made a preliminary presentation to a buying committee and have a second appointment in which you plan to make a close. How would your approach differ from selling to an individual? Which of the approaches discussed in this chapter would be most or least likely to get the order? Report.

Mini-case

Rich and Maureen were carpenters. When the energy crisis began they formed a partnership and bought a franchise to install a new type of foam insulation, designed primarily for installation in uninsulated older homes. Selected pieces of siding are removed and holes drilled in the underlayment. The foam is pumped through the holes into the air space where it expands to fill the space. Then the siding is carefully replaced.

The main selling point is the foam's effectiveness in cutting both heating and cooling costs. The business is in Wisconsin, where natural gas prices had increased 25 percent each of the last two years in their market. News stories of future gas increases coupled with homeowner's fuel bills helped their business.

While Rich and Maureen's advertising produced many prospects, they feel they are not closing enough sales. Their presentations usually go quite well. The prospect is normally very interested in this new product's features and how it is installed. It costs about $600 for an average house. Most objections are to the price. While people agree they will eventually get their money back in reduced fuel costs, most say they just don't have the money now.
Questions: How should Rich and Maureen handle this objection?

Define these key concepts

added incentive
assumptive close
emotional close
financial close
minor-point close

paired-choice close
positive affirmation
SRO
trial close

11 Follow-up and evaluation

Key terms

customer file
follow-up
selling-through
*Consumer Protection
 Act of 1968*
cash flow
account management

Overview

Today many salespeople devote large amounts of time to activities required to deliver the sale. Closing the sale sets in motion activities that are considered the salesperson's responsibility. Paperwork, delivery and installation supervision, customer training, complaint handling, and working with slow paying accounts all require time. It is also important to analyze your accounts regularly and set new goals.

After the sale is made

The length of time between making a close and actually completing a sale can be minutes or months. In most selling, the good or service is not delivered on the spot but at some time in the future. Sales can be lost during this time period.

After the close, all the details are entered onto the order. Some details may need to be discussed. This step is an opportunity to provide this and other information that may be necessary to ensure that the customer is completely satisfied. Some salespeople carry a copy of the guarantee or warranty, which they use to detail the steps to be taken if the product fails to perform. Instructions on proper operation and maintenance at this step and again at delivery may save both time and frustration in the future. Past customer problems are good indicators of what information should be covered for both your benefit and the satisfaction of the customer.

Keeping records

With most selling, record keeping is associated with closing a sale. These records should be completed as soon as possible so they reflect events accurately. Notes made at this time will remind you of promises for some future action. Company forms are filled out according to policy and submitted promptly.

One set of records should be of your own design: your **customer file,** containing information about the sale itself and about the customer. A 4-x-6 inch box of file cards works quite well (See Figure 11−1).

customer file
salesperson's file containing information about each customer and their purchases.

There is no better time than immediately after closing a sale to record information that can be helpful in the future. Idiosyncrasies, habits, birthdays, likes and dislikes, and perhaps even philosophy should be noted on the customer card. A record of the purchase also should be noted.

One furniture salesperson keeps meticulous customer records. Using the information from the file he sells over half his volume over the telephone during storewide sales. While using the price appeal of the sale as the reason for calling, he has previously selected items that have a high probability of selling to that customer.

Providing atmosphere

Other postsale activities can set the stage for future sales. A large amount of customer turnover at the retail level is caused by the treatment people receive after a purchase. Many salespeople find it easier to get lost in paperwork and other details of the transaction without giving customers the attention they expect.

Figure 11-1.
Customer file card

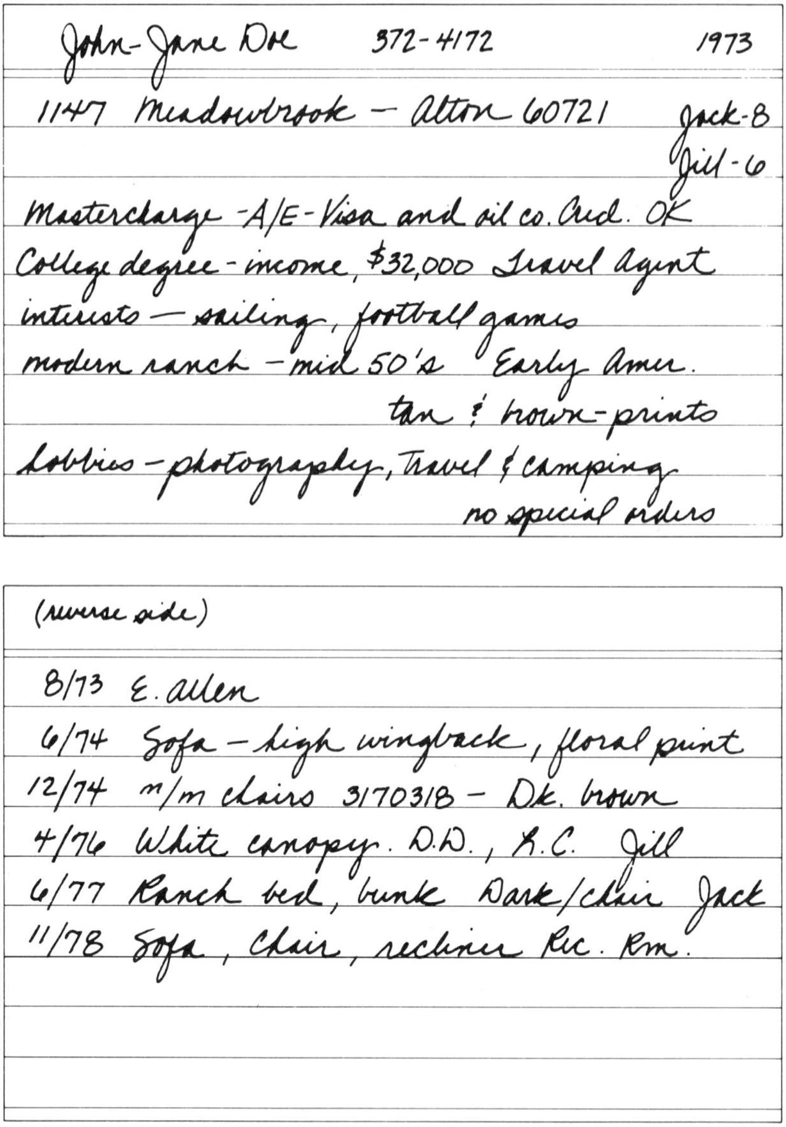

John-Jane Doe   372-4172   1973

1147 Meadowbrook — Alton 60721   Jack-8
                                                      Jill-6

Mastercharge -A/E-Visa and oil co. Cred. OK
College degree-income, $32,000 Travel agent
interests — sailing, football games
modern ranch - mid 50's Early Amer.
                    tan & brown-prints
hobbies - photography, Travel & camping
                              no special orders

(reverse side)

8/73 E. allen
6/74 Sofa — high wingback, floral print
12/74 m/m chairs 3170318 — Dk. brown
4/76 White canopy. D.D., K.C. Jill
6/77 Ranch bed, bunk Dark/chair Jack
11/78 Sofa, Chair, recliner Rec. Rm.

Others have not learned how to say good-bye graciously. All charm and warmth during the presentation and close, they turn cold once their objective of a sale has been reached. A handshake and a thank you are in order. In commercial and industrial selling similar recognition should be given to secretaries, receptionists, and assistants. A smile and a nod of the head may be all the effort that is required to be remembered the next time you call.

Prospecting is another postsale activity for many types of selling. Someone who has just made a purchase usually is enthusiastic about it and is quite willing to suggest the product to others who may seek similar benefits. The endless chain and other referral methods (see Chapter 6) make use of this human trait. Some salespeople wait until the customer has actually used the product for some time before calling back to obtain referrals. They may request letters of introduction or ask the customer to call the prospect to set up an appointment.

The last area of postsale activity is the follow-up, made some time after the sale. **Follow-up** has two dimensions. The first is some form of thank you sent through the mail. This is particularly useful in big-ticket retail sales and in consumer services like insurance. Unfortunately, far too often the company provides a form letter or a card with a rubber stamp signature. As with all relationships between a salesperson and customers, some personal touch would be much more meaningful. The time required to jot down a personal note is insignificant when compared to the goodwill it can generate.

The other area of postsale activity uses both the telephone and the mail. It is important to know if the customer is satisfied with the purchase or if any problems have been encountered. The majority of customers will not complain. They simply take their business elsewhere. Regular telephone contact to solve developing problems can prevent many cancelled sales. The mail can be used to provide additional information to customers at a much lower cost than a personal visit. (This subject is covered more thoroughly in Chapter 12.)

In an increasing amount of selling, the salesperson must make regular personal postsale calls. These calls to seek out trouble spots are quite common in wholesale and industrial selling as well as commercial services such as printing and advertising. They also function to keep on top of changes in the industry and to funnel information back to the company. For many salespeople, closing the sale is just the beginning of their work.

follow-up
using either telephone or personal call to determine customer's satisfaction with a purchase.

1. **What should you take into consideration after closing a sale while making your exit? How would you avoid making the customer feel they had made a bad deal?**

2. **Given your selected selling area, how would you express your "thank you" some time after a major transaction? Would it be incorporated with other postsale activity?**

Delivering the product

For much of selling today the close of a sale sets in motion the activities of many other people inside the firm. Many of these people will have actual contact with the customer in person, or by telephone or mail. Their activities should be monitored, coordinated, or supervised as necessary. The role of salespeople now takes on a dual nature. They are representing the company to the customer on one hand. On the other they represent the customers' interests to see they receive what has been promised. Where there is conflict between the two groups the salesperson will be expected to serve as mediator or arbitrator. It may be quite similar to walking a tightrope.

Certain employees in the customer's firm will need attention as well. Wholesale salespeople, manufacturers' agents, and those selling commercial goods and services usually sell to an account over a relatively long period of time. The salesperson generating a new account for one of these firms will be expected to know the new account's operating procedures. This would include knowing their paperwork process and how deliveries and invoices are handled as well as working out details of installation, maintenance, and servicing.

Another area that has fallen on the shoulders of many salespeople is training. Increasing technical sophistication now requires more instruction to a buyer's employees, especially in instances where the purchaser is not the one who actually uses the product. When the product is delivered the salesperson is expected to come back in order to provide operating instructions to one group and service instructions to another if a support team is not provided by the salesperson's company. The purchasing agent should be expected to inform the salesperson of the appropriate procedures.

Manufacturers' agents and salespeople selling through wholesalers and other sales intermediaries (traditionally called middlemen) may be also called upon to provide sales training for the users. In the automotive area it has been common for manufacturers' salespeople to hold sales seminars for retailers in their wholesalers' showrooms, for instance. This is called **selling through.**

selling-through
to provide services on behalf of an intermediary customer to one of their customers.

Delivering the sale often also means servicing the sale. The professional salesperson is a *consultant*. If the seller's own firm cannot meet support needs the customer expects the salesperson to find others who can. You need to maintain a large number of contacts that can be called upon to supply information and/or training. Your contacts may include firms involved in financing, warehousing, interior design, sales promotion, and management consulting.

Even at the retail level the professional salespeople know what the competition is doing. They know where customers can find goods and services their company does not provide. Those who provide this level of service to their customers will be pleasantly rewarded with future business. Being a consultant is part of the job of being a salesperson.

Credit and collections

We live in a society built on credit. Even in the retail sector more purchases are being charged to bank cards and credit cards. The amount outstanding on homes, auto, furniture, and appliances— fueled by inflation—has jumped significantly in the past few years. Firms in the commercial and industrial sectors have routinely done business on account, with rare cash purchases.

Firms at the retail level must conform to the **Consumer Protection Act of 1968** (often called *truth-in-lending*), requiring the details of financing to be spelled out in the contract. The rate must be in annual terms, and in almost all states there is an upper limit to the rate that can be charged. In 1977 the Federal Trade Commission ruled that firms who sell to foreign-speaking customers must provide a translation of the contract.

All states now have their own "truth-in-lending" acts with provisions for in-home selling. The cooling-off period usually specified is designed to counter high-pressure tactics, but there is some question as to whether this provision has been as effective as the disclosure of the annual interest rate.

In the commercial and industrial sector business bankruptcies have risen in the last few years. Competition from imports has had

Consumer Protection Act (1968)
also known as the Truth-in-Lending Act; requires disclosure of interest, service, or other financial charges in credit sales to consumers.

The ABC's of the Collection Call.

How to be successful collecting your money by telephone.

A. Plan your call

1. Was Your Company at Fault?

2. Were Any Previous Steps Taken to Obtain Payment?

3. Make Sure You Have the Name of the Person Who Can Authorize Payment.

4. Set Up a Scheduled Payment Program.

5. Prepare an Opening Statement and Fact-Finding Questions.

B. Make your call

1. Identify Yourself and Your Firm.

2. Give the Reason for Your Call.

3. Make a Strategic Pause. (Listen to What a Customer Has to Say.)

4. Ask Your Fact-Finding Questions.

5. Suggest the Payment Program.

6. Overcome Any Objections.

7. Get A Firm Commitment.

8. Close Your Call.

C. Follow-up your call

1. Record Your Notes.

2. Update Your Records.

3. Call Back If No Payment Was Made.

If you have any further questions, call a Bell System Representative at 800-821-2121. (In Missouri, call 800-892-2121.) We'll be able to give you more information on how you can make your collection efforts pay off.

Courtesy of Illinois Bell.

serious effects on autos, steel, fashion, shoes, TV sets, and other goods. Business and the population continues to migrate, leaving scars in urban areas. As part of the prospecting and qualifying efforts the salesperson should check out aspects of a new customer's credit before establishing a business relationship. The procedure may be difficult with firms just starting up.

The salesperson must also monitor existing accounts for signs that things are not going well, and this may cause some conflicts. On the one hand you seek to develop and maintain a friendship with your accounts; on the other hand you must act as a spy. Many firms will go to extreme lengths to cover up a shaky situation, especially if they plan to initiate bankruptcy proceedings. Part of their smoke-screen may include the appearance of affluence, even increasing their orders. Large orders may be a clue that a firm is on shaky ground. Use tact to find out the facts before writing what appears to be a lucrative order. Although turning down such an order is difficult for salespeople on commission, at times it is entirely necessary.

All salespeople who build a clientele will have to deal from time to time with slow-paying accounts. This is the province of the credit or accounts-receivable department. In many firms they deal directly with the customer, and the salesperson should be informed. Ideally after the first overdue bill notice the salesperson should contact the customer by phone. A variety of discounts are used in selling today and there could easily be a disagreement on how the bill was computed. Incomplete shipments, in-transit damage, and wrong merchandise can all lead to witholding of payments.

cash flow
actual cash income minus actual cash expenditures, made during a period, commonly a month.

Firms may find themselves in a temporary **cash flow** bind because their expenses in one period exceed their income in the same period. This is especially true of small firms and new businesses. It is often to the customer's advantage to work out a payment schedule rather than create hostility by repeated notices. This job is often assigned to the salesperson.

When people find themselves in a position where they cannot pay their bills on time, they often tend to do nothing but wait until the selling firm makes the first contact. This is especially prevalent in retail sales. When the contact is made by the salesperson in a warm and helpful tone, future business may not be placed in jeopardy. Nevertheless there are businesses and consumers who are not profitable customers; they pay slowly or never. It takes good judgment to deal with borderline cases.

3.   Your credit department has notified you that one of your largest accounts is now over 30 days past due. Yesterday you wrote a very large order for them. What action would you take?

4. A good retail customer of yours with a revolving charge account has begun to pay late and make only minimal payments. Rather than go to the credit department they approach you for help. What would you do?

Handling complaints

All salespeople receive complaints from customers. Some are about goods or services they have purchased, others are about the performance of the company's personnel. Some customers do not complain, they simply take their business elsewhere. The way complaints are handled by a salesperson can greatly influence future sales.

Customers who approach a salesperson with a complaint are usually upset. They may have agonized for some time over whether or not to make the complaint. Some will be so mad they will be visibly shaken. Others will be abusive with their choice of words. Improperly handled, these people have been known to resort to physical action.

Complaints are best handled by listening, a skill that may escape you in the heat of the moment. The first thing to determine is whether the complaint is of major or minor importance *to the customer*. The magnitude of the real problem is frequently overemphasized or underemphasized rather than stated as it is. Aggressive people tend to blow things up larger than they are; submissive people may appear apologetic about having to complain and feel very uncomfortable.

Ask questions to get to the real problem. Especially in heated situations, other unimportant side issues are brought into the conversation—watch for key words like "always" or "never" to spot an emotional complaint. Only when the real problem has been discovered can any corrective action be taken. At this point the focus should not be on placing blame (a negative viewpoint) but on finding an agreeable solution to the problem (a positive approach).

One proven method of settling complaints is simply to ask the customer what they would like you to do. This approach has two merits: first, it forces the customer to suggest a solution rather than wait for one from the salesperson. An antagonistic atmosphere is changed to one of cooperation. Tempers tend to cool and the real problem is more rationally considered. Second, in most situations the customer will ask for less than the salesperson might have offered. Money is saved for the company, and otherwise complex problems are given simple solutions. Of course a few people will try

Figure 11-2.
Complaint follow-up form

COMPLAINT FOLLOW-UP		DATE	
NAME		TELEPHONE	
ADDRESS	CITY	STATE	ZIP
SALESPERSON	ACCOUNT #	SALES MANAGER	

COMPLAINT — DATE

_____
_____
_____
_____

ACTION TAKEN — DATE

_____
_____
_____
_____

FOLLOW-UP REQUIRED

cc: HOME OFFICE   BY WHEN   PERSON
    SALES MANAGER
    SALESPERSON

to take advantage of this approach to ask for far more than they deserve. Negotiation may be necessary for a settlement.

Where complaints involve others in the firm, it may be necessary for you to perform in the dual role of company representative and customer representative. Others' activities may have to be monitored to see that the corrective action is made as promised. In some instances a customer's employee or the consumer is at fault. Here the blame may be laid to the salesperson who did not give proper instructions or properly follow up the sale. Preventive medicine is much cheaper than providing a cure.

5.   In the selling area you have chosen, what complaints would you expect to be faced with? List five and explain how you would deal with each. Include alternate strategies for different personalities. Report.

Building volume

In the profession of selling one of the goals you will probably set for yourself is to increase your sales volume at regular intervals. In this section we will explore four sources of additional sales volume. You can build volume successfully in four primary ways: by encouraging repeat business, by writing larger orders on each call, by adding new accounts, and by reclaiming lost accounts.

Repeat business

In most selling the greatest volume comes from established customers. Even at the retail level it is important to treat these customers well and encourage repeat business. Often a firm's advertising and promotion efforts are insufficient to maintain this steady flow of repeat business. Salespeople may be required to pick up the phone or send out a reminder—to tell customers they have been missed. Keeping customers coming back is a salesperson's responsibility.

One of the dangers in the day-to-day dealings with established customers is giving them more or less time than the account volume warrants. While future potential business must be kept in mind, giving equal time to all customers ignores the true profit potential of each. Selling to customers that you have a good relationship with is obviously more pleasant than calling on customers that give you a lot of grief. As we will see in later chapters, there are some customers who do not merit a personal call. The telephone and mail is sufficient to service their needs, thereby keeping costs in line with volume sales.

One should not assume that customers will return just because they were satisfied with the last transaction. Your competition tries to lure them by advertising and sales promotions just as you do. Competitive salespeople are making telephone and personal calls to arrange presentations for their goods and services.

An effective follow-up plan is needed to assure repeat business for your company. Just remember that it is normally less costly, in both time and money, to keep a customer than to develop a new one.

Larger orders

One method to capture larger orders is to pursue the sale of related items and accessories; this is commonly called *add-on* or *suggestion* selling. Most retail selling offers ample opportunity to increase the average transaction significantly. When a suit is purchased, for example, suggest a scarf and blouse or shirt and tie. If selling is too aggressive, of course, it turns people off, casting a bad light on an otherwise satisfactory transaction. To overcome this problem, stores use displays drawing goods from several departments. Salespeople are urged to draw from these areas for *cross selling* (see Chapter 2). A salesperson from the other department might assist in making the add-on sale.

The principle of seeking larger orders per call by add-on selling can be almost universally applied. An insurance representative, after writing a policy on the family's breadwinner, may suggest other policies on spouse and children. A furniture salesperson may suggest a lamp or wall decoration to go with upholstered furniture. Stock brokers can suggest that a client also start an investment fund for a child. Real estate people are now selling inspection, appraisal, and surveying services, as well as several types of insurance policies.

In the commercial and industrial sector, writing larger orders is usually a process of building. The key to writing larger orders is that the increase is relatively small in comparison to the order already written. You would not normally sell someone a typewriter stand and then ask them to buy the typewriter, but the reverse works well. When the additional money the customer is asked to spend appears insignificant in comparison to the purchase already made, the customer is much more likely to buy.

Writing larger orders through add-on sales techniques should be

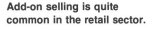

Add-on selling is quite common in the retail sector.

Courtesy of Vertel's of Evanston.

a planned activity, not an afterthought. Using the suit and tie example cited earlier, almost all sales of either a suit or sport coat should include the showing of shirt and tie combinations. A nonverbal assumptive approach in this case works quite well. Notice that both the good and the service has received forethought, as well as the method of presentation. Larger orders do not fall into your hands from the sky. Selling them takes as much preparation as selling your regular volume.

Adding new accounts

As we saw in the chapter on prospecting, satisfied customers are often the source of new leads. An integral part of follow-up activities is securing new business. In some selling situations this happens right after the close; in others, during delivery of installation; in still others, only after a friendly relationship has been built over time. The timing of follow-up is up to you.

An effective follow-up plan includes prospecting on either a regular or intermittant basis. Again it is a matter of conserving time and money.

Reclaiming old accounts

Volume can also be built by reclaiming accounts that have been lost to competition, to changes in economic conditions, or changes in management. Rarely will a salesperson be able to keep all his or her accounts over an extended period. That does not mean that an account that has been lost must necessarily be considered lost for good.

The business climate is constantly changing, with new products, new markets, new management, and new government regulations. By maintaining records on old accounts as well as current ones you can discover how these changes affect past customers' current purchasing. Allotting time for this activity is also part of follow-up.

You can use phone calls, mailing pieces, and even personal visits to keep you and your firm in mind. Absence in this case does not make the heart grow fonder (nor the commission larger).

It is necessary to be selective in allocating time to this activity. Some accounts you don't want back. When you are selling some items, such as automobiles, the time between purchases may be long. In these instances timing is critical. Attention must be paid to this overlooked detail.

6.   In your chosen area, what products would you consider as add-on sales? List them. What primary objections to additional buying will you encounter and how will you meet them? Report.

Account management

account management
classifying and analyzing
accounts according to
past and potential sales to
determine how much time
and effort should be
directed toward each
account.

Salespeople in many ways are their own managers. **Account management** is the regular evaluation of accounts to determine future sales and service requirements. Before calling on an account the salesperson should ask the question, "What do I want to accomplish with this call?" Textbooks call this *management-by-objectives*. After each presentation the question should be, "Did I achieve my objective?" Without specific objectives to be accomplished many selling presentations are a waste of time and energy. Without evaluation of goal-reaching the same mistakes may be repeated.

Managing accounts usually means finding some way of classifying them. This is necessary because while the needs of present and potential customers are unlimited, your selling time is limited. Certain groups of customers offer more sales or profit potential than others. Through classification and evaluation, time can be allocated more wisely.

Through evaluation of customers as a group, basic patterns will emerge. At retail, for instance, credit customers are more likely to buy add-on or suggestion merchandise than cash customers. You probably will discover that purchasing behavior is different when two persons shop together and when a person shops alone. From these analyses you can make changes in your approach, presentation, and your closing techniques.

Those selling outside the firm must also classify accounts and evaluate them. The most time will be allotted to those customers who are the most profitable or have the potential of being very profitable. It is quite common today to classify customers in three or four groups based on either volume, as in Figure 11–3, or on profit. Those in the bottom class rarely receive a personal visit. The telephone and mail are used to meet their needs.

Accounts are also classified by two types: the type of business or customer and the personal characteristics of the buyer. When classifying by business, in real estate for instance, a given home could be sold for two different purposes: as a residence or as a rental property investment. Insurance is classified as personal or commercial, and each type has further breakdowns. A gift or novelty salesperson will call on a wide variety of stores. All should be classified and evaluated.

The second type class, by personality types or other personal characteristics, relates back to the chapters on the social and psychological aspects of selling. Factors such as sex, race, income, education, and hobbies all relate to selling; they should be evaluated as to their effect on selling a given good or service.

Total Sales Volume	Over 1,000,000	500,000 to 1,000,000	250,000 to 500,000	100,000 to 250,000	Under 100,000	Total
Major Department Stores	6	—	—	—	—	6
Local Department Stores	3	4	—	—	—	7
Regional Chains	7	4	1	—	—	12
Large Local Units	—	4	3	—	—	7
Small Local Units	—	—	—	49	18	67
Total	16	12	4	49	18	

Figure 11-3.
Accounts classified by volume and type

These evaluations and classifications of accounts should be continuing processes. Over time, good accounts become poor accounts and poor accounts become good ones. Both economics and sociology change. The way you sell today may not be the most fruitful strategy two years from now. Account management will help you to continue making the best use of your time and efforts.

7. Interview a person who has sold for one firm for longer than ten years. How has her or his accounts changed? How has selling strategy changed? Report.

8. Given your selling area, what ways would it be practical to classify your accounts for analysis purposes? What value would you derive from this evaluation? Report.

Mini-case

Anne has been selling for an office supply firm for fifteen years. She has developed a solid customer base with several accounts buying from her for over ten years. In the past few years a greater proportion of her sales has come from the newer technologies, primarily electronics.

While her firm has long had a service department, the current technician has been with the company only three months. The two previous technicians stayed less than six months. Although Anne knew their service wasn't the best, she hopes the new technician will improve with time.

There has been some grumbling from accounts, but nothing she has not been able to smooth over. One morning, however, she received a call from one of her old, established accounts. They asked her to come to their office the next day at two o'clock to discuss the service on their machines. They indicated that they wished to cancel their service contracts and take their business elsewhere. Another company had made a presentation asking for the business.

Question: What do you recommend Anne do to retain this account?

Define these key concepts

account building
account classification
account management
cash flow
collections
customer file

evaluation
follow-up
management-by-objectives
paperwork
selling-through
suggestion selling

Sales support activities

4

12 Telephone and direct mail as sales support

Key terms

call rate
call frequency
marginal account
beeper
radiophone
card dialer
WATS (wide area telephone service)
direct mail
bulk mail

Overview

Selling costs are climbing constantly. Many salespeople have discovered that selling by both direct mail and telephone can greatly increase productivity. Customer contact can be doubled or tripled with little output of either money or time. Some firms in both the industrial and retail sectors employ no outside salespeople at all, conducting all their business with these two methods. Both are important selling tools that are frequently mishandled by salespeople.

Using the telephone

Today virtually every home and business is equipped with a telephone and that puts all potential customers literally at your fingertips. About seven million calls are made daily by people trying to sell something. Almost half of those called will listen to the presentation; approximately one out of fifteen will purchase. When one considers that a great number of these calls were picked at random from telephone directories rather than carefully compiled from lists of prospects, the potential becomes obvious. It's great.

Of course direct selling like this is not the only way to use your telephone. In this section we will consider six additional business uses of the telephone: prospecting, scheduling appointments, screening prospects, advertising follow-up, servicing after the sale, and information gathering. Our treatment is necessarily brief, and additional reading on this subject would be profitable. One recommended book is *How to Build Your Business by Telephone* by Murray Roman (McGraw-Hill, 1976).

Prospecting

Many firms use the telephone as a prospecting tool. Using circulated lists of people or businesses, the telephone yellow pages, and other assorted directories, they simply start with the letter *A* and begin dialing. Callers, called *telephone solicitors*, are trained and scripts are carefully prepared and tested, and most of these firms enjoy moderate to great success. Three different approaches to prospecting are commonly used.

The first approach attempts to generate enough interest to secure an appointment for a sales call. In some organizations this task falls on the sales force; others employ a separate sales group to sell the appointments. This approach is common in selling home remodeling, carpeting, encyclopedias, and other products.

Another telephone prospecting approach is also concerned with generating interest, but appointments are often not made. Instead, those who express interest are mailed further information about the good or service along with a cover letter, calling card, or both to remind the prospect that this material was requested and is not just part of a mail promotion. Those with a desire to purchase will contact the salesperson. When time permits, those who asked for materials but have not responded to the print advertising are called again. This method is very useful where prospects are geographically dispersed and each personal presentation is costly. Presentations are confined to those who express interest.

A third approach uses the telephone to prospect and close sales with the same call. Current state and federal legislation requires many of these sales to be made on approval, but firms with good products can be sure the returns of merchandise will be few.

Screening

Another function of the telephone is screening. A great deal of direct mail and media advertising also asks potential customers to write for more information—it is a prospecting activity. But all inquiries are not good prospects; many people write for anything and everything. Using the telephone to qualify prospects before making an expensive and time-consuming personal call can provide considerable savings. The call has the double benefit of collecting information prior to the first visit so the presentation can be better tailored to the needs of the individual or firm.

The telephone is an excellent screening tool for both the buyer and seller. Firms get responses from many sources, often from people who are not in a position to purchase but are just seeking information. Frequently calls are made in response to your directory or yellow pages listing. This information can often be provided on the phone rather than in person. The mail can deliver supplemental materials to answer questions. All firms must do some screening since no firm can be all things to all people.

Scheduling appointments

call rate
number of sales calls that find the customer in and willing to meet with the salesperson. May be improved by making appointments by phone.

The telephone is not as widely used as it should be in territory routing to schedule appointments with existing accounts in a salesperson's territory. A former student of mine doubled his **call rate** (visits that found the prospect in and willing to meet the salesperson) simply by calling in advance and making appointments along specific routes at *his own* convenience. Prior to that time, making each appointment at the account's convenience, he found himself crisscrossing his territory wasting both time and gasoline. Appointments also eliminated wasteful cold calls where the person he wished to see was either involved with other business or was out of the office. A great deal of unproductive time spent in waiting rooms was also eliminated.

With acceptance of the marketing concept's idea of the consumer as king, we often lose sight of profitability—an integral part of the concept. Making appointments by telephone can be to the customer's advantage as well as yours. When you arrive he or she is willing to give you full attention, and will have reserved enough time to explore alternative buying decisions fully. Both of you will profit.

Advertising follow-up

A major use of the telephone is to follow up advertising response received by mail. The use of advertising to elicit response from potential customers has increased greatly in the past few years. Much of this advertising does little to screen out the "only looking, thank you" types from the true potential customers, as we have seen in the two previous chapters on prospecting and on buyer decision making. Where the advertising method does not screen, the task falls to the sales force. Typical problems encountered by salespeople are receipt of prospects' names long after the company received them; receipt of names only, with no information on which advertisement generated the response; and receipt of only part of the responses. If you encounter this problem, talk to your supervisor about the problem.

Telephone selling

The telephone, as we have seen, is an excellent tool for selling. Many firms do all of their selling by telephone. Others have set up a separate inside selling unit to handle routine reorders from established customers (see Figure 12–1). Hallmark, the card manufacturer, uses this system for calling certain individual retail outlets weekly for reorders. Salespeople use their time to introduce new products, cultivate new accounts, and build individual store volume.

Retail stores, in catalog sales, are now using a similar inside telephone sales group to sell discounted merchandise to established customers. Customers who do not buy are nevertheless reminded of the firm's products; this serves to maintain or increase their regular business. Many salespeople in furniture and appliances keep accurate records of customer's purchases. They are able to sell additional items by phone at regular intervals, especially when they know items their customers want are on sale. Creative salespeople in all fields can use the telephone to sell with minimal cost in time and expenses.

Service after the sale

The telephone is also underutilized in follow-up. It is here that the marketing concept is often not put into practice. A sale should not be considered complete until the customer is completely satisfied. This implies satisfaction with the product, instruction, installation, and all aspects of taking delivery of the product or service. Satisfied customers are great business builders through word-of-mouth advertising.

Today more business requires service after the sale than ever before, and the telephone is an economical way to ensure this service. Checking on delivery, installation, and other factors often does not require a personal visit. In many selling areas where the salesperson coordinates the activities of sales support personnel, the telephone can substantially cut the time required.

Gathering information

The telephone is also a very good research and information tool. The majority of dissatisfied customers will tell you nothing. They simply avoid you. Only a minority will complain loudly. Yet most are only too willing to speak negatively to others about you and your service or about your firm's product—and probably about both. By regularly calling customers a few days after completing a sale you will stay on top of problems. Small misunderstandings can mushroom into big headaches. Small adjustments immediately made, where justifiable, can build small accounts into big ones. They can keep some problems from going to court. Salespeople need the constant *feedback* that telephone contact can provide.

1.   **Contact a firm that sells only by telephone or has an inside group for telephone sales. What are its policies regarding call lists, print advertising support, qualifying, etc. Report.**

2.   **Contact two or three firms that make heavy use of advertising to generate leads. How is the telephone used in following up these responses? Report.**

3.   **Contact a sales manager in a firm that uses salespeople covering a relatively large geographic area. What role does the telephone play in effective territory coverage? Report.**

Advantages of telephone use

Efficient telephone use can save you two increasingly valuable commodities—time and money. Transportation costs are mounting steadily, and the expense of keeping salespeople on the payroll is increasing. Your personal contacts can be every bit as effective in many cases when maintained at least partly by telephone rather than by in-person calls at the customer's location. We will examine these areas in which savings can be effected: call frequency, marginal accounts, and control of selling expenses.

call frequency
number of times a customer is contacted during some time period.

Call frequency

Perhaps the greatest advantage the telephone can provide is **call frequency**, how often the salesperson contacts the customer during a time period—once a month, for instance. Not all customers require the same level of service. Many need only infrequent personal visits, in some cases only once or twice a year. Contact can still be maintained between personal calls with regular use of the telephone.

This factor is especially important when the customer comes to the salesperson. People selling securities, automobiles, furniture, and similar retail items need to maintain the contact the telephone can provide. This applies equally to those selling commercial services whose customer's needs are *intermittent* and *irregular*.

There is a direct relationship between number of customer contacts and sales. Regular planned telephone contact with current customers, former customers, and prospects can multiply the personal call frequency two or three times. It's a matter of using time effectively.

Marginal accounts

Another place where the telephone can produce very good results is in servicing a **marginal account**, that is, one whose level of purchases may not justify the expense of an in-person call. Usually the majority of customers a salesperson serves offer limited volume; only a few customers truly have high profit potential. It stands to reason that giving all customers equal time has to waste a lot of effort.

marginal account
small account that produces little profit or one that costs too much in relation to volume of sales.

Time can be maximized and expenses minimized by ranking accounts by either volume or profit potential. The more customers you have the more important this approach becomes. Those with the highest potential for profit or volume are contacted regularly in person and on the phone. Those with a lower level of potential are contacted less frequently in person, but may be given equal time with use of the telephone. Those at the lowest level are contacted only by telephone. This concept is applicable to almost all selling but it is obviously more important the wider the geographic area served. It can have great value as a time and expense control tool.

Control of expenses

Salespeople are interested in maximizing time. Companies are interested in minimizing expenses. The telephone can significantly reduce sales expenses. Recent figures estimate the cost of an average industrial sales call at about $80 and rising. For salespeople who use automobiles and motels extensively expenses will probably climb faster than in other selling areas. Many firms are looking much more closely at sales expenses. Obviously a sale that can be completed by telephone has expenses measured in pennies.

Some managers tend to be short sighted, looking at monthly phone bills as an expense to be reduced, not increased. The truth often is that doubling the monthly telephone bill may save many times that amount in other expense areas. It's simply a matter of applying the synergism concept to controls of selling expenses. Telephone contact following an answer to a phone solicitation equals more sales than the solicitation without the following contact or the whole presentation made to everyone on the call list regardless of whether interest has been expressed.

4. Using your selling area of interest, devise a method for ranking customer potential in three or four categories. What frequency of personal or telephone contact would be appropriate for each group?

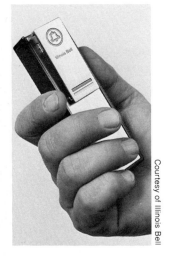

beeper
a devide that signals a person by an electronic tone sent from the base unit which is usually located in the office. To respond, the person being paged must go to a telephone.

Modern telephone equipment

Telephone companies and allied manufacturers nationwide engage in research to improve the capabilities of telephone service and thereby improve their profits. As a result we frequently see new developments in telephone communication. Among those that are applicable to your efficiency in sales are mobile telephones in automobiles, paging devices and **beepers**, automatic card dialing devices, WATS line service, and connecting devices for electronic data processing (EDP) equipment. Two-way radios provide an inexpensive alternative to telephones for communicating while on the road.

Communication while in transit

Mobile telephones, or **radiophones**, are not yet in widespread use among salespeople because of their great expense and limited availability. Although administered by the telephone companies they operate on radio frequencies controlled and assigned by the Federal Communications Commission (FCC). Priorities are given to medical use where life-or-death emergencies are likely to arise. Companies will not usually pay the high price required for mobile phones unless the profits generated by the salesperson make the investment worthwhile. In the metropolitan Chicago area in 1977 about 1,000 instruments were in use.

One less expensive alternative is not truly a telephone at all. It is a two-way radio that communicates with the salesperson's home office on an assigned radio band in much the same way CB radios do. Within a limited distance the salesperson can communicate with the office while traveling. The salesforce can maintain frequent office contact while servicing accounts. Salespeople can be quickly dispatched to solve customer's problems; when necessary these people can request service technicians or inventory to be sent to customers. One application is for a firm serving the construction industry where telephones may not be available at the site. This form of communication is widely used by messenger, delivery, and repair services.

Another popular alternative is the pager or beeper a person carries. The signal can be activated by someone in the home office or by an answering service. The person signalled must reply by telephone in order to communicate verbally. These devices are used primarily where the sales force is on 24-hour call and where travel time is significant.

Automatic dialing

One modern telephone installation, the **card dialer**, employs punched cards to dial customer's numbers. When a card is picked from a small rack and placed in a slot behind the phone cradle, the number is automatically dialed. These are most often used by inside salespeople who service regular accounts by phone.

The key contribution of these units is accuracy—no more wrong numbers—and speed. They also increase efficiency by classifying accounts. Customers can be called routinely on a daily, weekly, biweekly, and monthly basis keyed to *color-coded cards.* Customers too can use automatic dialing for order entry by connecting with the seller's computer and inserting order cards into the dialer.

WATS

Another service now provided by telephone contracts is widely used by salespeople when calling to or from the home office. **WATS** is the name given to **Wide Area Telephone Service**, in which all long-distance calls from the subscriber's location are made for a set monthly charge, rather than each call being charged separately. Customers or others calling the location may dial the prefix 800 and the number for toll-free calls as an extension of the WATS line service. The service is designed primarily for those who make a large number of long-distance calls and whose selling area covers a large portion of the country.

Machines that talk to each other

Recent telephone advances have been seen in electronic data processing (EDP) interconnects. Similar to the card dialer for order entry mentioned above, currently marketed units of several types

radiophone
mobile telephone that uses a radio signal for communications with a regular telephone through telephone company facilities.

card dialer
telephone that accepts plastic cards with pre-recorded number for rapid dialing.

WATS (Wide Area Telephone Service)
a service that bills long distance calls at a flat monthly rate.

The Transaction* phone is
being used increasingly by
salespeople for order entry.
*Trademark of American
Telephone and Telegraph
Co.

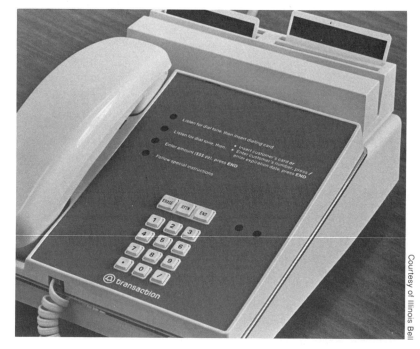

Courtesy of Illinois Bell

connect with a standard telephone for rapid data entry, primarily
orders. This equipment is discussed in the next chapter, which covers computer applications to professional selling.

**5.   Contact a commercial accounts representative with the local
telephone company. What uses of this equipment, and perhaps new
equipment, have firms in your area made? What effects were seen
on the sales force?**

**6.   Contact a firm that sells two-way and radio telephone
equipment. What firms in your area use the equipment as sales
support? What is the cost?**

Direct mail as sales support

direct mail
*mailings that ask for a
customer response,
usually by telephone or
return mail.*

As selling costs escalate, many firms are turning to **direct mail** as a
way of increasing productivity for the salesforce. Like the telephone
service just discussed, the mails can deliver information at a much
lower cost than a personal presentation. Salespeople are
permitted—even forced—to think about time use. A great amount
of information customers may need can be communicated with
printed materials as well as or better than in person.

Mail can be divided into two areas: *direct mail* pieces a firm sends either to individuals or in *bulk* (to everyone on a mailing list) and pieces the salespeople themselves send. Since the salesforce is normally not involved in either type of company-generated direct mail, this section will be concerned only with materials sent out by salespeople, as they are used for prospecting, product education, qualifying activities, and follow-up.

Prospecting

One major use of the mail by salespeople is prospect development. Often, in feast-or-famine fashion, too many prospects are generated at one time. When this occurs a salesperson may do some screening by mailing brochures, specification sheets, flyers, and other company produced materials, along with his or her calling card, to all current prospects. Interested prospects will contact the salesperson and ask for a presentation. With this feedback a salesperson can concentrate energies on high potential presentations, leaving the nonrespondents to call on in leaner times.

Many firms have used specialty items (see Chapter 15) as part of a campaign in developing prospects. Although these are usually handled by an advertising agency, in some cases the items are given to the salesforce to mail as new names are generated. The mailing frequently consists of a series of three or four pieces. A few days after the last piece has been mailed the salesperson either telephones for an appointment or makes a *warm* call in person.

Product education

Another function of the mail is providing information before making a call. Much time can be saved in making presentations if the customer has information about the product before the salesperson calls or the customer visits an office or store. The material sent is primarily educational, and is most helpful in selling unique new products.

Another direct mail application is in selling products to new markets where most potential customers are unfamiliar with the good or service. When the mail is used in this manner only a few pieces are sent at one time. Records are kept on each piece sent, and the prospect is telephoned after allowing time for delivery. Some suggest timing the mailings so the pieces are not delivered on Mondays when mail is the heaviest and people are the slowest. A standard routine of five pieces per day followed by telephone contact five working days later has proven very productive in working new markets. The method is slow, methodical, and thorough.

Keeping customers informed

Salespeople often keep current customers informed of products and services by regularly mailing new company materials. Reprints of advertisements, new product announcements, results of research, and even industry information not directly connected to one's firm are often sent. While not usually faster than a personal call, it is much cheaper. Also customers can read the materials at their leisure when they can devote full attention to them. Many salespeople seek out all possible materials of interest to their customers, including magazine articles and newspaper clippings, to maintain regular mailings. A handwritten note personalizes the materials and keeps the salesperson and the firm in the front of these customers' minds.

Follow-up activities

Mail is also widely used in *post-sale follow-up*. Thank-you notes are the most common form, although far too many are company-printed and not personalized by the individual salesperson. Computer-printed thank-you messages may create more negative than positive feelings.

Other postsale activities include delivery of guarantees, service manuals, operating instructions, and similar materials to ensure that the customer receives satisfaction. This includes reminders at regular intervals that service may be required. Many service stations and auto dealerships have successfully used this device to keep their customers coming back. Retail people can use it to announce sales with a personal memo. Absence does not make the heart grow fonder; it makes the mind forget.

Personal communication

The last major function of the mail is a personal one. Cards sent on anniversaries and birthdays, cards to congratulate someone on a promotion, and get-well cards to those who are ill serve a dual function. From a professional point of view it shows a concern for people; from a business point of view it keeps your name and company in the customer's mind. Both are of value. As with the thank-you cards, make sure they are personalized.

7.   Using the selling role you have selected, how could you use mail to lighten your selling load? Give one example for each of the four areas mentioned above.

Telephone-mail synergism

For many areas of selling today the telephone and the mail are part of a campaign approach to selling. The presentation and the close are the end of a series of activities of which generating a prospect's name is only the beginning. Telephone and mail can be used in many different combinations. For example, one firm may respond with a personal telephone call to screen the prospect. This may lead to no further contact, to an appointment, or to the mailing of materials. In the latter case the mailing may not be one piece but a series of pieces. Further action is abandoned if the prospect does not respond.

Another firm may proceed with only one mailing to a prospect to be followed by a personal telephone call. If an appointment is secured for a presentation, it is made far enough in advance for a second, customized mailing to reach the prospect before the sale's presentation is made. Those prospects who are only lukewarm may also receive another mailing to be followed by a second personal telephone call.

Another area where telephone and mail work well in combination is in *marginal account* servicing. This was covered in the section above on time and money advantages of using the telephone, but in most cases mail is also used. Catalogs, product sheets, and other necessary information is mailed to those accounts that merit only infrequent personal calls. Many well-designed programs have the mail carry the major burden of the selling effort. Telephone calls serve only to maintain some personal contact and seek out any customer dissatisfaction.

Salespeople covering large territories that call on accounts only two or three times a year, in apparel for instance, can use mail and the telephone to maintain contact with their customers. In these cases the salespeople often get **bulk mail** permits (200 pieces minimum) and make regular mailings of newsletters, trade magazine articles, research summaries, and personal letters to maintain between-call contact. Use of a WATS line telephone contact is made between mailing for continuity.

bulk mail
mailing of pieces presorted by zip code in lots of 200 or more; requires a permit.

Both mail and the telephone are greatly underutilized by salespeople. These tools can cut selling costs, increase contact frequency, screen prospects, and support other selling activities. Almost every type of selling can profit from using them more often. Then why are they not used more?

One major reason is lack of company support. Effective use of both mail and the telephone takes training, which few firms provide. It calls for planned strategy, support materials, and implementation procedures including personnel and a budget. In the absence of these tools it is a rare salesperson who will develop them. This chapter, however, has given you many ideas you can easily incorporate into your selling plan. The phone is at your elbow. The envelopes are in the drawer. The rest is up to you.

8.   Develop a synergistic plan using both the telephone and direct mail to accomplish the entire selling task with a selected target market group. How would you monitor its effectiveness? Report.

Mini-case

John is a manufacturer's representative for 22 women's wear firms. He covers Minnesota, North Dakota, and South Dakota. About 80 per cent of his business comes from small local shops. He serves a few multi-unit retailers and several medium sized department stores. Only six of his customers could be classified as big accounts.

Last month he replaced a manufacturer of women's belts with a new firm. The new line supplies a very attractive display unit with an order of a gross (12 dozen or 144 pieces). The company's research shows that their unit will increase belt sales at least 35 per cent compared to most traditional fixtures.

John wants to get these units into as many of his stores as he can in the next three months. To make a personal visit to those accounts where he thinks they will buy that many belts he would have to alter his normal call pattern. He would rather not do that since his customers expect his calls to be made as he scheduled them on his last visit. Changing his call pattern would involve calling too many customers to reschedule his next call.

Question: What plan would you suggest using a combination of telephone and mail for John to achieve his goal?

**Define these
key concepts**

beeper
bulk mail
call frequency
call rate
direct mail

marginal account
radio phone
service level
telephone-mail snyergism
WATS

13 Electronic sales support

Key terms

EDP
inventory control
EOQ
territory analysis
account analysis
optical scanner
CRT
order processing

Overview

Computers earlier were considered strictly a management tool, but this is no longer true. Electronic data processing (EDP) technology is now applied to selling including sales support for both preparation and delivery of the presentation. The computer is a tool the salesperson can use to increase both efficiency and effectiveness. It touches every selling field.

EDP as sales support

Businesses have invested billions of dollars in computer equipment and software programs for a very simple reason. Correctly used, **EDP** produces more work at less cost and increases profits. It can perform calculations with incredible speed and with great accuracy, reducing to less than a second work that would take a person hours to complete. Current equipment not only deals with mundane matters like payroll and inventory but can create new designs and run whole factories.

EDP
electronic equipment used to handle and store information related to a company's business.

As our society becomes more complex, so does our selling process. More and more data is needed for decision making and planning for the future.

EDP serves the professional salesperson with its ability to handle the large amounts of data now required. In the past only department managers used this tool, but today the salesperson needs the available information in order to sell effectively. New equipment makes this data readily accessible to all selling areas.

Inventory controls

One of the earliest major uses of EDP directly by the salesforce was for **inventory control.** Only recently has this use been established to any significant degree in the retail sector, services, and small manufacturing. Currently, adoption of the Uniform Product Code (UPC) eases the transition for manufacturers and many retailers who are developing basic standard models for some articles of clothing, home furnishings, and other products not already standardized. The UPC, with its code of bars of various sizes, has been in effect in grocery stores for some time. Its universal adoption should force a national standard on all nongrocery consumer goods and pave the way for rapid conversion to computer-controlled inventories at all levels.

inventory control
includes record of stock on hand, incoming and outgoing shipments, plus the analysis of cost factors for each item.

The Ford Motor Company has embarked on a plan to tie together a total parts-supply system that would include all its dealers. The nationwide system would put all parts of the combined inventories in computer storage. The economic advantages are enormous. Individual dealers' inventories could be significantly reduced, flow of parts would be smoothed with fewer instances of items being out of stock, and production would be more closely coordinated with demand.

At the wholesale level, at least with medium and larger firms, computerized inventory controls are now standard. The salesforce needs to know instantly what inventory is available for shipment. End users and retailers seeking lower inventories and higher turnovers keep shifting the storage back to the wholesaler. Changes in *physical distribution* (storage, materials handling, and transportation) have resulted in smaller, more frequent shipments. This in turn requires high-speed inventory controls for replenishing stock and delivery orders.

Order processing

With computerized inventory controls comes computerized order processing. Newer sophisticated systems link the buyer's computer to the seller's. Reorders can be based on economic order quantity *EOQ* —the order size with the lowest cost per unit, including cost factors that are fixed and those that can change. These orders are automatically transmitted and processed without an order book or salesperson. The huge (one million square feet) Sears catalog fashion warehouse in Elk Grove Village, Illinois, sends automatic reorders to Japan via satellite. To say that this will have a great impact on professional selling is an understatement.

EOQ
order size with lowest total costs, including physical distribution costs.

The area of salesperson-computer teaming for inventory control purposes is expanding to new areas. Similar to the much publicized computer dating, placement agencies are doing profile matching to fill jobs. Realtors are connecting into nationwide inventories of property and similar matching processes for clients.

The computer has long been used to sell an inventory of seats by airlines. Federal, Emery, and other air-freight companies now track each shipment from pickup to delivery. This same concept has been growing in both truck and rail carriers. The new generation of minicomputers will expand this capability to the smallest firms.

The future of sales

At first glance it may seem these interconnected systems will replace the salesperson. To a very minor degree, they may, but total selling jobs will actually be expanded. The major results of these new methods are changes in the sales task, and some new problems that will arise.

First, the salesperson must become knowledgeable about data systems to aid in developing and modifying the controls. Human judgment must be injected into inventory standards, safety stock, and reorder points.

Newer systems for the retail sector not only control inventory but also allocate shelf space, and this leads to a second change factor. Many new products continually come to market. Criteria must be established for product elimination, new product additions, and realignment of displays. It has been very difficult for some firms to get new products into stores with inflexible systems. The sales-person who can understand and work within the limitations of exist-ing computer programs will benefit.

Introduction of data systems for both inventory control and order processing will not be without problems for the salesforce. These problems will be both external—in dealing with other firms' systems—and internal—in your own system. Salespeople must learn to communicate with a new group of people, the computer programmers, who have their own technical jargon. It is necessary for you to learn programmers' shop talk in order to deal with them effectively—to solve your problems as well as theirs.

1. Visit a salesperson from a medium to large wholesale firm. Discuss the problems they have with computerized inventory control and order processing. How does it help them? Report.

2. Visit a grocery store with electronic point of sale terminals. What merchandise is on the system and what is not? Discuss with the store manager his or her perceptions of the benefits. Report.

Time and account analysis

Only recently have individual salespeople begun to use the com-puter as an analytical tool to improve productivity. For this purpose the use has been primarily in account and time management, and primarily by manufacturers and wholesalers. **Territory analysis** is concerned with routing of sales calls and assignment of time to accounts according to their profit potential. **Account analysis** is con-cerned with purchase patterns and profitability of individual ac-counts.

Work in both of these areas stems from a proven principle: 80 percent of the profits comes from 20 percent of the accounts (*80-20 principle*). This principle has frequently been applied to *time* and *account management*. With the help of the computer one can isolate marginal accounts, that is, customers whose sales do not pay back the selling costs. Not all products carry the same profit contribution. Close analysis may show that a customer buying a high volume is buying only low-profit goods. Where commissions are tied to profits (as they should be) both the firm and the salesperson suffer in this situation.

The concept of account analysis can be extended to manage-ment of customer's inventories. The computer is invaluable in de-termining EOQ reorders by handling data concerning storage costs, transportation costs and time, materials, handling costs, rate of use

territory analysis
determining best method in terms of time and money management for covering accounts in a geographic area.

account analysis
determining purchase patterns and profitability of each account.

"As we see it, the broadcast rep who can supply reliable data instantly has an enormous selling edge.
"That's why Blair backs its salespeople with the three most advanced computer systems in the industry."

"A lot of people still look upon the computer as just an accounting tool.

"But at John Blair & Company, we view it as the most remarkable marketing tool ever invented.

"Information is the raw material of every marketing decision. And today, brand managers, agency account executives, and media planners must support their decisions with increasing amounts of data.

"A properly designed computer system answers this growing demand for data, and can deliver it in the most sales-effective form—all in a matter of minutes.

"We have just such a system at Blair. Or, perhaps I should say 'systems', since there really are three.

Blair Tel/Avail: precise & targeted sales proposals in minutes

"In television, our goal is to make informed multi-market spot buying as quick and easy as a single network buy. Through a system called Blair Tel/Avail, we're almost there.

"Blair Tel/Avail can generate complicated multi-market sales proposals in minutes. It enables the Blair salesperson to instantaneously supply the broadcast buyer with any of 125 different demos on any program, on any station Blair represents —with GRPs, CPMs, current share trends, three rating sweeps and more.

"Tel/Avail even has the capability of printing out a sales rationale for the recommended buy, to underscore why it is the best way to reach the buyer's target audience.

Blair Brain: radio revelation

"For radio we've developed what we believe is the medium's most comprehensive information system.

"We call it 'Brain', and central to it is a highly sophisticated reach and frequency planning system.

"Through the wealth of information this system provides, we've been able to demonstrate something thought to be impossible a few years ago; the economical use of radio to obtain broad reach as well as frequency in a market.

"Advertisers and agencies are using the system now to determine how they can buy radio to attain their reach and frequency goals most productively, whether in one or a hundred markets.

Donovan Reppak: instant contracts plus management information

"Just as Tel/Avail and Blair Brain are designed to help our salespeople on the street, a third system, Donovan Reppak, generates computerized contracts and helps cut back-office paperwork time.

"Reppak is the counterpart of Donovan's Spotpak, which now processes over a half-billion dollars in spot billing for agencies. Blair is the exclusive subscriber to Reppak.

"Reppak is also the industry's most advanced management tool. With it, we can retrieve instant sales performance data for our stations, our offices, and individual salespeople, by agency, by client, by brand.

"We can compare current sales activity with any previous period, observe changes in spot buying patterns, and know precisely where, when, and to what degree, extra sales pressure should be applied.

**Jack Fritz, President
John Blair & Company**

All systems
for all offices

"All 15 Blair offices have on-line access to all three computer systems. Our people in Los Angeles, for instance, can generate exhaustive proposals with the same speed and accuracy as our people in New York. And every office has the advantage of instant contract printouts.

"We've literally invested hundreds of thousands of dollars in these systems. And we'll be investing even more in the future as new computer technologies are introduced.

"Blair's leadership in this area provides our represented stations with the most advanced sales and support service in the broadcast industry. It assures them of maximum sales productivity now and in the years that lie ahead.

"As we see it, our job is to give our stations that selling edge."

BLAIR TELEVISION
BLAIR RADIO
Divisions of John Blair & Company
Reliable people, reliable data.

by weeks, months, or quarters, and similar information. With these data in hand before making a sales call, the salesperson will know at least as much about a customer's inventory as the customer does. This is powerful sales support.

The retail sector has begun applying similar analysis to their accounts. Combining information from credit applications and purchase records of individual accounts, market segments can be better defined. A salesperson can obtain a profile of his or her customers (age, income, education, occupation) as well as a profile of purchase behavior (price, styles, seasons).

Time management

Use of the computer in time management is important in controlling the allocation of time to different accounts. It is wasteful to spend too much time with marginal accounts that either buy only low profit lines or have low profit potential. Programs are available that can arrange accounts in order on either basis. Since market economics are fluid, this program must be rerun at regular intervals.

Territory routing has proven quite beneficial for rack jobbers and distributors. Combined with account analysis it can also specify what product assortment to load for each route. It is also beneficial in determining call frequency. All customers do not need the same level of service. This may require different call patterns each week revolving around a monthly or quarterly routing plan. While daily and weekly plans may be left to the salesperson's discretion, the computer data are very valuable in preparing a plan.

Forecasting

Although some people purchase to meet current and even crisis needs, most selling activity will be to meet future anticipated needs. In our complex society, many variables affect the forecast of future sales. The computer is our only tool capable of manipulating the huge quantity of data now available. Forecasting is usually the function of sales management, not of the salesforce. Frequently, however, salespeople supply part of the *input data* used to develop the forecast.

Some of the information you will submit for the data bank (information storage) will be based on judgment and observation of forces at work in a given territory. Since most territories have some unique aspects, each must be treated differently. In addition, no market stays the same; each is ever-changing. These perceptions are important in preparing market *projections* —forecasts of future buying and product needs.

The sales forecast affects most salespeople; it will determine each one's quota or goal. This fact is important since bonuses, incentives, and other rewards are frequently tied to the forecast. This in turn puts pressure on the salesperson to know whether the goal is realistic in view of the perception of current market factors. For this reason enlightened sales managers are involving their people in forecast preparation, even though it adds to the salesperson's job responsibilities.

Prospecting

The role of the computer in prospecting was mentioned briefly in Chapter 6. Consumer mobility offers great potential for the retail sector, especially regional and national chains and franchises. Mobility of the commercial and industrial sector has been on the increase as well, and this can be a problem for sales. For example, some experts estimate that ten thousand businesses have either gone out of business or moved from Chicago in the past five years. Suburban shopping centers have taken $2 billion in retail trade from downtown Chicago stores. Computer technology today can identify both consumer and industrial moves that change markets.

The computer has found many ways to identify prospects after the need develops, but even more important is development of prospect lists before the customer has identified a need. For example, retail chains can obtain lists of people planning moves to new areas. The name, new address, and other data, as well as expected arrival date, would be sent to salespeople in the store closest to the new address. A "friendly hello" from an appliance or furniture store can produce great sales results. The computer can even mail a letter in advance of the move to advise the prospective customer of the store's location and phone number and to provide a salesperson's name.

Similar activities can be applied to the commercial and industrial sector. Since these moves often take much longer, even more advance planning can be done. Some firms now offer the service of finding and qualifying these particular prospects. Architects, engineers, contractors, and development companies, as well as state and local development commissions, are being tapped for data on these major, nationwide moves. Normally these lists can be purchased already sorted by both SIC code and ZIP code as well as by Standard Metropolitan Statistical Area (SMSA).

As the migration continues to the south and southwest from the north, to the suburbs from the city, and to the rural areas from urban communities, computer-based prospecting will have greater importance. Unfortunately, few firms provide their salesforce with sophisticated information even though the technology is available.

3.   Contact the local IBM, Burroughs, NCR, or other EDP salesperson. Discuss examples of local firms' applications of computer techniques as sales support. What new technology is being tested? Report.

4.   Write a supplier of prospect information such as F. W. Dodge, Dun & Bradstreet, or trade publications. See Standard Rate and Data Service (SRDS) publications for other sources. Report on their services.

EDP and other techniques

Much recent emphasis has been placed on equipment that linked the salesperson directly to the computer. Many devices permit the salesperson to add input, or information, into the system. New equipment now permits the field sales force to receive output as well—information *from* the EDP system. Not all of this electronic equipment is computer based. ERA, the real estate franchisor, sends pictures of property over telephone lines with facsimile machines.

Keyboard, voice, and optical input

Inside salespeople communicate with a data system most often with a keyboard similar to that of a typewriter. In many stores point of sale terminals replace the old cash registers. A video display provides output when required, but many also use printout units if a hard copy is needed.

Voice input and output units are being used by some retailers for credit checks on their own credit cards. The salesperson reads the card number and amount of purchase verbally over the telephone after dialing a special number. If the credit is in good standing, an authorization number given verbally by the computer is recorded on the salescheck. If the credit is poor or the amount is over the customer's limit, a prerecorded message instructs the salesclerk on what action to take.

Voice input is sometimes used for inventory reorders. This method is not in widespread use because the expense for writing the computer program is high. By using code numbers, an order can be recorded on magnetic tape with a battery-operated portable unit. The information is replayed via telephone.

For routine reorders many firms today are adding a portable data entry terminal similar to the one pictured here. The small keyboard, about the size of a hand calculator, is connected to a magnetic tape recorder. Company, item number, and quantity can be quickly re-

Courtesy of MSI Data Corporation.

A sales representative using an optical wand to read a product identification number for order entry.

corded and then played back from any telephone at high speed. If the proper format is used there is no need for additional keypunching, verification, or other handling. The computer automatically generates order lists and billing.

One unit from MSI Data Corporation can record up to 250,000

characters on the recording tape and transmit the data at 120 characters per second. Input is provided by manual keyboard or **optical scanner**. The product's identification number is read by the scanner either from shelf labels containing a bar code or from numbers in the salesperson's order book. This system is most useful where large volume data is required and fast order writing is important.

Some of these units have solid-state memory and a visual display. Information recorded on the tape can be verified by search and display. Orders can be changed, if necessary, prior to transmission to the data center.

optical scanner
an input device that reads magnetic codes on grocery products; it also reads graphite marks.

Card input

An older entry system that is still used packs prepunched cards with each order. When stock reaches a certain level the card appears and is pulled and mailed to a data center for processing. Larger concerns have on-site card readers and transmitters which send the order at a predetermined stock level without a person handling the order at all.

New systems have coded plastic cards with reorder information. A special telephone unit reads and transmits the information after an individual dials a special number. Larger users have a hot line connected to a reader. Much of this selling uses the supplier's computer. American Hospital Supply, for a monthly fee, will put buyer's inventory reorders into their system. Many other wholesalers are now providing similar services.

Western Electric's "Transaction Telephone" has several methods of input. The twelve buttons can act as an input keyboard. The device can also read the magnetic strips on credit cards for credit checks. With magnetic codes on plastic cards for any standardized information, inputs can be entered from remote sites.

These are only a few examples of input devices available.

Visual output

Some of the newest portable data bank units feature both input and output. Carried in a briefcase, they have a keyboard for input. Output information is displayed on a small cathode ray tube —**CRT**— or similar visual display device. Some units even have a small printer.

CRT
equipment used to display data on a screen similar to a television screen.

Portable units are now available with color CRTs for playback of stored film, videotape, or other visuals. Because of high cost these systems are not yet popular. One venture attempted to use this equipment for booking entertainment talent. Each performer or group made a three-minute video recording that was stored in the computer with data about their fee and available dates. A nightclub

1 Credit	Salesperson reports information; computer provides checks on new and existing customers.	**Figure 13-1 How salespeople use EDP system**
2 Inventory	Location and quantity applied to both your firm and your customer's. Perrhaps the most rapidly expanding computer area of importance to salespeople. Now being applied to service businesses such as real estate, employment, advertising, travel, transportation and banking.	
3 Order Entry	Applies not only to entering an order but to tracking during processing. Permits rapid changes or expediting as necessary. Of use to every business, whether goods or service.	
4 Prospecting	Variety of methods for identifying target market segments. Can generate data for both screening and presentation preparation. Useful in almost every type of selling.	
5 Personal Management	Used to aid in time management. Helpful in determining call frequency, routing where territories are assigned, and customer profiling. Can significantly reduce paperwork burden with electronic input units.	
6 Presentation Support	Output devices can either give current data or process input data to generate new data during a presentation. Used not only for inventory search but for engineering design, advertising media schedules, and similar applications. Will also store and replay media (film or videotape) materials.	

owner would specify type of entertainment, price range, and open dates. The computer would select groups with these qualifications and each group's audition would be replayed on the remote color CRT. This system combined both electronic and visual selling. Unfortunately, the firm went bankrupt.

More sophisticated devices are entering the market daily. Even so, teaming the salesforce with the data system will continue to be slow. Most effort is concentrated on data entry or order entry.

5.   There are many firms now producing input or output devices or both for data systems. From the Yellow Pages find two offering remote units. What benefits are they selling? Report.

order processing
work associated with processing an order—sales, accounts receivable, order packing, transportation, insurance, and inventory controls.

Time-saving advantages

The primary purpose of teaming the salesforce with the **order processing** data system is to increase speed and accuracy. Many firms defeat this purpose by using complicated, lengthy forms for input; they are transmitted through the mail by salespeople. When received, the forms require further processing before the data can actually be fed into the system. Although this procedure may help management by producing more refined information, it costs the company valuable selling time and may mean loss of sales because of slower delivery.

Most recent devices and systems are directed at freeing the salesforce of much of their routine duties (primarily paperwork) that may demand 50 percent or more of their time. Figure 13–1 lists several areas where the salesforce and computer have been linked for increased productivity.

As you can see even from this incomplete listing, electronic data processing can touch almost every aspect of personal selling but it has affected only a handful of firms; for others the problem is a matter of time and money. Some new technology is of little or no use as sales support because the high cost has produced insignificant gains in productivity. It is only a matter of time, however, before virtually all salespeople down to those in the smallest profitable firm will be plugged in to some type of data system. EDP should be viewed as a sales support tool and should be used as such. In professional selling it offers great potential.

6. Interview a data processing instructor at your school. How much material in the introductory courses deal with EDP as sales support? Is any time given input/output devices that would be of particular interest to a professional salesperson? Report.

7. In what way is computer-developed information used at your school by counseling, admissions, and other personnel to identify and sell prospective students? Report.

Mini-case

Gladys just bought a franchise to sell a computer matching service. Her territory is Arizona, New Mexico, and Nevada. The service, for heavy construction equipment dealers, initially will provide a storage bank for used asphalt road construction equipment.

In order to sell new equipment, these dealers often must take as trade-in an old piece of equipment, which they then must sell. If

demand in their market is light, the trade-in may sit on their lot for many months tying up capital. Most dealers are interested in keeping their used equipment to a minimum.

Each dealer will pay $1,700 for a terminal and its installation. They will also pay the monthly line charge to the telephone company to connect with the computer. After the installation the dealer enters information about all trade-ins into the terminal. Each dealer can use the service to locate available used equipment.

Gladys receives a 15 percent commission, which she must split with the franchisor. She estimates an average transaction will be about $2,500.

The franchisor is also paying Gladys a bonus of $200 for each new dealer she signs up during the first year since the system needs many dealers putting information into it to make it of value. The franchisor has given Gladys a list of all known dealers in the three-state area.

Question: How can Gladys sell the first dealer first when the system is of use only when many dealers are on line?

---

account analysis	optical scanner	**Define these**
C.R.T.	order processing	**key concepts**
E.O.Q.	territory analysis	
80–20 principle	time management	
inventory control	Uniform Product Code	
keyboard		

14 Visual materials as sales support

Key terms

visual selling
flip book
slides
filmstrips
videotape
videodisc
micropublishing

Overview

Visual support can add impact to sales presentations. As some tools become simplified and are more widely used, others are becoming more complex. This chapter examines some reasons why use of visuals in selling is increasing and studies the impact they have on certain selling areas. We will investigate major types of visual selling techniques, equipment, and applications.

Effects of visual selling

Effects on the customer

Only recently have salespeople begun to understand the effect *visual selling* aids can produce, although many studies have shown that visual communication is powerful. Customers not only receive more information when visual devices are added but they also retain it longer. When visuals are employed, information is communicated faster and better; the visual presence forces the prospect or customer to concentrate on the particular message. Visuals can increase productivity considerably.

Visuals have the advantage of adding credibility to your presentation. Spoken words may be doubted, but statements and figures have more believability in pictures or print. Testimonial letters and movies of products being tested are very convincing support for a presentation. They also make those parts of a presentation believable where visuals are not used.

A sales presentation that effectively uses visuals is viewed by most customers as more professional than one that doesn't. It lends status to the salesforce that uses it and to the firm. It can make the difference in the final sale.

Visuals can help with both sales presentations and supplemental activities such as customer training. Specific training courses include maintenance and repair of equipment, operating instructions, and setting up product displays. In many areas of selling more time is spent on after-the-sale servicing than on selling. A good audiovisual program using print materials is an effective substitute for a busy salesperson.

Effects on the retail salesforce

Not all salespeople welcome the support of audiovisual materials. Some workers in the retail sales area see this support as a technological threat to their jobs. Continuous-play movies are being used to replace people selling many types of goods. In one test by J. C. Penney, for example, significant sales increases were made with four different products (rototillers, bathing suits, scarves and jewelry, and a game).

There are other signs that *media*—use of visual presentations, film, or television—may actually replace some retail sales personnel. A retail buyer takes merchandise sold by these movies to a cashier serving several departments. A rising proportion of these

visual selling
use of models, media, and print materials as sales aids.

cashiers are part-time employees, saving the store not only wages but, more important, fringe benefits.

This trend at the retail level will put pressure on manufacturers and their salesforces to provide traditional P.O.P. (see glossary) materials *plus* media. In turn, manufacturers will adopt media to support their own selling efforts to both retailers and wholesalers. Photography, including video, is primarily for end users, but retailers and wholesalers respond better to graphs, charts, and other graphic presentations. They are more interested in inventory turnover, space allocation, consumer buying patterns, and related statistical information, than in product advantages.

Effects on commercial, industrial, and service sales

Some industrial and commercial areas have been using visual selling tools for some time, especially engineering. In several engineering areas drawings, cutaways, and cross sections, combined with charted data, have long been a mainstay. Recently, however, this material has been converted from print to media for added convenience. A tray of 80 slides, for instance, can combine several different kinds and sizes of print materials into one small package.

In the commercial and industrial area where after-the-sale servicing is required, media will play a larger role. Media is an effective and efficient training tool for both operators and service technicians. The continued technological change will require media based instruction.

The services sector will also be forced to make more use of visual selling. The area has lagged behind in generating any significant productivity increases while charging higher and higher prices. Visuals can produce faster and greater sales in this area by providing more effective presentations, thus slowing the rise in prices.

Not all service areas are lagging behind. Advertising agencies sell a visual product; obviously they use visual selling. A few insurance companies have experimented with videotaped presentations played back on a customer's home TV set. Real estate firms, through franchised networks, have developed new techniques to use visual selling electronically.

The level of sophistication in using visuals to sell seems to depend not on the type of product but on the size of the organization using them; this is probably a result of the expenses involved in production. The major expense in visual-based selling is initial production and equipment costs. Reproduction cost of materials is minimal. Competition will force the largest firms to make the investment in media as its sales productivity is proven.

1. **Visit a retail store using point-of-purchase visual selling with continuous movies. Review the presentation. Interview the store manager for data on the machine's sales productivity.**

2. **Visit several franchised real estate offices. Compare and contrast the print and media support from the parent franchisor.**

Sight sellers

Flip books

Most salespeople are provided with some type of visuals, including product photos, data sheets, catalogs, brochures, and similar print materials. Usually these materials are not part of a planned presentation but are introduced as the need arises. Far too often they remain hidden in a file or briefcase, and the presentation never gets the visual support it needs.

As we discussed earlier in presentation planning, every salesperson should know what materials are available and how to use them effectively. "Sight sellers" should be so organized that incorporating them in the presentation is smooth and natural. Rummaging around for a lost item reflects very poor planning.

Where presentations to different prospects and customers is somewhat standardized, one might consider making a **flip book**. Most flip books are three-ring binders that include most, if not all, of the visual support materials provided. The layout of each page has three elements. At the top left is a statement of a product benefit. The center of the page supports the statement, using photographs, testimonial letters, graphs, charts, or drawings as proof. Often there is more than one possible method to support the statement. In those cases you must decide which will be the most effective method.

In the lower right corner of the page is a printed question the salesperson uses to ask the prospect to agree that the stated benefit is of value. If customers show agreement, there are two courses of action: a trial close may be attempted or the salesperson can move on to another benefit page.

A flip book provides several selling tools in one unit. It contains a comprehensive list of customer benefits arranged in order of importance or interest. The benefit support materials should answer the most common objections against buying. With appropriate materials these objections are overcome in a convincing fashion. The flip books also forces the salesperson to continue to look for closing opportunities during the presentation.

flip book
prepared presentation in ring or spiral binder; each page is part of a sequenced delivery.

Several cautions are in order. All listed benefits are not of value to all prospects. You must take care to select only those pages needed for a specific presentation tailored to the prospect's needs. For the same reason you need not feel obliged to cover every page before asking for an order. Avoid skipping back and forth through the flip book. If a question is raised that is answered later, ask that the client wait, but assure him or her that it *will* be answered.

Color slides

The next level of sophistication in visual selling concerns using **slides**. In addition to the standard 35 mm slide there are super slides, with more film surface, or minislides from cartridge film. Most are mounted in standard cardboard or plastic mounts. A deluxe model by 3M has a magnetic sound-recording surface circling the transparency. Special equipment is needed to use these slides.

The most popular types of equipment are those that are easiest to use. For portability, many of these projectors come housed in a briefcase with its own pop-up rear screen. This is ideal for individual

slides

color transparencies viewed on a large screen or wall. Some slide projectors are available with audio synchronization.

Movies can help increase the effectiveness of your sales presentation.

Courtesy of Charles Beseler Company

or small group presentations in the prospect's office or home. Usually these projectors may be removed from the case to allow the slides to be projected on a wall screen for larger audiences.

In some instances the customer comes to the salesperson, as, for example, in sales of portrait photography, interior design ideas, new homes and remodeling, or real estate. Equipment for these locations, while less portable, is still compact. The slide projector illustrated here is one example.

Design advances have reduced the size and weight of this equipment, and now it is possible to add a recorded selling message. Several units now on the market, including the 3M model mentioned above, use different methods of delivering a standardized story. One compact model now uses a minicartridge. The unit houses a record and playback component, complete with speaker. You can put the sales message on recording tape and set the machine for automatic slide changes to coordinate the presentations.

There are several other reasons for the growing popularity of the slide-supported presentation. Slides are significantly easier to produce than ever before. Automatic 35 mm cameras, many with built-in flash units, have reduced photography to three-step simplicity: aim, focus, and push the button. Many salespeople carry these cameras to photograph evidence to support their claims.

New graphic arts tools, such as press-on letters, make preparation of titles and other flat art relatively easy. While this has affected all visual media, the conversion of these materials to slides still is the simplest and least expensive method. Existing print materials can be easily converted to slides.

Nevertheless it does take some time to create a custom presentation for one customer but this disadvantage is more than offset by the realism gained and the compactness (80 to 140 slides to a tray) of the tool. Creation of a slide show forces you to give serious thought about the ingredients of the presentation that will tell a complete and convincing story.

3. Collect visual material for a product and prepare a flip book in the suggested format. Where materials are lacking create your own. Have you covered all major benefits and answered all major objections likely to be encountered?

4. Visit with the production manager in the audio-visual department of your school. Report on the materials and techniques for preparing flat art. How much would it cost a firm to set up this kind of facility for its salespeople?

Sight and sound

In the previous section we discussed tools that were primarily visual and that are best used with your own personal presentation. Flip books are basically pictures to illustrate your comments. Color slides may be used in the same way.

Other tools, such as movies, filmstrips, and videotape almost always incorporate sound as an integral part of a professional presentation. In these formats the narration is normally not your own but is prerecorded. In this section we will take a look at how these formats are used in selling.

Filmstrips

filmstrips
single strip of film with many frames, often synchronized with audio tape.

The primary advantage of selecting *filmstrips* instead of slides is cost. Almost all filmstrips begin as slides that are "animated" into one master piece of film. Although the master is expensive, copies made from it are very inexpensive. Filmstrips are used primarily where many salespeople are telling a standardized story. The Mormon church, for example, purchased more than one thousand filmstrip projectors for their house-to-house missionaries to use.

Unlike slides, where the verbal selling is usually delivered by the salesperson, filmstrips often have a prerecorded audio track complete with music. This added professionalism usually extends to the photography and graphics as well. There appears to be a direct relationship between the number of people who will see the filmstrip and the investment in the master print. In some cases this includes using professional actors for the narration.

Many lightweight, compact filmstrip projectors on the market are intended for use by salespeople. Like the slide projectors, some can be easily housed in a briefcase with a small rear projection screen. One of the major innovations in filmstrips is the plug-in cartridge. The LaBelle Courier contains a continuous film loop and the audio cassette. For convenience, there is a built-in carrying handle on top.

Movies

Eastman Kodak has recently been advertising heavily the advantages of using movies in selling. The primary drawback of slides and filmstrips is the lack of action. Where motion is a vital ingredient of a concept or product, either movies or videotape is required to convey that action.

Major technical advances have been made in equipment to produce the movies and to play them back. Many new cameras have built-in zoom lenses, automatic focus and shoot features, and microphones for on-the-spot sound recording. New film permits shooting in low light so extra lighting equipment becomes unnecessary.

Playback is the most important aspect of visual equipment for the salesperson. Super 8 film is probably the most widely used in selling; normally it is housed in a continuous loop cartridge. Its simplicity allows the salesperson to simply plug it in and play. For easy portability the playback equipment has been redesigned into a small compact deck about the size of a slide projector. Some models play the movie back on a television monitor, while others project it on a small rear screen for individual or small group presentations. The movie has become quite a versatile selling tool.

Like filmstrips, movies are economical to use only when they are to be shown repeatedly to many people. Initial production costs are extremely high, especially if a professional crew is employed. Costs may run over $1,000 per minute for movies of professional quality.

Small firms that want the motion of movies but cannot afford the great cost can produce their own presentations. New cameras have reduced costs significantly. Many salespeople carry movie cameras to film product testing and demonstrations to produce their own movie presentations.

5. Refer to the Yellow Pages to find a local firm that prepares filmstrips. Prepare a report on how slides are converted to a filmstrip and give cost ranges for different sizes (half-frames, 35 mm) of filmstrips.

6. Visit a local camera store for a demonstration of a Super 8 camera. Have the salesperson compute the cost for producing ten seven-minute films a year. What is the initial investment in equipment? Prepare a report.

Videotapes

In the last few years TV manufacturers have been producing small hand-held TV cameras at a more reasonable cost and reduced size. This breakthrough has expanded the use of TV considerably. The fairly complete package of lightweight portable equipment illustrated here, including a color camera, can be purchased for less than $5,000, and the price is falling. Like the Super 8 camera, its use has been simplified so even amateurs can operate it with minimal instructions.

Videotape is much more versatile than movies. Special effects, computer graphics, and electronic creations can generate more impact. In an age where everyone has had a steady diet of television for over a generation, people have become accustomed to this level of sophistication. It must, however, be done skillfully to be effective.

videotape
a television recording system that can be played back immediately after recording.

Video equipment has become quite popular in recent years. It is used often in retail store settings and by salespeople in their presentations.

Courtesy of Sony Corporation of America, Video Products Division

Most salespeople are not involved in the production of these video-based selling tools. One exception can be found in real estate, where the hand-held camera is used to videotape tours of houses and buildings. In other instances great volumes of materials are needed but the materials have a very short life. In these cases no special effects or graphics are used and occasionally there is no sound. Processing is not required; the video material can be used to sell immediately. Using real estate as an example, a house listed in the morning can be videotaped on the spot and shown in the office to a prospect immediately upon return of the salesperson, who narrates. Travel time is reduced considerably.

Competition has brought rapid changes to the playback equipment industry. In addition to the now standard ¾-inch cassette widely used in educational and industrial training, the ½-inch EIAJ, ½-inch Betamax, and the **videodisc**, a flexible disc that looks something like a phonograph record, compete for market share. By the time this book is published the battle will have intensified even more.

videodisc
similar to videotape but uses a disc (like a phonograph record), instead of a tape cassette for recording.

While it may seem somewhat futuristic to discuss video-selling, video is a rapidly maturing industry. New equipment and techniques as well as competitive factors will produce a further increase in its use. It is estimated that over a thousand firms have been established to produce video materials (software) for business and industry. While the majority of these firms have begun by producing training materials, the sales support market is large and lucrative; it will no doubt be aggressively pursued.

7. Visit a television station, local video production firm, or advertising agency. Report on the equipment and techniques of video production.

8. Visit with a salesperson for a manufacturer of video hardware. Report on recent applications of video to selling.

New developments in micropublishing

Microfilm is no longer the exclusive province of the super spy, but has lately come into use as a sales support tool. Libraries have recognized the value of its compactness for storing records. Files of all types have been stored on microfilm by libraries and business concerns.

A major drawback to its use in sales has been the large, bulky reader that is required to make the microfilm material accessible to the user. With the development of microfiche and small, portable readers, nothing stands in the way of the widespread use of this visual tool for selling.

Microfiche is a film that holds 98 color images mounted on each 4 x 6-inch card. Individual frames are viewed on the portable reader illustrated here. If needed, a small tape cassette player can provide professional narration.

Microfiche has many applications to retail and commercial industrial sales as well as sales of services.

Micropublishers have adopted their facilities to produce product catalogs, the major use of microfilm today. Catalogs on microfiche are computer generated and they regularly reflect price changes as well as product additions and eliminations. Where catalogs had been bulky and difficult to update they now can be carried about on a few microfiche cards and viewed on a small reader.

Catalogs of parts available can also be kept in this way by retailers and wholesalers for both sales and repair services. Diagrams and printed information can be generated by the computer.

Training programs are readily adaptable to this method. Yamaha uses the format for more than 40 programs to train motorcycle mechanics. The trainee, while working, places the reader next to the motorcycle for step-by-step instructions.

The use of micropublished materials in sales support will probably increase. Compact and lightweight, they are ideal for outside salespeople. Now that color is also available the opportunities are expanding. When coupled with computer generated materials as well as traditional photography, sales will find many applications.

Courtesy of Eastman Kodak Company

micropublishing
recording in miniature on film cards. A 4" x 6" card may hold 98 color frames.

Courtesy of Bell & Howell

Visual support material are an indispensable part of a successful sales call.

Changes in the selling role

Visuals are changing the role of the contemporary salesperson. In the medium and large firm that can afford it, more media will be produced either to reduce face-to-face selling time or to increase volume for the same investment of time. Visuals can increase productivity, a commodity firms are always looking for more of.

Advances in technology will require salespeople to spend more time servicing an account than selling it. Media is also very effective in providing service, especially in training and other educational information. Shortages and environmental factors are producing long-term relationships between businesses. This also puts more emphasis on the service aspect.

For the small firm to remain competitive, its salespeople must become involved with media production and use. As newer, more efficient, and less expensive visual equipment come to the market, few firms will be able to ignore the advantages of media use.

Both the nature of selling today and the use of media materials are changing the responsibilities of the professional salesperson. In some areas media will permit the salesperson to make many more presentations and sales simply by reducing the time required for preparation and face-to-face selling time. In other areas media will require the salesforce to keep current on new media materials and also to become involved in media production.

Whenever media is used, more thought goes into the presentation and more professional results usually occur. This contributes to increasing competition. To be competitive the salesperson must make use of some form of visual-based selling. It sells.

9. Visit a local audio-visual equipment distributor. Prepare a report on applications by local firms of each media method discussed. What failures have occurred and why?

Mini-case

Jeri has about had it. Since she took this job selling minicomputers she has only made one sale in the past four months. Many presentations; no sales.

Jeri is selling new minicomputers to retail stores, primarily family-owned, single units. She offers packages that range from $6,000 to $30,000. The computers will handle inventory controls, payroll, and bookkeeping. On paper she believes she can show that the computer will pay for itself in eighteen to thirty-six months,

primarily in better inventory control. Out-of-stock items and slow-moving items can be monitored.

Jeri has a firm that will finance the purchase. Also, she will spend one week with a buyer to see that the system works smoothly. She has testimonials from other users. Jeri is convinced she has a good product at a good price.

Yet these people seem afraid to step into the computer age. She thinks if she could prepare a slide package to dramatize the cost savings, the increased turnover, the reduction of out-of-stock items, and the payback period she could make a more convincing story. *Question:* Limiting yourself to eighty frames, can you design a slide package to help Jeri sell?

---

filmstrip
flip book
media
microfiche
micropublishing

movie
slides
videodisc
videotape
visual communication

**Define these
key concepts**

15 Using sales promotion to sell

Key terms

premium
specialty
contest
fairs
trade mart
exposition
trade show
convention
vertical promotion

Overview

The role of sales promotion activities as sales support has increased considerably in recent years. Most selling positions require interaction with a variety of sales promotion efforts—all those activities a firm uses to stimulate sales. Some promotion activities are directed at customers, but some are directed at the salesforce, to stimulate their efforts. These promotions are designed to help the salesforce do a better job of selling. Yet many salespeople react negatively to the involvement required because they do not understand the role sales promotion currently plays. The purpose of this chapter is to provide basic knowledge about these diverse sales support tools.

Expansion of sales promotion

When competition intensifies, when advertising does not produce as expected, or when sales become sluggish, most firms look to sales promotion for help. More and more people are becoming convinced that well designed and executed short-term sales promotions have exceptional sales-producing power. As promotion grows, it will be the rare salesperson whose selling life is not touched by these activities.

Two types of promotions

The first type of activities are promotions that a firm produces specifically for the salesforce on a regular basis. Normally included are the production of sales support materials such as catalogs, brochures, samples, and other items that would be used on a day-to-day basis. As we saw in the last chapter this may include the regular (or irregular) production of media materials. An example now used by some firms would be a weekly microfiche edition of a catalog or price list. Most materials, however, are produced annually, semiannually, or quarterly. Although the materials usually are not part of any special promotion, they are considered necessary tools for efficient selling.

The second type of promotions are part of a special effort designed to achieve some particular objective. These projects are usually combined with the firm's advertising for added impact. Examples are attendance at a series of trade shows or pursuance of one-shot programs such as a contest or incentive program. Advance planning and continuing coordination is required both for a specific event and for programs that will run for given time periods. Because of all this extra effort, these projects are usually run by a promotion manager, an advertising agency, or a public relations firm. The wise sales manager normally does not actively design and execute these plans but coordinates them with the salesforce.

Purposes of sales promotions

Sales promotion activities may be undertaken in response to competitive pressure or as a means of gaining a competitive advantage. Both involve the salesforce, but in different ways.

One example of the first type of activity is regular exhibition at trade shows and conventions that are attended by your customers. Because all your competition has exhibits, your firm will exhibit too. Even though orders may not be written in quantity at the show, the goodwill generated will have a subtle but positive effect on later selling.

The second type of promotion, aimed at developing a competitive advantage, is exemplified by a promotion campaign to support a new product introduction. Promotion campaigns may also be used to stimulate sales during slow seasons, to encourage customers to order larger quantities or a wider variety of products, and to stimulate the salesforce to work harder. While a few promotions are aimed at generating goodwill, most are designed to increase volume and profit.

Your involvement

To what degree is the salesforce actually involved with these sales promotion activities? This varies greatly, depending on the situation. There is no direct involvement when the promotion is part of a direct mail campaign or is handled by a special agency. In these instances the promotion takes a supportive role much like that of advertising. In most instances, however, the salesforce will be directly involved and an active part of the promotion plan. This would range from using a special offer as an incentive to close sales to giving salespeople several days off from regular selling to work with exhibits and displays or engage in other nonselling activities.

Specialty items and premiums

premium item
item given as an incentive to place an order.

specialty item
items imprinted with the company name or trademark given free as reminder advertising.

Each year firms spend millions of dollars on a variety of **premium** and **specialty items** designed to stimulate sales. Some are dispensed by salespeople to serve as reminder advertising and to generate goodwill. Common items are calendars, key chains, matchbooks, and pens. It is estimated that the specialty advertising industry now generates more than *half a billion dollars* a year in sales of these items.

There are differences between the specialty and the premium. For one, the specialty is imprinted with the firm's or the salesperson's name; the premium is not. For another, specialties are given out freely, while the premium is normally given as an inducement to buy.

Premiums are tied directly to closing sales, and this makes them more important to salespeople. Business recognizes this by spending a much greater amount on premiums than on specialties. Premium sales now total *over $3 billion a year*. The largest amount goes to consumer package goods in return for box tops, labels, and other proof of purchase. The cash rebates widely popular a few years ago to move cars, cameras, and appliances is also a type of premium. In 1976, for example, American Motors tied in with American Airlines and American Tourister Luggage for a premium offer. The benefit of premiums to salespeople is that they help close sales. Most premium offers are backed by advertisements that use the offer as their theme. Manufacturer's salespeople and representatives find wholesalers and retailers much more receptive to their products when premium offers are included. Some of these premiums may be directed at intermediaries (middlemen). For this group both merchandise and services can be used as inducements to buy.

1. For your selected selling area, what package of materials should be provided, exclusive of audio-visual aids? How should they be organized in your desk or briefcase for efficient use? Report.

2. Would reminder or specialty advertising be useful in your prospecting or maintaining contact with marginal accounts? What item(s) would be most welcome and displayed?

Contests and incentives

Contests and incentive programs may be directed at the customers, the salespeople, or both. A specific time period is indicated, and the goal may be to sell a certain quantity or dollar volume of a particular product, to introduce a new product to the market, or merely to increase the visibility of a product or firm.

contests
at the retail level these are usually games of chance; in wholesale, commercial, and manufacturing firms', contests and prizes are usually tied to sales or profits.

Contests for the ultimate consumer

Contests and incentives directed at the customer are often supported by massive advertising to give sales support and call attention to them. Because of state and national laws that control them, contests must have few if any strings attached; they are used primarily as a prospecting tool. Retail stores frequently have contests to attract new customers, sometimes in conjunction with local radio stations. These are designed both to attract new customers and to keep old customers coming back. Retailers know there is a definite relationship between traffic and dollar volume.

In any contest the prize for the sponsoring firm and for their salespeople is increased sales and profits. For this reason many national and regional firms selling through intermediaries will sponsor contests directed at the *ultimate consumer* to stimulate sales. The effect is actually to "pull" the merchandise through the wholesalers and retailers. If sufficient demand is created, the salesperson merely writes the orders and is free to concentrate on servicing accounts without spending time on fruitless presentations.

Contests and sales are directed toward maintaining and increasing customer patronage.

Courtesy of Walgreen's

Contests directed at other businesses

While contests directed at the ultimate consumer are primarily for prospecting and repeat business, contests directed at businesses who are your customers can be tied to sales volume. These require direct involvement by the salesforce and can be very stimulating. They are aimed primarily at wholesalers and retailers. Prizes, usually awarded for increasing volume or for meeting quotas, may be exotic vacations, automobiles, appliances, luggage, and television sets. A key factor is that everyone has an opportunity to win, and all who actively participate receive at least a small prize for their efforts.

Contests such as these normally run for at least a month, and sometimes longer. They provide excitement before, during, and after the actual contest. They serve to strengthen ties with established customers as well as to increase volume. If they are well designed and executed they can develop goodwill and a close working relationship between salespeople and their accounts. The big winners often are indebted to their sales representative for help in achieving their goal.

Incentives for the salesforce

Contests in the last group are aimed at the salesforce, and they are widely used. New product introductions are often accompanied by a contest as an incentive to speed distribution. Off-season sales, slow-moving products, and products with high profits are also good bets for a contest. Salespeople usually welcome these contests. For one thing, selling work can become tiresome; the contest is rejuvenating and adds some spark. It also promotes healthy competition between the salespeople. Where the rewards are substantial, both ego and income receive a good boost.

While some incentives offer luxurious vacations or fancy luggage, more often they consist of a check and a trophy. The money may soon be spent, but the trophy on the mantel or plaque on the wall long proclaim one's competence. Placed in an office, they convey professionalism to customers. Everyone benefits.

3. Interview a sales manager on both the positive and negative aspects of contests directed at the salesforce. Report.

Product exhibitions

The role of the professional salesperson in shows, exhibits, **fairs**, expositions, clinics, and conventions has been expanding dramatically. There are many signs that this situation is not restricted to the commercial and industrial area but now applies to the retail sector as well. State and county fairs especially have been attracting record numbers of local businesses as exhibitors. Growth in the number of **trade marts** has altered the role of many salespeople. The new Apparel Mart in Chicago, for example, is aimed at "regionalizing" fashion shows. It adds to the already established fashion centers of New York, Los Angeles, and Dallas. As we shall see, some of these changes are subtle; some are dramatic.

fairs
exhibits which are primarily county and state-sponsored. Most are still agriculture-based but draw significant urban crowds.

trade marts
office buildings where many related firms maintain sales offices and display areas.

Retail shows
In the retail sector you may have noticed an increase in "show" activities. Part of this is right in the stores. Demonstrations are now a popular promotional tool. Usually the store's salespeople do not stage the demonstration. Instead, they are provided by the manufacturer. Either their salesperson becomes the demonstrator or individuals are trained to go on a demonstrating "circuit." In most cases, however, the local store's salespeople benefit from the promotions: they ring up the sales—and the commissions.

How-to demonstrations
An offshoot of the demonstration is the wide variety of in-store clinics we now see. They have been most successful in do-it-yourself areas

The Chicago Apparel Center is located next to the long established Merchandise Mart in Chicago's loop.

Courtesy of The Apparel Center

such as fashion sewing, plumbing, heating, electrical wiring, paneling, and air-conditioning. One of the top three pattern companies employs women to go from one fabric store to another showing off their latest designs. They give helpful sewing hints to sell not only the patterns but fabrics and trims as well. Many fabric shops have offered sewing classes as a source of both income and extra sales.

These clinics and classes have also been widely adopted in the arts and crafts area. In one recent month a midwest chain offered no less than one hundred classes covering a wide variety of crafts to move their merchandise. Courses such as these prospect and sell at the same time. Retail photography supply firms have been using "authorized factory representatives" for in-store demonstrations more aggressively the past few years. In these cases the representatives usually do more than demonstrate: they also write orders.

Specialty expositions

Not all show selling is in the store. As a professional photographer, I participated for several years with six other firms in a large bridal show held in a rental ballroom. Although the fashions were the show, each participant was assigned a display booth that was seen by more than two thousand guests. Participants shared all advertising, promotion, and other costs. Attendance was limited to engaged women, their mothers, and some guests. Salespeople from the firms attended the booths in tuxedos and formal gowns. This lucrative show, held in February, usually filled the books with May through

August weddings, even though our studio sold the highest priced photography in town.

Perhaps the biggest boom in multi-store shows has been the local **exposition**. Usually with the backing from manufacturers, and the support of their salesforce, these shows are now widely used in boating, home improvement, automobiles, motorcycles, snow-mobiles, skiing, and other recreational pursuits. Recently they have been expanded to hobbies and crafts as well. Some retailers partic-ipate partly as a prospecting method: others show new merchan-dise to keep customers coming back: a few join in reluctantly be-cause competition forces them to be there. For the last reason, if no other, more and more retail salespeople will find themselves staffing these displays.

exposition
large show with many exhibitors displaying goods or services in booths.

Attendance at county and state fairs has increased in recent years, and in response more and more exhibitors are participating. These run the gamut from small local retailers to major national firms, alongside public service groups and colleges. Yes, colleges have begun to recruit students with fair booths. In our language it is prospecting: faculty members are asked to be a salesperson-for-a-day to help staff the booth.

Trade shows and marts

There are two kinds of **trade shows,** both of which have grown con-siderably over the past decade. One kind is open to the public; the other is restricted to the trade, or businesses engaged in the field.

trade shows
expositions limited to wholesalers, retailers, or other qualified buyers.

The first type is very similar to the local exposition put on by retailers, but is much larger, is used by manufacturers, and is held only in major cities. The boating industry has a series of these in late winter (primarily February) to introduce new models. The car indus-try runs its shows in the fall. These shows try to produce glamour and excitement. Name entertainers are usually booked for shows, displays tend to be lavish, and attractive women are used to dem-onstrate the products. The salesforce serving the region will often be there, too.

The second type of show—the more important to most salespeople—is open only to the trade, which means primarily wholesalers and retailers. Selling—writing orders—is a primary goal at these shows. Most of these shows are put on in conjunction with a market week near a regional trade center. In Dallas, the world's largest complex, the apparel mart produces fifteen major fashion shows each year to attract buyers for their tenants.

The success of these trade shows connected with marts has caused a spurt of new building. Most major cities now have exposi-tion halls that aggressively seek bookings.

"Open" trade shows, like the car show illustrated here, provide a showcase for new consumer goods.

Courtesy of McCormick Place

In much the same way the growth of mart buildings has forced the restructuring of many salesforces. Exhibits at trade shows are expensive and as firms feel compelled for competitive reasons to exhibit at smaller and smaller shows they find their costs escalating without corresponding sales increases. Since the salesforce usually staffs these shows, they end up losing valuable time they should spend servicing accounts. Salespeople therefore become reluctant to attend shows when they feel more orders can be written by working their territory. In consequence a few major national firms have abandoned all but a couple of *major shows*. This may have a ripple effect that will seriously hurt the trade show complexes. The effect on sales will be watched.

Similarly, the growth of mart buildings has taken many salespeople out of the field, but for different reasons. The trade mart today is very much like a regional shopping center for retailers. Firms have learned they can cut costs and still serve their customers by establishing sales offices in these central locations. The customers—retailers and wholesalers—come to the salesperson to buy. Between calls they are served by telephone and mail. New accounts are solicited the same way.

This development has significantly restructured much selling and buying. It has both advantages and disadvantages for the sales-force. First, there is little or no travel, since all selling is either at the trade show or in the sales office. Salespeople are selling on their own ground which is to their advantage since the physical environ-ment and distractions can be controlled. Usually they are provided with better selling tools such as samples, cutaways, displays, and media. The office tends to be fairly plush, creating a better psychological climate for buying.

The disadvantage is related to schedule. The majority of buying is compacted into a few mart weeks during the year. During buying weeks the pace is hectic; customers may not be given adequate time. Business can be lost when potential customers pass up a crowded office and forget to come back. They find what they want elsewhere or do without. In the rush, tempers may flare and ill will may be developed. The pressure is more than many salespeople can cope with. Between mart weeks, however, the selling is primarily a desk job. Orders have to be executed and followed up. Much time will be devoted to telephone contacts, mailing materials, and pa-perwork. Customers will be invited for more leisurely discussions of their needs.

Courtesy of McCormick Place

Most industrial trade shows are closed to the public. Consequently the salespeople can concentrate building their sales volume.

convention
meeting of a group with similar business or educational interests.

Conventions

The last area of show selling is **conventions**. Literally tens of thousands of associations and interest groups hold regular regional and national conventions. These conventions have exhibits for two reasons: to raise money by selling booth space and to provide an attraction to attend. Companies with products to sell are the primary exhibitors. This book, for instance, has been displayed by Rand McNally at several academic association conventions around the country. These conventions attract primarily business instructors and professors from colleges and universities. Since conventions attract a high proportion of innovators and early adopters (see Chapter 4), they constitute a good place to display new products.

Despite this attraction many salespeople resist having to work conventions. They usually have to oversee moving the materials, actually set up and tear down the exhibit, and spend much time staring into space when the group is in session. Often the majority of their traffic is on one day, but the exhibit must be staffed for the entire convention. Cocktail parties and hospitality rooms are used to promote goodwill, with the salesforce sometimes doubling as bartenders and afterwards as janitors. Those doing a good job in the

Major publishing firms regularly exhibit their products at academic conventions.

Courtesy of Rand McNally Trade Division

field will see few new faces and write few additional orders. The goal is primarily to keep up with competition and maintain prestige.

All conventions do have advantages, however. For the small firms with a salesforce inadequate to cover a market fully, they provide visibility. Unlimited opportunities can be found to combine them with other sales promotion devices. A well-designed contest may secure names to be followed up—by phone or mail if time limitations prohibit personal visits. Specialty advertising can be used as reminders to generate later inquiries. Hats, buttons and bags, as at the public trade shows, can enable a firm to stand out from the crowd. Conventions also provide a good opportunity to shop the competition and build product knowledge.

Show selling requires hard work and long hours. As with any production it requires advance planning and time management. How productive the show is depends partly on the support provided by management, but it also depends on the salesforce using the opportunity to their advantage. Wherever crowds of people gather, whether they are consumers or businesspeople, there is opportunity to use show selling. Most factors are to the salesperson's advantage. The key is using those advantages.

4. Have a retailer or other business person take you to a closed trade show. Report on your observations.

5. Visit a fair or exhibition open to the public. Interview a salesperson from a medium to large firm on his or her involvement with the exhibit. What advantages and disadvantages do they see to this use of their time. Report.

Vertical promotion: the salesperson's role

The objectives of economy and efficiency in recent years has led to emphasis on establishing strong vertical relationships. These are the internal relationships that allow a company to control both production and distribution by dealing through wholesalers, retailers, agents, and brokers. When manufacturers sell through wholesalers to retailers their salespeople and agents may spend as much time with the retailers as they do with the wholesalers. Much of this activity centers around *vertical promotion*. We have already seen that these salespeople are often used for in-store demonstrations and clinics on behalf of their wholesalers. Other activities include coordinating new product introductions and point-of-purchase displays, signs and banners. The growth of co-op advertising has also placed part of the burden of policing advertising abuses on the salesforce.

vertical promotion
coordinated selling effort by a manufacturer and a wholesaler or retailer.

To take some pressure off their salesforce, firms now hire merchandisers to perform many of these promotion related tasks. Merchandisers may be viewed as the salespeople's assistants, although their activities may be directed by either a sales manager or a promotion manager. Some of their work will be for primary customers, but much of it is carried on for the benefit of secondary firms and ultimate purchasers. It is the responsibility of the salesperson in these situations to be aware of the activities of the merchandisers, as well as their talents and limitations. Some services fit into an entire promotional campaign: some services are requested by the salesperson to meet the needs of an individual customer.

Another technique aimed at building stronger vertical relations is the multi-company road tour. Using exhibits in trucks, motor homes, and specially constructed trailers, these tours usually feature a half dozen or more businesses. Moving from city to city, they set up in the parking lots of the major firms who are their target customers. While some firms sell directly to these buyers, others strive to gain distribution in new territories. Any sales written will be credited to the agent, broker, or wholesaler who has been assigned the territory, who will also service the account after the salespeople and their exhibits leave.

Firms who have been disenchanted with the great proliferation of trade shows and exhibitions often prefer this approach. Customers are isolated from distractions; the exhibits are designed for selling specific merchandise; and the salespeople can go into the prospect's firm to deal directly with their problems. The U.S. Department of Commerce has used the same approach quite successfully in foreign countries to sell U.S. products.

The range of sales promotion activities that today's salesperson can be involved with is now quite great. Promotional tools can be used to meet many objectives, from building goodwill to closing sales. Working with the firm's promotional activities quite frequently takes a significant part of many salespeople's time and energy. While much of this activity may not be pleasant, it is usually productive, especially for those who take the long view. Salespeople who can only see as far as this month's commission check will probably be reluctant to be involved with a firm's promotion activities. It is unfortunate that these people only welcome the short-term sales stimulus designed to pump up sales—and commissions.

6.   What vertical selling relationships—either forward or backward—would be beneficial to your selling choice? Would this relationship shift some of your selling load to others? Report.

Jack sells carpets for a major mill and is currently assigned to the showroom/office in the Dallas Mart. The showroom looks much like a major carpet store, with both floor and wall display units. The lighting is soft with dramatic accents and the carpet is fairly plush.

His firm just introduced a new look in carpet at the mart week that closed yesterday. They had sent mailers to all retailers in the area announcing their new designs and the response was tremendous. All the first runs of the carpet were sold out.

On the first day the showroom was mobbed. Jack was writing orders just as fast as he could take them. Late the second day one of his major accounts was finally able to see him, even though the room was still packed. He wanted to place a large order for the new carpet, but unfortunately several of the colors were now sold out. He reminded him that he knew it was first-come, first-served. He countered that he tried several times to get to him but was pushed aside by the crowd.

He asked that he find some way to take his order for the carpet or he would give his business to other mills. Jack was now worried about losing a very good account.
Question: How could Jack have avoided this confrontation?

**Define these
key terms**

caravan selling	trade mart
clinic	trade show
contest	fair
exposition	vertical promotion
premium item	sales incentives
specialty item	trade incentives
convention	customer incentives

Management of contemporary selling 5

16 Sales management

Key terms

sales manager
orientation
vestibule training
motivation
quantitative analysis
qualitative analysis
budget

Overview

For many professional salespeople the move from salesperson to sales manager is a career path development goal. In this chapter we will look at the duties and responsibilities of these managers, whose performance usually has a direct bearing on the financial health of the firm.

Although the position is primarily a desk job, it offers more variety and challenge than other management positions. Sales managers must be able to deal with functions like recruiting, selection, training, and compensation normally associated with personnel. The ability to motivate others is critical. The sales manager must develop budgets, make sales forecasts, and assign quotas. There must be close coordination with sales promotion, advertising, and publicity. They are also responsible for providing their salesforce with adequate support and selling tools. It is a job that requires many talents.

Should you choose management?

A sales career is an excellent training ground for those interested in management careers, not just for sales management. In fact, as we noted before, many firms use the sales department as a temporary training ground for those hired into a management training program. Approximately one-fourth of all corporation presidents have had some sales experience during their careers.

Job similarities

Many skills learned while selling are used by a **sales manager**. The primary skill among managers is the development of good human relations ability. Managers have to sell too; they sell ideas, budgets, forecasts, and organizational changes to higher levels of management. The salesforce will have to be sold on changes in territories, quotas, and compensation. Much of the planning and problem solving will require similar skills; only the types of problems and objectives will differ.

sales manager
one whose primary responsibility is the supervision of salespeople.

Job differences

The decision to enter sales management should not be made lightly, however. *The move is not as natural a step as it might appear at first glance.* Many people who have excelled in professional selling have performed poorly as sales managers. While some skills and abilities are similar, others are quite different.

Salespeople usually complain about the amount of paperwork. For those who enjoy personal contact and dislike paperwork, sales management may not be the right choice; managers do more, not less, paperwork. Paperwork is done at a desk in an office, and salespeople who find it disagreeable to sit at a desk for many hours each week should not be managers. This paperwork also places different demands on managers' time than on salespeoples'. In most areas of selling the use of time is largely under the salesperson's control. In management, however, there are always deadlines to meet—for budgets, reports, and sales forecasts, to name but a few—that some people find very confining.

The sales manager may also require some skills for which the sales career has not adequately prepared the salesperson. These would include recruiting, selecting, and training the new salespeople. In most firms these activities are not performed by the personnel department but by sales management. The following nine task areas shared by most sales managers illustrate the diverse nature of the manager's job!

1. Recruiting and selecting
2. Developing effective training programs
3. Supervising and motivating
4. Developing compensation and incentive programs
5. Setting quotas and budgets
6. Defining territory boundaries
7. Coordinating advertising and sales promotion
8. Coordinating support services
9. Qualitative and quantitative evaluation of the salesforce.

Sales managers' responsibilities

To explore these problem areas let's use as an illustration a professional football coach as the sales manager and the football team as the salespeople. You will see many similarities as we go along.

Recruiting

The beginning of a great team begins with an effective *recruiting* effort, that is, attracting people to fill positions. This is true with both existing and new teams. Teams will lose players because of old age, or injury, to the entertainment and broadcasting industries, to business, and because of nonperformance. The sales manager must assume that some salespeople will leave voluntarily from time to time and some will be asked to leave.

The proportion of people who leave can be tied largely to the effectiveness of the recruiting effort. The poorer the recruiting the higher the turnover. While I have no figures on how much it costs a professional football team to recruit and sign a player, it surely runs into several thousand dollars. To that cost must be added a training period. Very few rookie football players become superstars their first year in the pros. The money spent on recruiting, selecting, and training a new football player is viewed by management as an investment to return money to them in the future.

The same is true for professional salespeople. Most salespeople take several years to mature and develop their top potential. The cost to recruit, select, and train a new salesperson today often totals more than twenty thousand dollars. Included in this figure is the salary paid until the individuals are selling enough to pay their way. This period may be longer than one year in some technical and specialized areas, where costs of more than thirty thousand are not uncommon.

It should be clear, then, that poor recruiting is expensive. It leads to poor overall sales performance by building a team that will not produce a winning season. It can also be very expensive if a high number of rookies leave before returning to the firm the money invested in them. This problem is compounded in most firms since accurate statistics are usually not kept on the costs involved.

Training

In all but the larger firms the job of sales training falls to the sales manager. This is a new role for the sales manager—one of educator. In our professional football team, special coaches are employed to further develop already evident skills. The team also uses trainers for body building and body repair. In major corporations you will find similar specialists to assist in the training function, but most sales managers in smaller organizations must provide the training themselves.

By rereading Chapter 5 you can review what is usually necessary in a training program. We can divide this into three areas: orientation, vestibule training, and on-going programs.

Orientation is concerned primarily with acquainting a new salesperson with a company and all its operations. In manufacturing firms, for instance, this would include trips through the factories, warehouses, and offices. The amount of time and money devoted to a good orientation program is usually directly related to the size of the firm. Smaller firms generally provide a poorer orientation program. Retailers, as a group, have traditionally provided poor orientation to new salespeople.

Vestibule training is giving new employees specific skills to do the job they were hired to do. Professional football players would be given play books to study. They would then have practice sessions to see if they knew their assignment on any given called play. Rookies come to training camp earlier than veterans primarily for this purpose. Since each team uses different strategies and tactics, a veteran recruited from another team would still need this training.

In professional selling there is a need to provide new salespeople with information about the firm's operating procedures—how orders are to be written, handling of credit, delivery procedures, and so forth. Often this is handled in formal classes with the sales manager as instructor.

Sales managers also must provide whatever product knowledge and other information is needed to sell successfully. Many vestibule training programs also include a miniature sales course covering prospecting, making presentations, closing sales, and customer service. The sales manager usually tailors these training sessions to emphasize those techniques that have proven successful with their specific market. Role-playing—acting out the parts of customer and

orientation
period immediately following hiring when new employees are given general information about the firm.

vestibule training
training given new employees in job skills.

seller in a defined situation—is sometimes used to provide practice.

Ongoing training is also a necessary part of a sales manager's job. People forget, develop bad habits that must be broken, and need new information. Some of the materials used in vestibule training are often repeated for the entire salesforce. Training of this type usually is approached by two methods. One is formal classes with prepared materials. The other is individual coaching, providing of materials for independent study, or sending individuals to clinics, workshops, and schools.

In response to the need by sales managers for many different programs for their salespeople, a very wide range of materials has been developed. Movies, videotapes, filmstrips, and slide packages as well as audio tape cassettes are available on all sales and sales management topics. Seminars and workshops, while usually expensive, are plentiful. Xerox Learning Systems and Wilson Corporation are two firms that have achieved good reputations in the training field.

In many areas the sales managers feel that they need special programs to fit their firm's unique needs. In response, many firms will develop custom-tailored programs using a wide variety of formats. In some cases the materials are for the sales manager's use in formal classes. Sometimes each salesperson must study individually.

Supervision and motivation

motivation
*psychological stimulation
to improve one's
performance.*

A major task of the sales manager is *supervision* and **motivation**. The amount of supervision varies with the kind of selling, as we will see later in the chapter. The motivation problem, getting people to do their best work, is present in all selling. Some of the sales training materials mentioned above are specifically directed at this widespread problem. It is interesting that many were produced with famous football coaches or players. Vince Lombardi's movie, *Second Effort,* is widely distributed by Dartnell Corporation (Chicago). Obviously others also have recognized the sales manager's similarity to a coach in supervising and motivating the salesforce. In the football example widely used in media, however, the players need to be "up" only on the day of a game. With a salesforce they need to be "up" every day. Motivating them is a much more challenging job.

Compensation and incentives

Part of the motivation used by sales managers is *compensation*. Compensation plans often use a mixture of salary, commissions, and incentives. The decision whether to use salary more and commission less is an internal one that is affected by many factors. Some firms recently have been going back to a 100 percent commission plan. It is interesting to note that some famous football players determine their salary in part on how much they increase attendance at a game. For example, if a player felt he could increase attendance by 15,000 each game for eight home games at $12 a ticket, he might ask for $1.4 million for the season.

To a degree sales managers face the same problem of determining a team member's worth and most managers are willing to pay more if the sales volume is produced. The problem is complicated where the salesperson spends a significant amount of working time in servicing accounts rather than writing orders. As we have mentioned, this kind of selling seems to be increasing. Other factors include what the person is selling and how difficult the task is. Some firms spend huge sums to create a demand for their product. The salesforce's job is to keep the pipeline from manufacturer to consumer flowing smoothly. In other firms the entire selling burden falls to the salesforce and the firm's entire future rests largely in their hands.

Determination of quotas and territories

Sales managers are also charged with developing quotas for their department, division, or territory. This responsibility was discussed

One of the major responsibilities of a sales manager is the determination of sales quotas and territories.

Photograph by Rohn Engh

earlier along with the salesforce's role in determining future sales. While input from the salesforce is becoming more widespread, there also seems to be increased use of statistics from both external and internal sources. Firms that were making one- and five-year plans last year are now making only one-, two-, and three-year plans. Market uncertainty is making forecasting riskier.

Sales forecasts that the managers make now are more important than individual quotas. Production schedules, purchases, and hiring are usually determined before goods are sold; production managers, retail buyers, or service managers must rely heavily on sales managers' forecasts.

The computer has made available an increasing wealth of data about markets. There is an increasing reliance on this type of data to determine where an unsatisfied demand exists and what the company's market share, should be. Individual quotas are set by dividing this total potential market into units.

As a result of these factors, territory boundaries are now changed more frequently than before as the potential market shifts. These boundary changes do present a problem for a sales manager with a field salesforce. Sometimes a changed boundary changes the sales potential for the person assigned to the territory. All of the salesperson's calling patterns are based on the territory and must now be changed to make effective use of time and transportation money. Losing some steady customers and having to find new ones to replace them may mean the salesperson may have to accept a reduction in income, at least temporarily. Convincing the salesperson that the change is for the best takes a skillful job of selling on the manager's part.

With some rapidly changing markets both quotas and territories must be reviewed and revised regularly, perhaps monthly. In more stable markets they should be reviewed at least quarterly or semiannually with an eye toward making some changes. That is to say, both quotas and boundaries should be considered only good "guesstimates," subject to change as new information becomes available.

Coordination with other departments

The sales manager also must work closely with other managers within the firm. Just as the head coach must supervise the assistant coaches, trainers, and other support people, the sales manager must work closely with those providing sales support materials. The range of tools now used in professional selling was discussed earlier. It is a rapidly growing area that must be managed with care. Adding a computer-based sales support system, for example, is a

Sales managers must communicate not only with their salesforces but also with their support personnel.

decision that requires a great deal of research and careful analysis.

Even the basic selling tools should be chosen with care. It has become obvious that the tools for both training and selling provided to most salespeople could be substantially improved without a great investment. This small investment would pay off handsomely in most cases. The smaller the firm the less likely it is that someone within the firm is knowledgeable about sales support. The total burden then falls to the sales manager.

There are other managers within the firm with whom the sales manager must also work effectively. Coordination with those in charge of advertising and sales promotion is critical, as we saw in earlier chapters. The company's plans to expand into new markets or to introduce new products has a direct bearing on future personnel requirements. In addition, some managers are expected to get out and sell with their salespeople, or at least to assist in some situations.

Those selling goods must also deal with those managers in production and distribution. Those selling services must coordinate their efforts with support staff to schedule work effectively. All salespeople are concerned with being able to deliver what they have sold. Seeing that they can is part of the sales manager's job, too.

Evaluation

The last area we will discuss is the job of developing ways to evaluate effectively the efforts of the salesforce. The volume produced by a salesperson often is not a true indicator of his or her effort. That must be weighed against the sales potential of the market in which one is selling. Often a sales manager doing this type of **quantitative analysis** for the first time has been surprised to find that the top sellers, when weighed against the potential of their territory, are actually the poorest producers. Sales managers also will develop other quantitative methods to evaluate the salesforce. This data is usually concerned with the number of new markets developed, sales gains over a previous period, changes in market share, and expense controls. For comparative purposes data are often then converted to ratios or percentages.

But sale managers must also conduct a **qualitative analysis** of the salesforce, using subjective factors that are based on observation. These factors include the salesperson's relationships with customers, willingness to cooperate with changes in operations or assignments, and dress and personal habits. When people are asked to leave a company, whether they are in sales or other careers, the reason most often proves to be personality and other subjective factors. Even in professional selling, the substandard producer is often not fired if he or she works well with people—both those within the company and customers. Sales managers should guard against this tendency since it affects both volume and profits.

1. See the latest *Sales and Marketing Management* magazine's "Annual Survey of Selling Costs" in your library. Of what value is this information to sales managers?

The sales manager in retail sales

Opportunities in sales management in the retail sector fall principally into three general areas: management of stores or departments of stores; management of groups of people selling big-ticket items such as cars or appliances; and administration of in-home selling. Very different kinds of duties are required in each area, as we shall see.

Store or department managers

These opportunities range from the small boutique to large depart-

---

quantitative analysis
judging a person or an activity by measuring against set objective goals.

qualitative analysis
judging a person or an activity on a subjective basis.

ment store chains. Most of these people do not consider themselves sales managers in the traditional sense. Especially in the smaller limited-line stores, for example, the job of sales manager is only one of many management jobs they perform. The majority of their time is spent with inventory planning and control, promotion and advertising, display, accounting, and handling complaints. Most of these jobs are with chain organizations such as franchises, regional chains, or national corporations. Here, much of the typical sales manager's responsibilities are determined at a higher level. Compensation and incentive programs, for instance, are usually outside their control. Normally, they have no voice in advertising or promotional support. Even training, what little is provided in this sector, tends to come prepackaged.

Big-ticket sales managers

The big-ticket area of retail sales takes on more of the character usually associated with sales management. These people are hired to manage the salesforce for such retail firms as automobile dealers, insurance and real estate agents, home improvement firms, and other sellers of big-ticket items. Some of this selling takes place in the retailer's facilities and some takes place in the customer's home. Firms that sell both ways often have separate inside and outside salespeople, sometimes with separate managers.

These managers take on most of the duties and responsibilities covered in the prior section. With the advent of franchising in the real estate industry, for example, has come a great increase in emphasis on sales management. Training is now increasing in importance and some firms are changing their compensation programs. The recent series of advertisements sponsored by the Hartford Insurance Company stresses the professionalism of their salesforce through training.

As consumers become more affluent more of their income is spent on items that in the past were considered luxuries. This promises an expanding market for managers of salespeople who sell second homes, motor homes, packaged vacations, furniture, carpeting, and entertainment systems. In this field commissioned sales are the rule; the manager is paid a salary, to which a bonus is added, calculated on total sales.

Management of in-home salespeople

In-home retail sales also has shown very good growth in recent years. This area includes those who manage the salespeople who sell in the home. These people primarily use two methods of selling.

One is the call on the individual customer in what has recently been named consultive selling, which is an extension of the salesperson's role as educator. Many firms selling cosmetics, clothing and jewelry, like Avon, use this approach.

The other widely used method is the *party plan.* Most commonly linked with Tupperware, getting people together to have a good time also is an effective way to sell toys, clothing, pots and pans, and decorative accessories. Both kinds of selling require skilled managers who perform most of the traditional sales manager's functions with a strong emphasis on training, supervision, and motivation. Since most in-home salespeople work on a part-time basis, the manager's performance is critical to total company sales.

In order to upgrade the quality of personnel, some firms have hired husband and wife teams to manage a given area on a full-time basis. These people usually sell as well as recruit and manage a salesforce. In some product lines this has worked very well.

Summary
There is ample opportunity in the retail sector for both professional salespeople and professional sales managers. Neither career should be overlooked. For good producers the monetary rewards can exceed $30 thousand annually. More important is the enjoyment and satisfaction the job produces. The great diversity of retail product areas offers something for everybody.

2. Interview a sales manager whose primary job is the supervision of an outside salesforce or a telephone selling group. (Some may do both.) What aspects of their job require the most time? How do they deal with the continual motivation of their salespeople?

The sales manager in commercial sales
Most commercial sales are made by an outside salesforce and therefore require a sales manager. However, the duties vary greatly from one firm to another and one industry to another. A district manager in insurance for one company may deal primarily with independently owned local agencies who have their own salesforce. Other insurance companies have their own salesforce to call directly on businesses. In a few cases insurance companies operate in both modes, depending on the market.

As was pointed out in Chapter 1 on commercial services, coordination of support personnel activities is of prime importance. While the salesforce often will work directly with these people, it is the sales manager's job to personally oversee the workload for scheduling purposes. Conflicts occur frequently about which salesperson's customer order has priority. Decisions on rush orders and the requirement by support personnel to work overtime are often the manager's responsibility. The ability to work smoothly with a variety of people, both in sales and in support, is crucial.

Managers in commercial services usually perform the normal functions of recruiting, selecting, training, and supervision. Since the majority of commercial services are produced by small firms, decisions on compensation, territories, sales forecasts, budgets, required reports and evaluation procedures rest with the sales manager. The larger the firm, however, the more likely it is that these decisions will be made higher up.

The commercial sector may also be defined to include wholesalers, distributors, and jobbers. It is difficult to define these firms as significantly different from those normally associated with commercial services such as printing, insurance, fringe benefits, and advertising. The reason is that those in the wholesale sector have been increasing the range of services they offer their customers. It is not uncommon today for wholesalers to offer their customers data processing services for inventory control, for example. Thus the sales manager in the wholesale sector must be increasingly involved with support personnel.

Perhaps the major distinction for those commercial firms selling goods is that their volume is normally tied quite closely to that of their customers. Also, firms do not tend to change suppliers rapidly; the salesforce concentrates on taking orders with established accounts more than on seeking new business. The sales manager concentrates on achieving smooth flow of merchandise and finding ways to increase their customers' volume. Managers must know both their own business and their customers' businesses equally well. Where customers are diverse and separate salespeople are assigned to specific customer groups, this range of expertise must be large indeed.

Job opportunities are broad. Consider the differences between a district sales manager for American Hospital Supply and a district sales manager for L'eggs (hosiery). Both firms perform a wholesale function. In the first case, the firm handles several thousand items, but sells almost exclusively to hospital purchasing directors. In the second case, the firm employs women to service a very limited line in a variety of retail stores. The time devoted to the tasks of supervision, motivation, and paperwork is significantly different.

3.   **Interview two sales managers in either goods or services in the commercial sector. How do they handle the coordination of support personnel and what major problems do they face in keeping work flowing smoothly?**

The sales manager in manufacturing

The duties of sales managers vary more widely in the manufacturing sector than in any other area we have discussed. One important reason for this variation is obvious: the great diversity of consumer goods, commercial goods, and industrial goods that are being sold daily. Further, in any of these areas distribution methods also vary.

For example, management of the sales function for an apparel firm that uses agents to call on retailers will differ significantly from sales management for a hardware manufacturer that employs its own salesforce to sell directly to wholesalers. Significant differences will also be found between an industrial firm whose engineers bid on larger special fabrication orders and one whose salespeople sell a line of earth-moving equipment primarily to dealerships. In the commercial area a similar illustration would involve differences between computer manufacturers, most of which employ their own salesforces, and office equipment manufacturers, who sell through local dealers.

All these differences make it impossible to describe a "typical" sales manager for a manufacturing firm. We will try, however, to state a few generalizations, based on recruitment, budget management, the relative importance of sales as compared to advertising and promotion, and the opportunity for any salesperson to become a manager.

Selection and training

Each salesperson in the manufacturing sector is generally expected to generate a significantly larger volume of sales than his or her counterpart in the commercial and retail sectors. Training is usually more extensive and, as a result, more costly. Therefore the selection process must be thorough: the hiring and training of a salesperson who quits after a year or less of service can be a very costly mistake for a company. A good manager cannot afford to make many such mistakes. The selection process should be able to match the person to the job accurately.

Importance of selling

The manufacturing sector normally places heavy reliance on the salesforce to sell while advertising and sales promotion are used primarily as support. The sales manager must be strongly motivated and be able to motivate the staff and inspire them to push ever harder. Since single orders can often be six- or seven-digit figures, competition is keen. This area is the "major leagues" of selling.

Budget management

Contact with the people in the field is often limited by the demands on the regional manager's time. A great deal of paperwork is required. Reports submitted by all salespeople must be reviewed and analyzed. Cost controls are crucial, and the manager is expected to justify his or her personnel's selling expenses. Managers are often rated on their ability to produce high sales volume while keeping expenses low.

Forecasts gathered from individual salespeople are submitted to the central or home office by regional or district managers. These forecasts, combined and evaluated, enable the company to establish related forecasts and **budgets**.

Comparison of forecasts with actual figures, often analyzed by computer, provides measures of performance for individual salespeople, for regions, for managers, and for the company as a whole. Discrepancies between actual figures and those that have been forecast may lead to discovery of incorrect goals or procedures, or both.

budget
estimated costs to perform certain functions during a specified period.

Opportunities

Obviously it is a good deal more likely for you to become a district or regional manager than a national sales manager for a large corporation. It is a simple matter of numbers. It is also true that the duties of these people differ considerably.

When one moves from sales into sales management, the initial management job is usually at the regional level, supervising a salesforce assigned to specific territories. Recruiting, selecting, training, and sales support usually come from the home office, and the compensation and benefit plan is also outside the individual manager's control. The major functions of management in this situation are to motivate and to keep track of the salespeople. In some firms the manager is also assigned to a few key accounts, but usually the duties are primarily related to supervisory activities and helping a salesperson solve a particular problem.

In small companies the range of duties required of a manager tends to be wider. This is also true the higher one moves in the larger companies. In small companies the managers may be expected to contribute to advertising and promotion; in larger firms the focus shifts to coordination of sales personnel with support personnel departments. Here such tasks as training provision sales support material, and promotion coordination are assigned to other managers. This structure is illustrated in the organization chart in Chapter 1.

Mini-case

Jim, the national sales manager, and Eleanor, the director of sales training, were discussing the budget for next year's training costs. Jim felt that costs could be slashed significantly without hurting their program—or sales.

Currently they bring each of the 129 salespeople in from the field for a one-week refresher course each year. The district managers are also given some materials to be used during the monthly district meetings. The direct cost per person including travel costs, meals, and accommodations is projected to be about $1,500 per person. Included is Eleanor's salary, the cost of purchased training materials and overhead charged to office and classroom space.

Jim wants Eleanor to shift more of the training burden to district managers. He also wants Eleanor to run the one-week sessions at the district offices to eliminate the travel costs back to the company's headquarters by the salesforce. On paper he figures they will save over $40,000 and still run essentially the same program.

Eleanor wants to keep things the way they are. She thinks a yearly visit to corporate offices and meeting the top people in the company produces more sales. It helps morale and contributes to productivity.

Question: If Eleanor and Jim are to make their proposals to the director of marketing next week, how should Eleanor sell her concepts?

Define these key concepts

budget	qualitative analysis
job description	quantitative analysis
job specification	sales manager
motivation	vertibule training
orientation	

17 Personal management

Key terms

build-up method
breakdown method
time management
career goal
personal assessment

Overview

In the field of professional selling your success or lack of it will be determined primarily by self-management. Your most important concern will be time management: making time, using time, and conserving time. On both a short- and long-term basis, goals need to be determined. Your activities should be goal directed: for tomorrow, for next year, and for five years ahead. Setting and achieving realistic goals is basic to self-management.

Setting goals

In some of the more enlightened firms the salespeople and their managers sit down at regular intervals and discuss their progress and their goals. Since these firms are still in the minority, you probably will have to go through this process on your own. Two approaches are available to you. You may work from individual account figures to determine your total sales goal or you may be more comfortable setting a total goal and then determining the part each of your accounts will play in reaching that goal.

Building up from accounts

The first approach we'll call the ***build-up method***. Using some form of classification such as account types, product lines, or territory, you analyze each group and set realistic sales goals for them. Consideration must be given to the level of competition, current economics, and buying attitudes or other external factors that influence sales. You should also give some thought to internal support and competitive advantages such as advertising, sales promotion, and new or unique products.

build-up method
the process of adding
together smaller units to
create a whole picture.

   It is very tempting, and often a mistake, to use figures from last year, last quarter, or last month. They are readily available. You can pick some percentage of increase out of thin air, use the ever-present calculator, and multiply that percentage by sales figures from some previous period. This is the easy method, not the realistic one. It is unlikely that the forthcoming period will be similar in any way to what existed a year earlier. Market conditions change too fast today, and the only person who will be cheated is yourself.

   After you have thrown considerable paper into the wastebasket, your completed goal may look something like this.

	Product 1	Product 2	Product 3	Total
Territory A	$10,200	$34,700	$62,450	$107,350
Territory B	$18,600	$24,700	$49,100	$ 92,400
Territory C	$24,300	$37,000	$37,900	$ 99,200
TOTAL	$53,100	$96,400	$149,450	$298,950

Notice that a total goal of $298,950 has been built, but it includes several subgoals which should be reached as well. Some salespeople would want to use other subclassifications, depending on the type of goods being sold.

breakdown method
*the process of taking a
whole and dividing it into
parts.*

Breaking down from the total

While the build-up method starts with individual accounts, products, or territories, the **breakdown method** starts with a total sales goal. Your primary concern here is those market-demand factors that have a bearing on your company's sales. Discovering these factors often starts with national or regional projections made by either the government, trade associations, or private firms. Such data may be organized by zip code and census tracts. Private firms may charge as little as $75 for such a report, getting them within the financial ability of almost every business.

With this information as a starting point, a sales projection is made in total. Using the breakdown method, you will then divide it by territory, product, account, or other classifications to arrive at sub-goals to be achieved. The end result will be identical to the illustration above, by the setting the total precedes setting subgoals.

While both approaches have merit, salespeople tend to use the build-up method. It seems to be more manageable, since most people are more comfortable with this method. Also, most firms do not provide salespeople with the data they need to use the breakdown method.

Monthly and weekly plans

Developing goals goes beyond setting sales quotas to be achieved. There is often a direct relationship between sales and prospecting as well as between sales and number of presentations made. This was illustrated in the chapter on prospecting in relation to telephone solicitation, presentations, and closes.

While salespeople normally use the build-up method to arrive at sales quotas, they tend to use the breakdown method for other goal setting. These goals include specific targets for prospecting, presentations, and sales follow-up activities.

Establishing weekly and monthly goals goes beyond these areas. With the great increase in prices, primarily from inflation, expenses have received greater scrutiny. Travel, lodging, meals, and entertainment costs can easily get out of hand without some controls. Some of this responsibility falls on the salesperson. As service selling increases, along with selling where account servicing takes much of one's time, expenses must be watched closely. Excessive use of maintenance and repair technicians, advisors or consultants, and other support personnel can quickly erase any profits from a given account. Part of goal setting, then, includes expense controls and levels of account service. Remember, too little service can lose accounts.

1. Interview a sales manager on goal setting. How much is within the salespeople's control and what is assigned by the company?

2. Interview a sales manager on the number of forms and reports their salespeople must prepare. What goals and objectives are under their control?

Account classification

Salespeople can maximize the use of their time by account classification—assigning value to an account to the basis of volume or profitability. The first is usually easier since figures are readily available. The second is much more difficult because fixed or overhead costs are assigned to each product arbitrarily by cost accountants. These figures may be realistic or unrealistic, and often are the cause of heated discussions. Of course, some firms have no method whatever to determine profitability of either a single item or an account.

Of the two methods, the second is preferable. Firms who have classified accounts on the basis of their profit potential have found to their surprise that some of their biggest accounts on a volume basis actually contribute little profit to the firm. Perhaps they demand such a high level of service that profits are eaten away. Small accounts may present the same problem if their service requirements are much greater than their volume warrants.

The professional salesperson must look at customers from two perspectives at the same time. First, he or she must determine what profit they may contribute to the firm. Then, the time investment required to acquire that profit must be estimated. Many salespeople have been amazed after doing this type of analysis to find they have been spending the majority of their time with marginal accounts. Accounts that were either contributing good profits or offering very good future profit potential were often receiving little of their time.

There are some good reasons why few salespeople regularly analyze and classify their accounts. First, as human beings we all tend to gravitate toward accounts where we have a good, friendly relationship. Even in retail selling, the regular customer who buys little but requires a large portion of time for idle conversation tends to be warmly received. Another reason is that salespeople tend to sell what is easiest to move and avoid those items that require most effort. This is amplified where commission schedules pay the same amount for everything sold. Another reason is that salespeople tend toward short-term planning; their focus is on daily, weekly, or monthly sales and the commissions to be received. Classifying accounts takes a much longer view; the focus is on *account building* over time, concentrating on accounts which will be more profitable over the long term. Restructuring the time invested in each account category will not usually result in immediate benefits of great significance, but gains will be recognized over a year or two.

3.   With time investment versus profit potential (or commissions) as your base, what criteria would you use in classifying accounts? Is the time and expense of support personnel a factor? Report.

Daily time management

Your best-laid plans will go awry if you do not manage time on a daily basis. In the majority of selling jobs *less than half* of any given day will be involved in direct customer contact. It is strongly recommended that each evening, or the first thing each morning, half an hour should be spent in planning and preparation.

Pocket notebooks with calendar pages for each day of the week, available in bookstores, are designed for this purpose. Previously made appointments, if any, would normally be the starting point. Other activities should then be built around the time these appointments will require. These activities should include whatever is necessary to meet one's weekly objectives. Some time must also be allocated to prospecting, customer servicing, precall planning, and preparing reports. In addition, you should regularly include time to build your knowledge by reading reports, brochures, newsletters, and trade publications. Where support personnel are an integral part of servicing the accounts, time must be regularly reserved for planning and consultation meetings with them.

Importance of time management

Lack of success in sales as well as failure to perform above acceptable levels can often be traced to poor time management. In recognition of this fact, more and more firms are stressing **time management** in their training programs. Many have found training sessions on time management more fruitful than skills training for the experienced salesforce. Materials on time management are more frequently found in training programs for new people as well. *It is important.*

time management
planned allocation of time to different activities.

Yet the harsh reality is that these materials reach far too few salespeople. In most retail goods and consumer services this instruction is rare. The same is true with the small firms in both the commercial and industrial sector. Such training seems to be moderately available only within firms with a sales trainer or training department.

Your responsibility

Lack of company planning means the burden falls on you to develop a plan to manage your time both efficiently and effectively. It means breaking down weekly and monthly goals into daily objectives. It means allocating time to different accounts or customer classifications based on their sales or profit potential. Time must also be budgeted for "housekeeping" chores, such as record keeping and report writing, order follow-ups and customer service.

It means finding ways to expand time by systematically routing a territory rather than criss-crossing it and using the telephone instead of a personal call. These two simple methods can multiply your customer contacts in the same amount of time. The mail can accomplish the same objective for much routine information. When practical, use support personnel to call on customers. This will enable you to handle two accounts at one time. Since so many of your activities are self-directed, control of your time is critical. Time is the easiest thing in the world to squander and one of the hardest to manage. That half hour or so spent planning is the key to successful sales.

Managing your career: personal assessment

Objectives and goals are an important part of management of our selling effort: they should also be used in managing a career. In reality, however, few people plan that far ahead. You may view college attendance as working toward some goal, for example, when in truth it may not be. Graduation from college is not an objective; it is only a step toward the real objective of obtaining a job appropriate to one's interests and abilities. Far too many students set a **career goal**—their long term objective—which is not in line with their interests or abilities. Their choice of a program might be influenced by factors other than appropriateness or the job market potential. For example, students stampeded to journalism schools following Woodward and Bernstein's highly visible expose of the Watergate scandal. The journalism field simply cannot provide jobs for all these graduates.

career goal
a job or position one is seeking to attain in the future.

personal assessment
evaluation of one's strengths and weaknesses as they relate to a career goal.

Personality factors

The starting point in the management of your career is your own ***personal assessment***, which includes a close look at your aptitudes and interests. Virtually all college counseling centers have an array of interest and ability tests normally provided free to students. The service also usually includes an interpretation of the scores. In recent years many colleges, especially community colleges, have been offering a short course or seminar in career exploration. Assuming that you have by now chosen a career in sales, the focus would then be on matching your interests and abilities with the variety of sales opportunities. As you may recall from Chapter 1, there are sales jobs for a fairly wide range of people.

Educational requirements

Personal assessment should also include the *education required* for entry-level positions in professional selling. Most medium and large firms require a college degree. While the college major most in demand is business administration, some selling areas prefer that the student major in some technical specialization. Many engineering and science majors begin their career in sales because a high level of technical sophistication is required there. Companies find it

An aspiring salesperson has a variety of types of selling to choose from. Sales of athletic equipment and health related products is a major market.

easier to provide selling skills than technical knowledge.

You can find out what educational requirements are necessary in counseling centers and college placement offices. But your search should also include looking at the help wanted advertisements in the major newspapers and in trade journals serving your field of interest. Some students respond to the job offers to practice interviewing for positions and to find out what qualifications are really needed. Firms have a tendency to overstate qualifications as part of their selection technique.

A high level of education may not be necessary for initial employ- ment in sales but will be very beneficial in the long run. Professional selling requires a wider range of both knowledge and skills than many jobs. At minimum, it will include some work in basic business principles, some work in the social sciences, and some work in your chosen technical specialty. Far too many students omit at least one of these three areas. Speaking and writing skills, of course, are mandatory.

Aptitudes and interests

The last area of personal assessment is your *social interests*. A successful career in sales can be quite rewarding financially, result- ing in many material possessions, but serious consideration must be given to future social relationships. Although it is nice to dream about luxury automobiles, summer homes, and elegant parties, the truth is that relatively few people from lower and middle class back- grounds can successfully adjust to that lifestyle after they attain it. Show business personalities offer examples. Greta Garbo, after achieving fame as a film star, has been a recluse for the past forty years. Elvis Presley, Freddie Prinze, and Janice Joplin are more contemporary examples.

The social aspect extends to your husband or wife—present or future—and family. While the majority of commercial and industrial sales time is concentrated in a regular Monday through Friday workweek, a career in retail sales and consumer services requires night and weekend hours. This schedule, obviously, will have an effect on family relationships and social relationships. Conflicts be- tween required working hours and personal social activities are bound to occur. If you prefer to have your time off during the week rather than the weekend, however, this may be the right area for you. Salespeople also generally work more than forty hours a week. Cus- tomer requirements come ahead of family or social commitments. Emergency calls and burning the midnight oil to finish a presenta- tion are not uncommon.

One social advantage of a career in selling is the wide variety of

Personal interests can be combined with a sales career. For instance, the sale of art is a possible career choice.

Courtesy of The Art Institute of Chicago

people you meet. Many of these people become friends in both the business and social sense. Different kinds of selling will expose you to different kinds of people. In selecting an area for a selling career, you might consider whether the people you will be selling to are compatible with your personal life style.

4. After selecting a selling area, learn the education and experience requirements for most advertised entry level jobs. Can you explain the diversity of requirements between firms in the same industry? What do most have in common?

Managing your career: opportunity assessment

It is wise to look at your first job as a stepping stone in a planned career rather than just a job. One consideration to keep in mind is whether to begin with a large or small firm. Both have advantages depending on your perspective.

Opportunities in small firms

The small firm tends to offer more flexibility for its salesforce. Rules tend to be less rigid than with the large firms; they are more frequently changed to meet market conditions. Usually all or almost all people within the firm are known by name. This provides fairly close cooperation in serving your accounts. Since the small firm can afford only minimal specialization, those supporting your efforts will be few, but this will result in more of a team spirit. Many find this kind of atmosphere rewarding in itself.

The small firm requires members of its salesforce to be more versatile. The main advantage for the neophyte salesperson is the exposure to a fairly wide range of problems. Lacking many support specialists, these responsibilities often may fall to the salesperson. Calling on a retailer, for instance, may require the ability to discuss finance, display, advertising, and sales promotion as well as facets of your product line. You may also have to become a mechanic to install point-of-sale fixtures and materials; you may be a delivery person on occasion. Many regard the wide range of duties usually associated with the small firm as valuable training ground.

Advantages of large firms
The large firms also offer several advantages to be considered, foremost among these being training. Most medium to large firms have a full-time trainer working just with the salesforce. In the largest firms, this individual will have some assistants who themselves may specialize in a few aspects of sales training. These firms also make regular use of sales training consultants, packaged sales training programs, and media (movies, videotape, and slides).

Many beginning salespeople prefer the larger firms because of their exposure to a variety of support specialists. They look upon it as an opportunity to expand their own knowledge. In the larger firm, the salesperson usually has more high-quality selling tools. Audio-visual materials are becoming quite widespread. Since virtually all of the large firms are computer based, electronic sales support is slowly but surely expanding. Keep in mind that very few small firms can offer these advantages to their salesforce.

These large firms have looked very closely at what tools the salesforce needs to do a better job. Prospecting, for instance, is important to selling since it often has a direct bearing on dollar volume and profits. It is not uncommon for medium to large firms to do the prospecting for its salesforce, with the leads given to them for follow-up. These firms also recognize the relationship between volume and the amount of time the salesforce spends in customer contact. As a result, they use more sales support personnel. Some selling may be shifted to inside sales, people who sit at telephones to take orders and to follow up on any problems. Some firms use this activity as training before assignment in the selling field.

In determining your *career path,* the sequence of positions you will hold as you reach toward your goal, that first job is quite important. Large, medium, and small firms all offer advantages and disadvantages. The smaller the firm, the less education and experience is usually required for that first job. The small firm also offers a wider range of experiences. The larger the firm you choose, the more opportunity there is for additional training and exposure to specialists. There are, and always will be, ample jobs to choose from in a sales career. Consider what each one has to offer you as well as what you can offer them.

Moving on

In the course of achieving the goal you set for yourself, you may find yourself in a dead end. For some reason or other the firm you are in will not provide a clear pathway to your goal. Perhaps it is a small firm and the position you aspire to is securely held by someone else. Perhaps you wish to become involved in marketing to broaden your knowledge, but the company or your superior is blocking that move.

This is the time to do some careful reassessment of yourself and your situation. Have you learned as much as you can in your current spot? Will you be satisfied to stay with a job that offers no growth? Does the job give you enough personal satisfaction to justify staying with it because of a secure paycheck, especially at a time when your family may need that security?

You will be able fully to answer these crucial questions *only* if you have given previous thought to a thorough self-assessment; only if you have already analyzed your career goal and your needs. Start now on the road to self-knowledge. It is a continuous process of question and answer.

Developing long-term goals

Relatively few people have long-term goals, yet they are very important. The fact is, if you don't know where you are going, you are likely to spend your life aimlessly hopping from one job to another. At retirement time all too many people look back and wonder what went wrong over the years.

Financial goals

One aspect of developing a long-term career goal is financial considerations. Different types of selling have different pay ranges as we saw in Chapter 1. Most people are not able to earn large sums of money selling women's ready-to-wear or taking orders for small wholesale firms. Yet many who do not aspire to great wealth find these careers very satisfying. Time and pressure demands are minimal and may be considered more important than larger sums of money.

Long-term financial goals should be kept within your interest and ability. Sales careers generally pay more than most other occupations although relatively few strike it rich in selling. Jobs that do provide opportunity for substantial income usually require some sacrifice in terms of family and social commitments. The tradeoffs must be weighed: you must make some decision as to what level or standard of living you wish. Setting a goal for your income at some future time will serve to direct your efforts.

Career paths

Another long-term decision concerns your career goals. Will you use the initial sales career as a stepping stone to a management career or not? If so, the experience you gain in professional selling will serve you well when you move into management. Sales provides excellent exposure both to the internal workings of the firms and to the market served, a perspective that tends to be lacking in those who go directly into a management training program. Indeed, many firms use their salesforce as a pool from which to select management personnel. Some argue that this use of salespeople results in a less than ideally productive selling team.

If a management career is in line with your long-term goals, then professional selling takes on a different dimension. You must evaluate jobs in terms of the widest possible exposure to different selling situations and the breadth of the training programs. Firms that use the salesforce as a training ground may be more attractive than

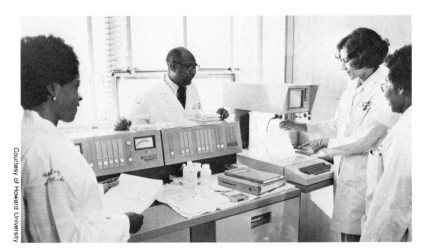

Courtesy of Howard University

The sale of medical technology requires specialized knowledge. However, the basic principles of selling apply in this field as they do in any other field.

those who do not. It is important to communicate your long-term goals to your manager. Failure to do so may have two results: you may not be considered for openings or it may affect the range of assignments you are given or the kinds of training programs in which you are offered participation.

While the decision ultimately to pursue a management path does not necessarily have to be made before beginning a sales career, it should be made early in that career. The sooner one begins pursuing long-term goals, the better. The paths to a long-term sales career and to a management career are significantly different. Both goals have financial and personal considerations to keep in mind.

Personal goals

Different sales careers have significantly different personal aspects. Some jobs require a great deal of travel and glamorous contacts. While the number of jobs requiring extended travel have been diminishing, there still are many. In some people's minds many jobs requiring travel are associated with wining and dining at fancy night spots and meeting exciting people. In truth, the majority of after-hours activity consists of watching TV alone in a motel room, picking up and returning rented cars, and waiting for planes at airports.

In developing long-term goals, such personal aspects should be considered. While the lure of travel may be great for someone young and single, perspectives may change if marriage and a family are part of your long-term goal. Each day in a sales career, unlike the factory or office worker's day, normally does not end with the five o'clock whistle. Usually part of the job is taken home and the family is involved to some degree. In fact an office at home is highly recommended for many selling jobs. Spouses and children of salespersons should know how to answer calls. They may also help with some of the paperwork and use both the phone and mail for prospecting and follow-up activities. This considerably expands the salesperson's time and potential income; the benefit to the family is obvious.

The long-term consideration must be weighed for different selling careers. The insurance industry, for instance, actively promotes its plan where its salespeople work primarily on account building while they are young and account maintenance as they get older. Residuals from renewals provide a good income in their later years while the hours spent on the job decline, so the fruits of their labor can be enjoyed. This example is one of the few where an industry actively promotes both short-term and long-term career goals for its salespeople. All people considering a career in sales should consider the same things.

Courtesy of The Apparel Center

Another possible career path is wholesale selling. Clothing wholesalers travel extensively throughout the United States and Europe.

5. What long-term considerations are most important to you? How do these factors relate to different selling careers?

6. What personal consideration do you have that may be in conflict with the requirements of some selling careers? Are these conflicts viewed as only short-term or long-term?

Putting your plan into action

Long-term goals are met through the achievement of short-term objectives. This takes us back to the breakdown method. Long-term goals for most personal planning are usually phrased in five- or ten-year projections. A five-year goal for a person under twenty-five, for instance, who is just beginning college, would be achieved in one to three years after graduation, depending on whether he or she is in a two-year or four-year program. Completion of a given program would be one short-term objective. Acquiring an entry-level position in line with the five-year goal would be another objective. Receiving some amount of experience and training in the last years of the plan would be a third goal.

Setting goals of ten years or longer is more tentative. Yet such decisions should be made as they give direction to a career. These decisions are made knowing that, at least to some degree, they will change over time. Both the environment we live and work in and personal considerations change over time. To deal with this, long-term goals should be regularly evaluated and revised—*in writing*.

As long-term goals are revised the short-term objectives will obviously change, but in most cases not radically. This decision should be viewed as a building process. Alternative career paths for those beginning a sales career are many. More than one door-to-door salesperson has become a company president, but the goal was achieved in short steps.

Setting your plan into action is mostly concerned with meeting weekly, monthly, and yearly objectives. You must determine your own long-term goals and break them down into manageable—and achievable—targets. You are your own boss.

If you are going to be successful you must take command of your life. You have to be honest with yourself about your abilities and your limitations. You must make decisions. Yes, you will make some wrong decisions, but they are part of learning about yourself. Success does not come without some risk, as you have seen in the book mentioned earlier, *Looking Out for #1* (Ringer, Funk and Wagnalls, 1977). Success requires a positive mental attitude that you can succeed. If there are some characteristics about yourself that you do not like, take some action to change them. You *can* do it. You *can* succeed.

7. **Prepare five-year and ten-year objectives in terms of income level, type of position, and family considerations. Break the five-year plan down into short-term goals necessary to meet the long-term objective.**

Mini-case

Dick has lost much of his enthusiasm for selling. He works for a supply firm that serves engineers, architects, and draftsmen with supplies. Drafting tables and drafting supplies are sold as well as transit instruments and related equipment for surveying. The firm offers a blueprint copying service; it also sells copying machines.

Dick knows all the firms in the area and sells to most of them. His company is the only one locally, though he knows some businesses buy from firms in nearby cities. He doubts they take much business away from him; he figures he has at least 80 percent of the market locally.

He first started with the firm when it opened. Then selling was a challenge. There was some competition but that firm has since gone broke. Because he has built a good relationship with most customers, now most of his selling is just order taking. Even with new products, customers rely on Dick's judgment on whether it meets their needs.

Since he makes over $35,000 a year he's reluctant to quit outright

and find another job. Yet he finds it harder and harder to get up and go to work each morning.

Question: How did Dick develop this problem and how can he now deal with it?

---

account management
career development
goal evaluation
goal setting
macro-planning
micro-planning

monthly plan
opportunity assessment
pr onal assessment
time management
weekly plan

**Define these
key concepts**

18 Legal and ethical considerations in selling

Key terms

*Securities Exchange
    Commission*
*Federal Deposit
    Insurance
    Corporation*
collusion
*Federal Trade
    Commission*
contract
consideration

Overview

To most customers, you not only represent the company, you *are* the company. Those you come into contact with every day will not likely see the home office or ever get to meet the president of your board of directors. They deal only with you; you are the only company representative they will ever see. It is clear that double-dealing and professional dishonesty can hurt you a great deal more than they can hurt your employer.

In addition, many laws have been enacted to regulate professional behavior in commercial activities. These laws pertain to particular practices in buying and selling as well as in the hiring of employees in the company's many spheres of activity. It is essential for each professional individual to know the laws that regulate his or her own activities.

Finally, if you become a sales manager you will find that your approach sets the style for those who are on your staff. Your handling of personal ethics and your expectations of those around you are important areas of self-examination.

Personal ethics

In an earlier chapter we stated that a professional code of ethics is important to each person who works in the field of sales. Table 1–1 shows a reprint of a sample code of ethics published by a professional sales organization. Your personal ethical standards must encompass three areas of responsibility: to your customers, to your company or firm, and to yourself. As you will see, the first two areas are inevitably intertwined with the last; if you fail to treat others fairly, you will probably be the one to suffer the most damage both personally and professionally.

Your economic livelihood lies directly with your customers, and with your mutual respect for one another. Both you and your company depend on sales of goods or services for income; further, you depend on repeat sales by satisfied customers for your income.

Will customers come back to you if you misrepresent the company or the product, or make service or delivery promises you cannot keep just so you can close a sale? It is not likely. To keep that continuity with your valued customers you need to show them repeated instances of promises kept.

Another aspect of fairness and honesty to the customer relates to your representation of the product's capabilities. There may be a very strong temptation to make false promises when you have invested a lot of time in making a sale and when you are anticipating a high commission on the sale. But these factors should be considered and measured against the consequences: Is the sale binding if it was based on false promises or misrepresentation? Will the dissatisfied customer return the goods and refuse to do business with you again? Will you lose your job if this kind of thing happens more than once or twice? Answers to all of these questions have a lasting effect on your future success.

Perhaps you know the competing products in the marketplace well enough to know that neither your product nor any of the existing products meets your customer's specifications completely. Make that fact known to your customer, selling your product's strengths, and let it go at that. But suppose you know that one product does, and that the salesperson has been trying unsuccessfully to get to your customer for some time. Naturally, you do not need to suggest this product to your customer if the purchase could lose you the account. If asked about the competing product, how much should you say? That is up to you to decide at the time. But one hard-and-fast rule should never be broken: Don't downgrade the competition or "bad-mouth" the competitive salespeople!

There are several good reasons why this rule should never be broken. First, some of the statements you make in haste or anger may border on slander or libel, either of which could get you into serious legal trouble. But there's an even better, more practical reason than that, and it pertains to your long-term future prospects. Most people who sell in one industry or product field are less likely to move out of that field during their lives than they are to change companies within that field. In practical terms what this means is that at some future time—perhaps sooner than you think—you may be working for the very competitor you were downgrading earlier. What happens to your credibility then? Better to be safe: Sell your strengths and ignore the competition's weaknesses.

Another ethical question, a little less obvious than those we have already discussed, relates to your evaluation of your customer's needs. Can you, in good conscience, oversell a customer—that is, put a higher than necessary price tag on a sale by adding extras and frills? In auto sales, this is where the highest profit margin lies. Only you can judge whether the lost repeat sales will justify the immediate profit, and whether such an inflation of the price is ethical under the circumstances or not.

Let's take a real case for illustration. A Chicago-area suburban home builder was trying to sell 200 homes in a subdivision at a rate of about ten per week. They hired Erik B., a strong seller with a high rate of closing, in the spring of 1969. For most young couples viewing these homes this would be their first home purchase. They came from city or suburban apartments and had no previous home-buying experience. Erik was a pusher and he knew that the highest profit margin for the builder lay in the expensive extras—central air conditioning, upgraded carpet and appliances, and so on. He sold his quota every weekend, managing to talk most home buyers into considerably higher monthly payments than they could comfortably afford.

During peak selling hours the company sent another employee out to the site to help show the houses. Kathy V., a bookkeeper for the company, had just received her real estate license and was very cost conscious. If a customer was able to pay the basic selling price of a house but hesitated to add the costly extras, Kathy offered helpful suggestions—a comparable air conditioner could be purchased at Sears and installed by the buyer. The basic carpet was serviceable and could be upgraded by the buyer in later years. The attic could be left unfinished at first, to be completed later. To the company's surprise, Kathy sold as many units as Erik did, although Kathy's commissions were smaller for each unit.

The real difference showed up about six or seven years later. The same buyers were ready to find larger or more prestigious homes because their professional positions and their income levels had risen. Those who had bought from Kathy came back to the same builder to seek more expensive homes. They felt they were dealing with a reputable builder who would treat them fairly. Those who had bought their homes from Erik, however, and who had been saddled with much larger payments than they could afford in their early years, harbored resentment against the builder. They looked for homes in an expensive subdivision built by a rival builder.

These effects, as you can see, are long term. But they are certainly real. A reputation for fairness can serve you well, in the same way that a reputation for dishonest dealings can hurt you and your employer in the long run.

1. Discuss the short and long term advantages and disadvantages of dealing honestly with your customer and his or her particular financial situation.

Legal and business considerations

In recent years the pressures of consumerism have caused Congress and the states to enact many new laws. The stated purpose of these laws is to protect unwary purchasers from fraud and misrepresentation. In addition, longstanding laws governing fraud as well as public health and safety affect the ways that companies and individuals can deal legitimately with each other commercially. You should be aware of these laws; if your company does not give adequate training relating to their existence and applications, make it your responsibility to take a college-level course in business law designed for salespeople.

Laws that protect consumers
Even before 1900, pressures were being felt at the federal level for laws to prevent firms from selling spoiled meat or other tainted products, a not uncommon problem in those days before widespread refrigeration was available. These pressures resulted in passage in 1906 of the first Pure Food and Drug Act and the Meat Inspection Act. The next big wave of consumer protective legislation had to wait for the Great Depression. As might be expected, these laws governed not food but finance, establishing the **Securities Exchange Commission** (1933) and the **Federal Deposit Insurance Corpo-**

Securities Exchange Commission
The SEC is an independent federal agency that was established in 1934 to govern the sale and purchase of stocks and bonds.

Federal Deposit Insurance Corporation
The FDIC was established in 1933. It insures approximately 97% of the banks in the United States. If an insured bank closes, the FDIC will pay up to $40,000 to each depositor.

ration (1934). In the 1950s, several different kinds of legislation were enacted, encompassing product labeling, pesticides, poultry inspection, and automobile sales. The climate of consumerism in the 1960s, however, led to a rush of new laws relating to almost every area of life in modern society. In addition, state and local laws governing in-home selling, door-to-door sales, and the licensing of those salespeople are facts of life that will affect most salespeople at some time or another. For example, the **Federal Trade Commission** (FTC) has ruled that a person who buys a product from a door-to-door salesperson is entitled to a three day "cooling-off" period during which time the contract may be cancelled.

People in business are affected at least as much by application and interpretation as by the laws themselves. For example, a sugar substitute popular with dieters was found to cause cancer in laboratory mice. Although the link between this substitute and cancer in human beings was never established conclusively, the product was taken off the market. Whether or not rulings such as this are fairly applied, they cost the producers a great deal of invested money and salespeople must abide by them.

Federal Trade Commission
Congress established the FTC in 1914. It is an independent federal agency that protects consumers from unfair business practices and oversees competition within the marketplace.

Laws governing commercial activities

In an earlier chapter we discussed certain kinds of sales tactics that have been outlawed by federal or state governments. It is illegal, for example, to advertise an inexpensive product as bait to attract retail customers, and then switch the sales effort to a more expensive product when the customer arrives. Other prohibited acts include:

Bribes

Collusion, such as price fixing or certain other conspiratorial tactics

Exclusive dealerships

False labeling

Fraud or other misrepresentation, even when the seller is unaware of the misrepresentation

Tie-in sales, in which a customer must agree to buy one product in order to buy another

Unequal pricing policies

Unfair trade practices, as defined by the Federal Trade Commission (FTC)

collusion
an agreement between two or more parties to obtain illegally or unfairly something from another party. Price fixing is an example of collusion.

Price fixing, mentioned in the above list, is an especially touchy issue. Like many trade practices deemed unfair under antitrust statutes, it is not well-defined in the law. Therefore, judgment in particular instances is often placed in the hands of the courts. Although it is generally the case in sales to have the price of goods established by some formula calculated by those in finance and manufacturing, you may at some time find yourself involved in an informal discussion with other producers of a product similar to yours. If the discussion turns to pricing policies, try to change the subject. If you can't change the subject, leave the group immediately. In a court of law, even this kind of casual situation can be interpreted as a price-fixing attempt, leaving you and your company open to serious legal action. Don't take the chance.

Other legal sanctions are covered in the Uniform Commercial Code (UCC), which was established in 1962 to regulate dealings between buyers and sellers. Articles of the code define when a sale occurs, especially when a contract has been written to cover the terms of the sale. A **contract** is an agreement, usually in writing, between two people or firms to do certain things. When the legality of a particular contract is in question, the standards of the UCC may be applied in court.

The body of law that applies to contracts is the legal foundation of America's business dealings. In order for a contract to be valid, there must be **consideration,** the amount of money or other value one party promises to the other for a good or service. Both parties must be *legally capable* of entering into a contract. It is said the Lord takes care of drunks and children, and where contracts are concerned the law protects them, too. A contract signed by a minor is not legally binding, nor is one signed by a person who is drunk or mentally incompetent. This fact can affect the seller if the merchandise covered by the contract is damaged then returned, by a minor for example, who is then not required to pay for it.

As a salesperson, you may at some time find yourself in the impossible position of being expected by your employer—or your customer—to act illegally in order to make a sale. What do you do, for example, if the customer indicates that he or she expects a payment, amounting to a bribe, in return for placing a large order? It is not uncommon for buyers to expect a salesperson to share some of the commission money resulting from a large order. How can you handle the problem tactfully, without either losing the account or breaking the law? First of all, you should find out whether your company takes an official, upfront position on the problem. The company should be able to provide guidelines for general and even for specific situations. In particular cases where you are genuinely at a loss to know what to do, you should be able to consult your sales manager. You may find that this is not the first such experience of this kind your company has had with this customer. With the manager's increased experience and, perhaps, a knowledge of that customer, a solution to the problem should be forthcoming.

contract
A legal contract is an agreement between at least two parties to do or not to do some particular thing.

consideration
Consideration is the amount of money or other value promised by one party to another for a good or service. For example, Joe promises to mow his neighbor's lawn every Saturday for $2.00/hour. In this contract, the promised pay of $2.00/hour is the consideration.

What if it's your company that expects you to engage in a prohibited business practice, as in the bribe instance just discussed? Then
you're on very dangerous ground professionally, as well as legally,
and you should probably start looking for a new employer at once.

In sales to foreign countries, however, some form of consideration
to government official is often seen as a cost of doing business,
even though our government and the Internal Revenue Service define the practice as illegal. A company that sells to foreign markets in
any quantity must formulate some guidelines for its employers selling there.

**2. Research and report on a recent case that involves
"consideration" to a foreign government by a U.S. firm. Do you
consider such actions ethical?**

Ethics for sales managers

For those advancing into management, it is important to know all the
information already discussed in the chapter. You must be aware of
any legal pitfalls you are likely to encounter. One of the best ways to
keep informed, in addition to your required reading of industry journals and daily newspapers, is to talk to the company lawyer. That
individual should have up-to-date information files on lawsuits and
court events that pertain to the industry.

With the lawyer's help you should be able to prepare a written
code of ethics for your own sales staff; the sales support staff should
also have copies of this information. Be sure all new personnel are
informed of your company's guidelines and monitor them so that you
are sure they are complying with them.

Hiring and firing

Federal and state controls applied to employment practices are very
rigid. They are covered by many statutes, including the Civil Rights
Act of 1964, enforced by the Affirmative Action Program administered by almost all U.S. employers, of all sizes. Your company's
personnel manager, or the staff member hired to coordinate Affirmative Action, is the person you should talk to in this connection.
Specific practices in hiring, firing, and promoting that are prohibited
relate primarily to discrimination on the basis of race, sex, or age.
Again, your company lawyer should make an effort to keep up-to-
date information on file regarding recent court decisions and current
issues. It's your business to know the laws as they relate to your own
professional integrity.

On another level is your own relation to your staff personally. How do you motivate the salesforce? With fear of losing the job if quotas aren't met? Most salespersons you hire will know that "peddle or perish" is part of the job requirement and will be working to satisfy quotas without belaboring the point. One of your primary responsibilities is to make certain that the quotas are in fact achievable or you will find yourself short-staffed in midyear as salespersons leave for firms with more realistic goals.

We have discussed how millions of dollars are spent in sales promotion—many of these dollars relating to the sales staff for training in the disciplines of their products and techniques of selling. Motivation for financial reward via short-term contests, product specialty pushes, Achiever-of-the-Month, have had a good history of producing returns. All these techniques are more attractive as motivators than fear or personal manipulation of one salesperson against another.

One opposite effect should be stressed: the salesforce should never become so positively motivated that they make promises to customers that cannot be kept. The motto, "We Deliver" has been used by many managers to remind their employees that a new product, a new service, or whatever, must enter the marketplace without the disruption of the good will already established between the company and the customer. A sale cancelled because of inability to ship on the date promised costs the salesperson and the company more than just the dollar volume lost.

The example you set personally is the best guideline of all. If you deal honestly and fairly with your customers and colleagues it will be easy for them to know what to expect of them. If they see that you are dishonest, they will respond in kind.

3. Prepare your own code of ethics.

Don is a door-to-door salesperson for the ABCDE Encyclopedia Company. He makes a sales call on Peg, a mother of five school-aged children. Don encourages her to purchase the 12-volume set of encyclopedias for $119.95, citing the advantages of the encyclopedias for school-aged children. Peg purchases the 12-volume set, signs the contract, and gives Don a check for $25.00 as the first installment. Two days later Peg reconsiders her decision to purchase the encyclopedias.
Question: Can Peg cancel the contract for purchase of the encyclopedias and can she receive a refund of her $25.00?

Mini-case

**Define these
key concepts**

bait-and-switch
collusion
consideration
contract
cooling-off period

FDIC
FTC
price-fixing
SEC

Appendices

Appendix A   Dress for Success
by John T. Molloy

When Gerald Ford was minority leader of the House of Representatives, he sold his product—himself—excellently. He was Jerry the nice guy and he dressed like Jerry the nice guy. When he became President, he had a different product to sell—leader of the country—but he didn't change his image in the beginning of his presidency and was still projecting Jerry the nice guy. Unfortunately, great numbers of people were ignoring him with disdain. Obviously, appearance was not the only reason, but he had to change his image—and he did, successfully.

The point is that if you are a salesman—and even the President is one—you are not what you eat; *you are your product.* And you must dress accordingly.

I was once disseminating this advice to a group of salesmen when one jumped up and said, "I sell computers. How do you dress like a computer?" I then did a very quick analysis of the audience. I first asked if there were men present who did not sell computers. I then asked those men what they knew about computers. They answered that computers are expensive and efficient; yet they break down a lot.

I then told the salesman that he really wasn't selling a computer. What his client was buying when he chose between computers was the reliability and integrity of the company. If he worked for Joe Schmoe computers, the only way the buyer could judge the company was by the way he appeared, and therefore it would be helpful for him to dress in a way that would insinuate that his was a very honest, reliable company that could back up its claims and give excellent service.

The main problem with most salesmen dressing to suit their product is that they don't know what their true product is. They make the very poor assumption that the product is what it physically is. This is wrong. Salesmen must dress to suit *not what they are selling, but what people are buying.* The difference can be large and crucial.

If you are really serious about improving your sales, you will also do the following:

For a period of 30 days, keep a running record of exactly what you wear every day. Keep your own record of the clothing worn by two other men in your company: one who does no better than you or does worse, and one of the more successful men in the company. At the end of 30 days, make a comparison. Is your clothing closer in appearance to the successful man or the unsuccessful man?

This simple test should change the dressing habits of half the salesmen in America who are not doing well.

When I speak before most sales groups, I can look out in a crowd and tell you who is selling and who isn't, merely by judging their dress. Sometimes I can even tell about a man by they way his wife is dressed.

The next test is a bit more complicated, but could be very enlightening. Have a friend take several pictures of you wearing what you usually wear, plus several of you in other clothes. Have the friend show it to people who do not know you. Ask them to judge your honesty, reliability, likability, etc. You may find that a change of wardrobe is definitely in order.

Never buy any article of clothing unless you believe that article will help you sell. I mean it should actively help, not just be neuter or of questionable value.

Test every suit you presently have by keeping a record of when you wear each one and how well you fare on those days.

How many doors were opened to you in your blue suit?

How long did you have to wait in the outer office in your gray suit?

What were people's reactions to you in your brown suit?

How much did you sell in your beige suit?

After six months of this, you may take a few of suits out and give them to charity.

I am frequently asked if there are any traits common to all successful executives. There most definitely are; they always have their hair combed and their shoes shined. And they expect the same of other men, particularly subordinates. If your hair is disheveled, even if it is short, it triggers very strong negative reactions from other men. Keep it neat, and if you have hair that happens to grow in every possible direction except the right one, then you had better find something that will keep it down, or a barber who can give you a cut that minimizes the problem.

I hate to tell you this, but thers is also a direct correlation between the shape of a man's face and his chances of success. The most successful face is masculine and elongated, neither too heavy nor too thin, without prominent features. In short, the perfect WASP face. Slight faces are judged as being effeminate and round faces are being ineffectual. That's the bad news. The good news is that hair can help, if you can find someone to cut it who knows what he is doing.

Large men, or men who have a foreboding or gruff appearance, have an advantage and a disadvantage. The advantage is that they tend to be extremely authoritative. Their tremendous disadvantage is that they frighten people. It is essential that a large man do everything in his power not to scare his client. One large salesman would "accidentally" fall down when meeting a small client; another would drop his papers; both were putting themselves on the defensive.

A third way is to do it with clothing. The large man should avoid all dark, high-authority suits and should never wear pinstripes or vest. He should wear very soft colors and textures; medium-range soft gray suits, beige suits, and very light suits in summer. He should avoid strong color contrasts and any articles of clothing that call attention to him. The large man should wear only very light shoes, avoiding the heavier shoes, such as wing tips, that are normally a prerequisite of any businessman's attire.

The authority problem for the small man is easily solved by wearing high-authority clothing; pinstripe suits, pinstripe shirts, Ivy League ties, vest. The best shirt for the small man is the white-solid; the best shoes are the traditional wing tips; the best coats are heavy and luxurious, such as camel hair. He should wear only rich-looking attire, and he shoud be neat to the point of being precise. Color contrast is very important for him, and it is easily attainable with a dark suit, white shirt and dark tie.

The small man should wear attention-getting devices, for example, a handerkerchief in the breast pocket of a suit jacket, a diamond stickpin, or a unique watch. He should carry the most masculine-looking attaché case he can afford. And under no circumstances should he carry an umbrella.

When the age of a buyer is over 48, it is essential that the seller dress in the following manner, assuming that he himself is over 33: He should have no long sideburns and no hair covering his ears. His best suit is a conservative solid or pinstripe blue, anywhere in the country. Solid white and solid blue are the only absolutely safe shirts. Ties that are always acceptable to this group of men are solid, rep, and club. These older fellows make very strong moral judgments based on clothing.

The prejudices of college students are violent and strong. They expect you to fit the stereotype they have of you. One no-no is the solid blue suit; so are pinstripe suits, and Ivy League and club ties. If you are recruiting or if you are selling something important, the best outfit is a solid gray suit, blue shirt, and rep tie. If you are obviously out of their age category, you should not attempt to emulate their dress patterns or styles.

If you're a black selling to white middle America, dress like a white. Wear conservative pinstripe suits, preferably with vest, accompanied by all the establishment symbols, including the Ivy League tie. If you are white and selling to blacks, you will fare much better if you dress in nonestablishment patterns. Whites selling to antiestablishment blacks do better if they wear mustaches, and they do even better than business suits, but no suit should be solid dark blue. For blacks selling to other blacks, conservative, establishment symbols of authority and success are the rule of the day. All blacks react positively to other blacks who have made it.

If you live in a sophisticated area and sell in a less sophisticated area, you must never wear items of apparel that are markedly more sophisticated than what's worn by the people to whom you are selling. On the other hand, if you come from a small town and are selling in a more sophisticated area, you must not wear items that will mark you as a rube.

The most conservative business areas in the U.S. are Wall Street, Washington, D.C., and Boston. The corporate headquarters of any major firm, no matter where it is located, fit into the same category. To sell in any of these places, you must be dressed in the standard Northeast establishment attire. Three dicta are basic: be conservative; be traditional; and be neat. It is also important not to be any more up-to-date in your clothing than the people you are dealing with.

The most acceptable clothing for these areas is dark and medium-range suits, with or without pinstripes. White or blue solid shirts are preferable, as are all conservative ties, with the exception of the Ivy League. When selling in the remainder of the country, it is best to avoid the pinstripe suit and Ivy League tie. Solid blue and solid gray suits are acceptable almost anywhere and are generally the safest.

Don't wear dark pinstripe suits when selling in the South; medium-range solid blues and grays are better than dark blues and grays. Outside of Atlanta and Dallas, you should avoid dressing in the latest fashion. In most of the South, the white shirt is still the safest shirt. Do not wear any attire that is peculiar to the area (for example, cowboy boots in the Southwest); this type of clothing is "owned" by the locals, and if outsiders wear the local uniform they are looked upon as phonies or put-ons. There are entire Southern industries in which short-sleeved shirts are acceptable because of the heat. I would suggest, however, that salesmen wear their long sleeves and perspire.

The midwestern tradition of conservative attire is exaggerated and somewhat misleading, particularly in sportswear. Men in the Midwest have very strong color prejudices. Wear no gold, gray, purple, or lavender, and make certain that you wear nothing that identifies you as a member of the Eastern elitiest establishment. But be careful—it is absolutely impossible to sell in the Midwest if you wear any clothing that indicates you are not doing well financially.

Like almost everything else in California, its dress code is distinctly its own. In San Francisco, the code is somewhat formal, but in the southern areas of the state, informality prevails and extends deep into the business world. The suits that work best in California are medium-range solids. Shirts may be much more colorful and patterns that are taboo elsewhere are perfectly acceptable. The tie designs are also much more lively. If you are selling to a California firm with very liberal dress codes, you should still dress as you would anywhere else, because people in certain professions are expected to dress in certain ways.

There are some rules that all salesmen should adhere to, all the time.

1. If you have a choice, dress affluently.

2. Always be clean; it is not always necessary to be obsessively neat, but it is imperative to be clean.

3. If you are not sure of the circumstances of a selling situation, dress more—rather than less—conservatively than normal.

4. Never wear any item that identifies any personal association or belief, unless you are absolutely sure that the person to whom you are selling shares those beliefs.

5. Always dress as well as the people to whom you are selling.

6. Never wear green.

7. Never put anything on your hair that makes it look shiny or greasy.

8. Never wear sunglasses or glasses that change tint as the light changes.

9. Never wear any jewelry that is not functional, and keep that simple.

10. Never wear any item that might be considered feminine.

11. Wear, do, or say something that makes your name or what you are selling memorable. Clothing or accessories are a very effective ploy in the identity game.

12. If it is part of your regalia, always carry a good attaché case.

13. Always carry a good pen and pencil, not the cheap, junky ones.

14. If you have a choice, wear an expensive tie.

15. Never take off your suit jacket unless you have to. It weakens your authority.

16. Whenever possible, look in the mirror before you visit a client. You'll be surprised at how many flaws you'll catch.

Appendix B *from* The Woman's Dress for Success Book

Theoretically, women should dominate the sales field. From early youth they surpass males in two of the most important skills required for sales: the ability to "read" people and verbal communications. Yet in sales roles, where those two critical skills are always operating, they often fail.

Research has proven conclusively that the clothing a salesperson wears will affect his or her chances of making a sale. Further, research by a series of experts has established that when a person gives off contradictory verbal and nonverbal messages, the nonverbal message is the one more likely to be believed.

My research indicates that most women, most of the time, give off nonverbal messages that would be negative in a sales situation. And this is the primary reason for their failure.

If the buyer is a man, his general appearance will fall into one of three categories:

1. **executive type** with an authoritative suit and tie

2. **nonexecutive suit-and-tie type** His clothes will be lower middle class or some other form that indicates that he is not headed for the executive ranks.

3. **nonsuit-and-tie type**

When dealing with executives, a saleswoman generally will perform best when she is dressed in appropriate executive attire. The skirted suit with contrasting blouse works best. If she feels that she must add authority to her presentation, she can keep her glasses on (if she wears glasses). She may also wear a hat in an office providing it is brimmed and not particularly masculine, and carry all the other appropriate executive accessories.

When selling to the nonexecutive type, the sales woman should realize that she is dealing with a conformist, but one who may be threatened by a very high .authority suit. She should wear a traditional conservative dress, and she will be far safer if her accessories don't pack so much power. A simple black attaché case would probably work better with this man than the expensive brown leather one that you would carry when selling to a top executive. Never wear a hat in this man's presence, since high-authority items on women might appear to be a threat to his manhood. And if you pose such a threat, it will be "no sale" time.

With the nonsuited or bluecollar man, you have a variety of choices.

Surprisingly, this man will often react well to the woman who wears a high-power suit, particularly if he is in a macho field, such as construction or the heavy equipment business, which doesn't require that he wear a suit and tie. But as a general rule, we would suggest that you wear a conservative dress with this man also, unless you know that he is a power figure in his own area. The only absolute negative rule with him is never wear anything that even resembles *Vogue* magazine.

Another man will have an advantage when selling to a man; he can build a relationship with him of comradeship. At first, our research could find no comparative advantage for women. When women attempted to become friendly with purchasing agents, there were almost always sexual overtones, and this hurt their selling.

In research we had conducted earlier for fund raisers, we discovered that a fund raiser wearing symbols of the prospect's youth was far more likely to be successful than one who was not.

One fund raiser who was dealing with a 57-year-old man looked up the Brooks Brothers ties that were popular when the man was in high school and college. Those ties were the early Ivy League look, with deep-colored stripes. He discovered that some of those ties were still around.

For another client he came up qith a hand-painted tie. In both cases he pulled down a lot of money.

We discovered that a woman could more than offset the male-to-male advantage if she wore, or included in her ensemble, elements of style that were part of the purchaser's youth. For a man 40 years old, a pleated skirt may well remind him of his youth in the early 1950s. However, the skirt cannot have a kick pleat or look dated in any other way. And, of course, this principle shouldn't be carried to extremes. Don't show up in bobby socks, saddle shoes, and a poodle skirt.

As potent a weapon as this is with older men, it will not work with men who are younger than the saleswoman or about the same age. Furthermore, when a woman wears clothes that are chic, "in," or "withit"—clothes that are attractive to a man her own age or younger—the implications are immediately sexual. And she will lose her authority.

A saleswoman must dress to match her product. This means she must look as if she is able to use it well. For a woman selling almost any business-oriented product, this would mean the standard skirted suit. But for a woman selling fashion, it would mean the latest look.

The best example of dressing to suit a product that I ever saw was a woman who sold highrisk securities in Florida. When she sold them at the watering stops of the rich and retired, she looked as if she were on a constant vacation. She knew that they were buying comfortable leisure. But when she sold downtown, she dressed in a conservative two-piece gray suit that was two shades darker than the grays the local stores were selling. She said that people in the downtown offices liked the possible high return, but they also liked to feel that they were buying a secure investment. Her pick of dark gray, gave them a sense of security.

There is a small bagful of tricks you can use to get across to other women the message that you are important.

Most women feel that certain elements of fashion are an essential ingredient for being well dressed. Therefore, if you are dealing only with women, your outfit should include something that would be considered high fashion. For example, in the early 1970s, when the fashion industry was pushing hardest on the midi, a midi-length skirted suit would have been the ideal uniform for a woman in charge of women.

Another way to hint that you're in touch with fashion is to wear this year's color. This is the best route if you have both men and women working for you. A blouse in the right color can be authoritative and chic. But if the "in" color turns out to be purple, green, or gold, don't wear it. Any positive fashion impact would be offset by people's negative reactions to those colors.

Male executives will think less of you for wearing designer scarves or carrying designer handbags, but women will not. And one-third of the women will give you a higher status rating if you have those items.

"Imitate men" advice usually comes from women in industry. Their articles appear in industry-oriented magazines. They tend to base their advice on their own experience. Their experience generally comes down to "I don't know what else to do, so I'll imitate men around me." And they wear things like pinstriped suits with vests.

My research indicates that a three-piece pinstriped suit not only does not add to a woman's authority, it destroys it. It makes her look like an "imitation man," and that fails.

The "imitation man" look does not refer to looking tough or masculine. The effect is more like that of a small boy who dresses up in his father's clothing. He looks cute, not authoritative. Rather than making him look larger and more grown-up, the father's clothing only draws attention to his smallness and kiddishness. The same thing applies to women. When a woman wears certain clothes with male colors or patterns, her femaleness is accentuated. She frequently looks more diminutive. And this reduces her authority. My testing shows that some men find the "imitation man" look sexy. Other men are completely turned off by it. In either case, a woman's authority is diminished.

If women today want the world to take off its hat to them, they would be better off if they kept their own hats on. For a man or a woman, a hat is a traditional symbol of power, authority, and position. A hat, particularly the right hat, adds height and substance to the wearer. Taking off your hat has always been a sign of submission, so it is ironic that women have chosen this moment in history to go hatless.

We put three different hats—large brim, moderate brim, and nonbrim—on a series of neuter faces. We asked the respondents to guess at the social status, corporate rank, and competence of the hat wearers. In every case, the larger the brim the higher the social status. However, in the other categories—corporate rank and competence—the hats with moderate brims tested best of all three types.

The hat that would work best for most businesswomen is a medium-brimmed fedora. One word of caution: If the fedora looks masculine, it will reduce your authority. I suggest a maroon fedora with a little feather, because men don't wear those.

APPENDIX C   Pricing policies and practices for salespeople

This section is provided especially for those who have not completed a college-level course in economics, marketing or business mathematics. It is a summary only, and is not an adequate substitute for these courses.

In legal terms, price is only an offer to sell some specific good or service for a specific dollar amount. The buyer has the right to decline the offer, to make a counter offer, or to accept the offer. Few firms would be so foolish as to price their goods or services so high that the majority of their offers were refused. Obviously, they would not stay in business for long.

Price is also relative. When a customer has the opportunity to purchase an identical good or service for a lower price, on the surface it seems they would do so. But costs are also measured in time and convenience. A quart of strawberries available for down the street at a supermarket and that same quart for $.69 in a farmer's field ten miles away have a price difference greater than $.30. From a time standpoint, the local supermarket offers much greater convenience. The 20-mile round trip at $.15 a mile takes 45 minutes and costs $3.00. But, the person buying berries from the field may have the advantage of selecting higher quality berries, since all berries are not created equal.

This brings up some important points. To what degree is your product identical to another in all tangible and intangible aspects? Probably, not much. Demand is often greatly influenced by many intangible factors such as your company's reputation, your own personality, and past experiences by the potential buyer. Each selling situation must be considered unique.

Price has strong psychological factors. You should understand that the less a potential customer knows about a given good or service, the more he or she accepts price as an indication of quality. As the range of goods and services expands in an expandingly affluent economy, price will more frequently be used as a measure of quality. These perceptions of quality can be altered by advertising and by changes in a firm's reputation and in its product offerings.

Seven pricing policies

Most firms have pricing objectives, although in many smaller firms they are not stated in writing. A good starting place in understanding your firm's prices is to find what your firm's pricing objectives are. They will usually fall into one or more of the following categories.

- Target return on investment
- Target percentage of net sales
- To stabilize prices
- To meet competition
- To prevent competition
- To maintain or improve market share
- To maximize profits.

Target return on investment, is receiving increasing attention as a pricing objective. People in the finance area are becoming involved in determining both prices and whether new products will be offered. Two approaches are commonly used. The first uses the total investment by the company's owners as the base. The second uses this method for each particular product.

The first approach is perhaps the most widely used. For sake of illustration let's assume the company's total investment is $100,000 and the company is selling four products. A reasonable return on this investment may be calculated to be 20 percent, either before or after taxes. Let's further assume we're looking for 20 percent return before taxes. Simple mathematics tells us the company wants to make $20,000 from the four products, collectively. Products are then priced, with all costs including interest determined, to yield this amount given different volume estimates at each potential price for each product. The result may look like this.

Product	Price	Volume	Total	Costs	Profit
Product A	$2.00	$10,000	$20,000	$18,000	$ 2,000
Product B	4.00	12,000	48,000	40,000	8,000
Product C	6.00	12,000	72,000	65,000	7,000
Product D	8.00	8,000	64,000	61,000	3,000
					$20,000

Since these projections are made in advance of actual sales, volume is at best a refined estimate. The target of this objective is return on investment. Obviously sales volumes above or below the estimates will affect the actual return the owners achieve on their investment.

The second method, using this approach for individual products, is used with increasing frequency with new products. Most firms, by the time they are ready to sell a new product, know how much they have invested in market research and the product research and development. They have also calculated how much they expect to spend in initial promotional costs to stimulate demand. The product is then priced to achieve some target return on that investment over some time period, not necessarily in one year as in the previous illustration.

This pricing policy has two things to recommend it. First, if the target is set within reasonable limits, usually 10 to 25 percent, the firm cannot be accused of price gouging by government or by consumer advocates or other interest groups. Second, it places the focus on profits, not just volume for volume's sake.

The second objective, to gain an amount of profits as a percentage of sales, is frequently used by retailers and wholesalers. A significant part of the costs for these firms is merchandise in stock that they resell, often 65 percent to 75 percent of sales for retailers and higher for wholesalers. Since these firms may carry tens of thousands of items, identifying the profit contribution of each item, as in the objective above, usually is not feasible without sophisticated computer technology.

After figuring the cost of operation, usually on a department or product-line basis, a markup is added to the cost of merchandise to yield a percentage profit. Typically, this percentage will vary from 1 to 6 percent. To arrive at their true yearly profit they multiply this figure by the inventory turnover. A supermarket may average only 1 percent of sales but turn its inventory 12 times a year. Profit as a percentage of sales is still 1 percent, but the 12 percent figure is a more accurate gauge of that firm's profitability. We must also apply some of the first objective, return on investment. For these firms, the major investment is in inventory.

Consider this example:

Inventory turnover	Average monthly inventory at cost	Average monthly inventory at retail	Monthly sales	Percentage of profit
6/year	$80,000	$120,000	$60,000	2%

This firm will net $1,200 a month profit, or $14,400 for the year, using the percentage-of-sales method. However, it has an 18 percent return on its inventory investment—$14,000 divided by $80,000. Notice that either of the first two objectives can be used, and commonly are, to arrive at the same results. Only the approach is different.

The third pricing objective is to stabilize prices. In some industries the costs of doing business fluctuate daily. While on the surface it might seem sensible to pass both cost savings and cost increases on to customers, it is actually easier to administer stable prices than those that change often. When prices do not fluctuate widely the salesforce can concentrate on product benefits, not prices. Stability also avoids the costly procedures of continually changing price lists and mailing change notices to customers. Firms who put prices in catalogs save costly printing charges, also.

This is a long-run objective, since in any given quarter a firm that follows this objective may experience losses. Similarly, year-to-year profits may fluctuate greatly. Its advantage is that is simplifies day-to-day operations.

A fourth pricing objective is to meet competition. Although widely practiced, the method is not highly recommended. First, the firm admits to taking the role of follower rather than leader in the industry. Second, it falsely assumes that its product is identical to its competitor's in all respects, both tangible and intangible. Only rarely is this the case. Further, with this method too much selling is directed at price rather than at benefits. Finally, it weakens the firm's main purpose of being in business, which is to make a profit. Nevertheless, it is widely used, primarily because it is easy to let someone else set price for you just as it usually easier to imitate another firm's products than to be innovative and creative.

Our fifth objective, to prevent competition, is primarily used either by new firms or by those with new products. Successful application normally requires that per-unit costs fall significantly as volume goes up. An outstanding example was the Bic pen, which was introduced at $.19. By asking such a low price for a good quality product the manufacturers effectively prevented direct competition for almost six years. This strategy is not widely used, however, because it takes great faith that the price will generate the volume required to make money.

Our sixth objective relates to market share. Markets are constantly changing in two directions at the same time, as we saw in chapter 6. They change as demand for a product changes and as the degree of competition changes. The great proliferation of private labels, for instance, has significantly altered market share for many product lines at the retail level. The effect of price on market share was very noticeable in hand calculators. When first introduced these items were priced at over $100.00; now one can be purchased for under $10.00. As the price dropped, the size of the potential market expanded. When the price dropped below $60.00, for instance, college engineering and mathematics students provided a lucrative submarket, and the slide-rule became obsolete.

A firm's objective may be to maintain its market share or increase it by its pricing policies. The success of this approach is primarily dependent on the role price plays in purchasing. It also requires a firm to identify its current market share. Many prefer this objective to the financial ones of return on either investment or profit. They have seen that when markets are expanding rapidly, a firm whose pricing policies are keyed to investment will suffer in the long run as market share decreases.

The last objective, maximization of profits, has probably been followed by more firms than any of the objectives discussed above. It is, of course, the basis of a free market system. Unfortunately, consumer advocate groups and those in some sectors of government have opposed this objective. They have failed to realize that relatively few firms can continue to make "unreasonably high" profits over the long run. Today, competitors can move in fairly quickly for a piece of the action when they spot some company enjoying high profits. And prices usually come down.

The concept of profit maximization has several advantages. First, capital for business flows to those firms that are very profitable and

Figure C-1.
Elastic demand curve

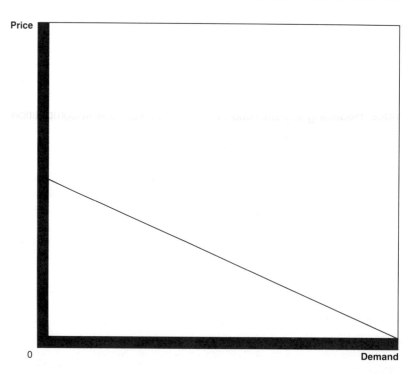

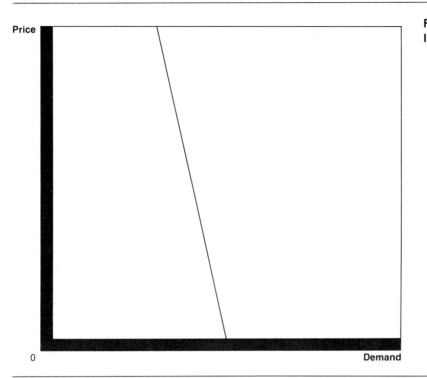

**Figure C-2.
Inelastic demand curve**

away from those that are not. Well-managed firms are rewarded while poorly managed ones die. Furthermore, the lure of profits produces a steady stream of new and innovative goods and services. Reducing this attraction obviously serves to limit competition to the detriment of our generally high standard of living.

A few final words on pricing policies. Some firms used more than one policy. They may use one for the short term and another for the long term. They may use one for new products during their first couple of years and another for the company as a whole. You should be aware of the advantages and drawbacks of each.

Economics of supply and demand

The relationships of price to the demand for a good or service is not widely understood. All too often it is falsely assumed that a reduction in price will result in an increase in demand. As noted earlier, in our impersonal society, with its staggering array of goods and services, price is often used to determine quality. Consequently, pricing a product too low may actually reduce sales rather than increase them.

**Figure C-3.
Positive kinked demand
curve (gasoline)**

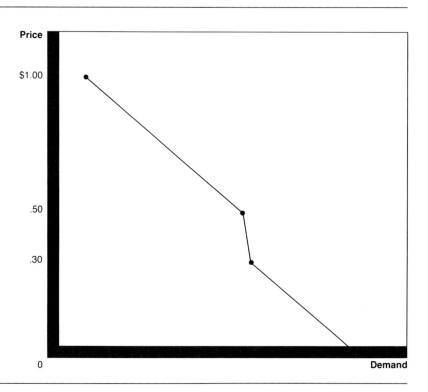

The degree to which price effects the sales of a product is called *elasticity.* If changes in price in small increments will results in similar changes in demand, the product is said to face an *elastic demand curve* (see Figure C-1). Conversely, if changes in price produce little or no change in demand, the product faces an *inelastic demand curve* (see Figure C-2). Graphically these two curves would look like this. Unfortunately, few products fit either graph, since the degree of elasticity may change at different price points. For example, the demand for gasoline for automobiles may have three different demands within three different price ranges, as illustrated in Figure C-3. Between the price range of thirty cents and one dollar there may be little change in demand for the product. It has been estimated that if the price of gasoline goes over a dollar consumers will make serious attempts to reduce gas consumption. Should the price fall below 30¢, however, demand may show some significant increase but within limits. It is highly unlikely that an ordinary driver would triple his or her consumption of gasoline. This kind of demand curve is called *kinked* because it has price points above and below which there is a significant change in demand.

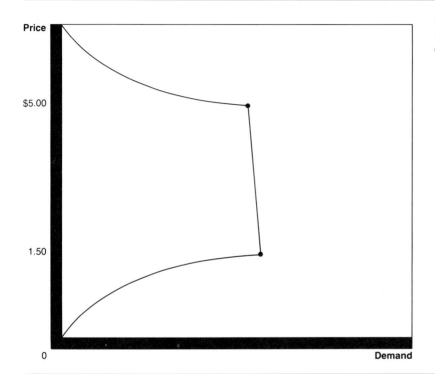

**Figure C-4.
Negative kinked demand
curve (lipstick)**

Another demand curve that has received increased attention is illustrated in Figure C-4. In this demand curve there is an 'acceptable' range within which a firm can price its products and achieve good sales volume. However, if the product is priced either above or below this range, sales will decline. My favorite example is that there is no glamor in a $.25 tube of lipstick and $10.00 is too high a price to pay for glamor.

While the average salesperson is usually not directly involved in the pricing of a firm's products, everyone should have some understanding of the type of demand curve the firm's products face.

Discounts and allowances in pricing

Pricing, especially in respect of discounts and allowances, are highly regulated by both state and federal governments.

Quantity discounts

To increase the size of an individual order or to increase the amount

purchased over some time period, firms often offer quantity discounts. This practice is not limited to firms that sell goods. Newspapers, radio, television, and magazines have long given discounts to
those who contract for large amounts of space or time. Bankers offer
better interest rates to their volume customers.

Legally, the size of the discount must be limited to actual savings
accrued to the selling firm through such savings as billing, packing,
transportation, order processing, and other factors. Currently a case
has been brought against the *Los Angeles Times* forcing them to
justify the rate difference between low volume and high volume accounts. This is a landmark case because the outcome will affect the
entire advertising industry.

Two types of discounts are common. The first is based on individual orders and is called *noncumulative.* The second method,
known as *cumulative,* disregards individual order size and is designed to keep customers over the long term. The size of the discount varies with the total volume purchased over a time period,
such as monthly, quarterly, or yearly. Some firms use two cumulative
discount schedules. The first may be on a monthly basis while the
second is yearly. The first is subtracted from the monthly bill; the
second often appears in the form of a rebate check.

Quantity discounts may be used where the firm can achieve significant economy through increased volume or where the firm
wishes to develop long-term customers to provide stability to their
sales volume.

Trade discounts
A trade discount is the price a firm is offering another firm to perform
some of its marketing functions. These discounts are based on the
manufacturing firm's suggested price to the ultimate buyer. This
approach is widely practiced in both retail goods and commercial
goods.

For illustration, assume a manufacturer wishes their product to
retail for $9.95. They then may offer a chain of discounts of 40-10-5
for retailer-wholesaler-agent. Selling prices then would be:

Discount schedule for $9.95 selling price
Retailer sells for $9.95; 40% disc. ($3.98) = $5.97
Wholesaler sells for $5.97; 10.0% disc. ($.60) = $5.37
Agent sells for $5.37; 5% disc. ($.27) = $5.10

Notice that the discounts are taken off the previously discounted
price. You cannot add the three together (55 percent) and subtract
that amount from the $9.95 to yield a price of $4.48. In effect they are

offering the retailer $3.98 to perform its services, the wholesaler $.60 to perform its services, and an agent $.27 to provide his or her services.

Trade discounts for each firm in the chain are usually computed on the value of the services provided. The amount should cover that firm's cost of providing those services and yield a profit. Since the manufacturer cannot control the level of efficiency of each and every member in the chain, the discount will then be an average of these firms collectively.

Cash discounts

Money has time value, which is usually reflected in interest rates. A dollar today is of more value to person than a dollar that may be received a year from now. Businesspeople recognize that it is important to a firm to collect money due them as speedily as possible. To speed up the cash flow, cash discounts are frequently offered.

A typical discount may be stated this way: 2/10 N30. This means that a cash discount of 2 percent will be subtracted from the bill if paid within 10 days of the billing date. If not paid within that period, the bill is due and payable without any discount in 30 days (read "net 30").

Some people see this 2 percent discount as a reward for those that pay promptly. Another view is that the 2 percent is a penalty. In any case, most firms do not expect all customers to take the cash discount. Suppose all products were priced without considering the cash discount and the firm then projected a 3 percent profit on sales. If all customers took the discount, profits would plunge to 1 percent, a drop of two thirds. A more practical approach to pricing might be to assume all customers would take the 2 percent discount. This assumption would be made when computing profits as well as prices. Those who paid late, that is, after the ten-day period, would be required to pay a 2 percent penalty as interest.

Seasonal discounts

Many goods and services are seasonal in nature and have periods when sales are very low. To stimulate demand in these periods some firms offer a discount from their regular price. The primary function is to even out production for the year.

Seasonal discounts are also used to encourage buyers to place orders and take delivery in advance of the season. A series of cash discounts then may offer the buyer more than two options for paying. In this case the discounts are not considered a penalty for late payment but as allowances for off-season storage. By helping the seller achieve a more even production schedule they help to reduce costs. In forward dating, a variation of seasonal discounts, a future date is placed on the order. In February, a toy manufacturer, for example, may write an order for toys to be delivered to a retailer in September for Christmas selling. For discount purposes, however, the order may be dated October 1.

Promotional allowances

Especially in consumer goods, promotional allowances, have become a major factor in recent years. In response, most major radio, television, and newspaper advertising departments have added a person to handle co-op advertising. Promotional allowances generally fall into two areas. The first is an allowance to pay part of the buyer's advertising costs. The second deals with the wide variety of sales promotion activities.

It should be pointed out that this is a highly regulated area, since there is extensive opportunity to provide special favors to select customers. For example, one firm developed an advertising plan in which it provided videotaped commercials and offered to pay half the store's cost of running them. This was ruled discriminatory against small accounts who could not afford to buy television time, especially in the urban markets. The plan could be offered only if an acceptable substitute was also offered to small firms.

As with quantity discounts, the amount of allowance to any one firm must be in relation to their purchases. Unlike quantity discounts, however, the buyer is not required to accept the allowance.

While advertising allowances have increased greatly as part of the average firm's promotional mix, sales promotional allowances shows significant growth as well. Refer to the text chapter covering sales promotion activities for more information.

Freight allowances

To be competitive in distant markets some firms take the option of paying all or part of the freight costs for a buyer. While this may result in selling to different buyers at different prices, it is often feasible for firms who have very high fixed costs. Any revenue over the variable costs of the product, plus whatever is absorbed in freight charges, can contribute toward those fixed costs. This pricing practice is legal as long as all buyers in a given geographic market are offered the same pricing.

Concept of contribution

In accounting procedure the costs of doing business are normally classified as variable or fixed. *Variable costs* are those that change directly with volume, such as the labor and materials in a factory. Where salespeople are paid on a straight commission, this cost would also be considered variable. Those costs considered *fixed* are rent, utilities, depreciation on buildings and equipment, and the salaries of executives. These are costs the firm would incur unless volume was to change greatly. If a firm decides to spend a specific amount for advertising during a period, this can also be considered a fixed cost.

In setting price, especially where a company has a large number of products, it is usually impossible to determine accurately the fixed costs for any one product; some costs must always be arbitrarily assigned. An example would be assigning some proportion of the president's salary and fringe benefits to each and every product.

On most items, to go through this process to determine the item's profitability is not worth the costs to the firm. Consequently, those who compute prices focus on the variable costs that are relatively easy to identify. Any revenue over the variable costs is considered *contribution to overhead,* which is a fixed cost. Obviously, all the products collectively must cover overhead and then yield a profit, at least in the long term. But another factor enters in at this level. Many retail stores and other firms decide to sell some products for cost, with little or no contribution to overhead, in exchange for the sales generated of regularly priced merchandise. Manufacturers may pursue this policy for different reasons. In some cases their customers demand a fairly complete assortment of merchandise at given price points. While most of the products may be quite profitable, others may be only marginally so. Elimination of the low-profit items, however, would result in loss of sales of the profitable item.

The concept of contribution looks at a division, a department, or the whole company when arriving at selling prices for individual products. The base for setting price is the total of variable costs for a given item. And the sale of any item is related to the rate of sale of other products. If selling one product for a price that only covers variable costs will significantly increase the sales of profitable items, the item will be kept, not dropped.

Appendix D   Duties of sales executives

The duties of a sales manager very naturally depend on the type of organization, the product it sells, the methods of distribution used, and, to a greater extend than may be realized, upon the sales manager's limitations. An analysis of salaries paid sales managers shows the highest compensation is in the speciality field—that is to say, in selling office appliances, insurance, advertising, real estate, automobiles, etc. In those fields sales management has reached the highest state of efficiency, and the duties of the sales executive encompass a wide range of responsibility. In general, he is charged with formulating sales policies, recruiting, training, and supervising the company's entire selling force.

An important responsibility of the general sales manager in some companies is known as "future demands." This has to do not only with the improvement of the products the company makes, but also the development of new ways of selling and using those products. Specifically, these duties as set forth by one company in its job description, are as follows:

Study new lines of business for the purpose of broadening our field. Devise systems for new or unusual lines of business. Suggest new improvements in present product. Introduce new improvements in present product. Introduce and promote sale of new type of machines. Apply present machines to unusual lines. Suggestion contest for purpose of securing suggestions for improvement of product.

In speciality sales operations, more than in the case of marketing staples through dealers, it is customary for the sales manager to actually devise sales plans and campaigns. Sometimes he has an assistant to do this, but in even the largest organizations that duty is considered so essential to sales production that it is assumed by the sales manager himself, although an assistant may follow through.

Indeed, only the most general sort of job description can hope to cover even a fraction of the duties and responsibilites of the many various types of sales manager. However, the following will serve as a starter for drawing up a job specification.

Title: Sales Manager

Organizational relationships
Reports to: Vice-President, Marketing
Supervises: District Sales Manager
Sales Training Manager
Sales Service Manager
Sales Statistics Clerk

Primary responsibilities
He is responsible for all field sales activities; for the maintenance of an adequate field sales organization; for obtaining maximum sales volume; for hiring of all sales and other personnel in his department, utilizing the facilities of the company's general employment department; for hiring of all sales and other personnel in his department, utilizing the facilities of the company's general employment department; for the adequate training and retraining of sales personnel; for sales service and engineering functions; for the flow-back of industry and marketing data from customers and on competitive conditions in the field; for maintaining an awareness for and acquaintanceship with those factors that influence sales opportunities and to plan asutely for their realization; for providing adequate forward stocks to assure proper sales and service.

Duties
1. To build, maintain, and direct an efficient, well-trained and effective field sales organization.
2. To develop and recommend to the vice-president, marketing, for his approval, policies and programs relating to:
   a. Size and type of sales organization
   b. Product lines
   c. Distribution channels
   d. Prices
   e. Sales objectives by product and geographical area
   f. compensation levels
   g. Personnel development and advancements
   h. Sales department budgets
   i. Advertising and sales promotion activities
   j. New product development and improvement of present products
   k. Credit policies
   l. Warehouse and deliveries

3. To establish and execute sales programs in accordance with approved policies.
4. To assign sales objectives to district, branch, and other sales terrritories; periodically to evaluate performance in their attainment; and to take necessary steps to bring results in line with objectives.
5. To organize, recommend to the proper executives, and administer procedures affecting sales, prices, terms, discounts, allowances on returned goods, sales service and field engineering services.
6. To plan and conduct periodic sales meetings for the purpose of educating, training, and stimulating the sales organization.
7. To supervise the formation and maintenance of an adequate recruitment, hiring, training, and development program for sales personnel.
8. To approve travel and selling expenses of district and other departmental managers, to review related monthly reports, and to institute remedial action when expense policies are violated.
9. To keep management informed of significant sales developments affecting the company.
10. To prepare and recommend selling cost and expense budgets and to strive to operate within approved budgets.
11. To recommend the addition of new products to the line or the modification or elimination of existing items.
12. To achieve adequate profit margins and sales volumes as required to maintain profitable operations.
13. To assist in the preparation of advertising and promotion programs, and to supervise the execution of such programs by sales personnel.
14. To supervise the preparation and interpretation of reports as to sales and markets, and the comparison of sales forecasts with actual sales and sales quotas.
15. To correspond with other company personnel and customers as required.
16. To travel in the field, calling on present and prospective customers, consulting and supervising district managers, branch managers, and salesmen as the needs require. Calls on present and prospective customers are to be made in conjunction with the proper field representatives and for the purpose of assisting them by the field sales manager's executive prestige, and in no way should the effectiveness of the company's local representative be impaired.
17. To attend such industry conventions and to participate in industry activities as the vice-president, marketing, may direct.

18. To participate in and contribute to such committee activities as the vice-president, marketing, may direct.
19. To handle all sales distribution problems as assigned by the vice-president, marketing, and to be his assistant and advisor in respect to sales coverage.
20. To interpret company policy in connection with questions arising in the field, and to consult with district managers on matters beyond their authority and experience.
21. To motivate field salesmen through the district managers, district officers, branch managers, branch offices, and other field facilities to see that policies and instructions are properly executed and customers are properly served, and to take remedial action when required.
23. To cooperate with all executives and other managers in the company, and to require cooperation of all sales, sales training, and sales service personnel with other personnel in the company.
24. To assume the obligations of good citizenship and to participate in worthwhile community and national activities as may be required for sound public relations for the company.

Other jobs closely related to the sales manager's may be outlined as follows.

Title: Merchandising Manager

Organizational relationships
Reports to: Vice-President Marketing
Supervises: Product Managers

Primary responsibilities
He is responsible for the development of merchandising programs; for furnishing functional guidance to the field sales organization on all matters pertaining to the merchandising and sale of company products; for maintaining awareness of and for recommendations concerning competitive quality, customer utility, price position, and sales volume of company products; for keeping informed on competitors' products, determining their strong and weak points, and observing customer acceptance of company products relative to competition; for acting as liaison between sales, research, development engineering, and manufacturing departments relative to the design, salability, and utility of company products; for the study of pricing data and pricing policies, price lists, discounts, and gross

margins in relation to competition and company needs; and for recommending changes in policy and practice, when required. He has no line authority over the field sales organization or other department; his is a functional staff department.

Duties

The duties of the merchandising manager may be summarized briefly as follows:

1. To advise and assist the vice-president, marketing, in the development of policies and procedures pertaining to merchandising, pricing, advertising and promotion, packaging, and new product development.
2. To supervise the development of necessary sales tools, including literature or manuals, as may be required by the firld force to sell the company's products.
3. To assist the sales training director in the development of training programs for the field sales personnel.
4. To work, and to cause the product managers to work, periodically with the field sales organization and customer personnel, through field calls, correspondence, or telephone, on current trends in industry, styling and customer acceptance. Field work should take at least 20× of his time
5. To recommend, on the advice of the product managers, the addition of new products to the line or the modification or elimination of existing products or lines.
6. To supervise the preparation of and to recommend sales volume budgets for company products.
7. To supervise the product managers in their attention to sales volume, product acceptance, quality and utility of company products, and the competitive situation for these products in the markets.
8. To supervise the accumulation of information concerning competitive products, features, specifications, prices, discounts, terms merchandising policies and programs, distribution channels and outlets, and customer acceptance; to maintain or direct the maintenance of displays of competitive products for ready comparison and company products.
9. To supervise the review of reports from salesmen regarding product complaints and to take appropriate action.
10. To consult, and to cause the product managers to consult, with factory personnel and engineers on company products.
11. To attend industry conventions and marketing meetings as deemed advisable.

12. To review, and to cause the product managers to review, publications containing industry and trade news.
13. To review pertinent costs of sales and other reports and budgets related to company products.
14. To supervise the preparation of, and give assistance in, the execution of merchandising plans to stimulate sales.
15. To assist in establishing prices for each product line, using price structure forms and percentage "mark-ons" as approved by company policy. Prices and terms are approved by the vice-president, marketing, and the treasurer, and copies are distrubuted to all principal executives. Once a price structure has been approved by management and the price published, changes may not be made without the formal approval of management.
16. To review sales quotas in cooperation with the vice-president, marketing, field sales managers, and market research managers.
17. To assist in the preparation of bids and proposals.
18. To supervise and direct the activities of all personnel in his department.
19. To supervise the preparation of any regular or special reports that may be requested of his department from the vice-president, marketing.
20. To recommend salary changes, promotions, demotions, or release of personnel under his control.
21. To cooperate with all personnel in the marketing and other divisions, and to cause the personnel of his department to cooperate with all other company personnel.
22. To assume the obligations of good citizenship and to participate in worthwhile community and national activities as may be required for sound public relations for the company.

Title: Customer Service Manager

Organizational Relationships
Reports to: Vice-President, Marketing
Supervises: Sales Correspondents
           Order Clerks
           Expediting Clerks
           Quotation Clerks

Primary responsibilities

He is responsible for handling all correspondence with customers and salesmen dealing with inquiries and quotations, with routing and interpretation of regular and special orders, specifications, prices, shipping dates and other matters of similar nature. He is also responsible for the maintenance of all records, files, preparation of reports that pertaic to the department. He has no line authority over the field sales organization or other department; his is a functional staff department.

Duties

The duties of the customer service manager may be summarized briefly as follows:

1. To supervise the activities of the customer service department.
2. To communicate with company customers and personnel, and others in regard to orders, prices, products, deliveries and other matters of simmilar nature as required.
3. To supervise and assist in expediting deliveries and in satisfying complaints as required for critical orders or special customer problems.
4. To act as liaison between customers and production on questions concerning orders placed, shipments, production schedules and inventories.
5. To direct the maintaining of records and the preparation of reports as required.
6. To assist in the preparation of production requirements based on sales and other pertinent data.
7. To review reports on shipments, inventories and production and to assist in sales planning in collaboration with the vice-president, marketing, market research manager, merchandising manager, field sales manager, and others designated.
8. To review the methods currently in use in the customer service department, and to make changes, improvements, and revisions as deemed advisable.
9. To delegate duties and work assignments to others in his department, to maintain and train adequate personnel to perform the functions of his department, and to assure good service and dispatch in handling customers' orders.
10. To cooperate with others in preparing the operating budget for his department, and to operate the department within the approved budget program.
11. To cooperate closely with product managers, sales managers, and other, and to handle special assignments as required to assure satisfactory order handling and deliveries.

12. To assume the obligations of good citizenship and to participate in worthwhile community and national activities as may be required for sound public relations for the company.

Title: District Manager

Organization relationships
Reports to: Field Sales Manager
Supervises: Branch Managers

Primary Responsibilities
He is the direct representative of management in the field sales organization.

Duties
The duties of a district manager may be summarized thus:

1. To direct and supervise the branch managers assigned to his district.
2. To see that all authorized policies, programs, and instructions issued from the general office are put into effect and carried out in all branches.
3. To review branch managers' reports, and to counsel, assist, and direct them as required.
4. To study market analysis figures furnished by the general office, and from them assist the branch managers in preparing sales coverage plans.
5. To review reports on sales activities and compare them with planned activities to assure close adherence to, improvements of, and maximal achievement of results.
6. To aid branch managers in controlling expenses, preparing budgets, call schedules, territory assignments and coverage, and in planning their work.
7. To aid branch managers in the planning of new distributor campaigns, and in the execution of such plans.
8. To make frequent and regular trips to the branches for inspection and counseling.
9. To accompany branch managers and salesmen when necessary in performing any of their duties, such as holding important sales meetings, making important distributor calls, and interpreting major policy decisions within his scope of authority. In all contacts with distributors, it is very important that a district manager build the prestige and recognition of the branch man-

ager and salesmen as the company's sales representatives in their territories.

10. To handle all necessary district sales correspondence.
11. To assist in the hiring of new sales personnel as may be requested by the field sales manager's office.
12. To plan and hold regularly scheduled district and branch conferences within the policy of the company.
13. To attend regularly scheduled district managers' conferences as called by the field sales manager, and to attend industry trade shows and conferences as directed by the field sales manager.
14. To perform required and necessary company entertainment duties with company distributors and prospective distributors.
15. To control expenses and costs within the district, approve expense reports of branch managers, and aid in the building of operating budgets and operating within.them.
16. To assist branch managers in determining distributor and sales territory quotas, and in programming related sales effort.
17. To counsel with branch managers and recommend to the field sales manager compensation changes for branch personnel.
18. To fill out and mail promptly and completely all required reports.
19. To maintain awareness for and keep the general office advised of all competitive distribution trends, policies, new products, sales campaigns, prices, discounts, profit structures and "special deals" as these come to his attention.
20. To train and develop branch managers as possible candidates for the position of district manager.
21. To cooperate with all company executives and department heads for the maximum achievement of sales, profits, and satisfied customers.
22. To assume the obligations of good citizenship and to participate in worthwhile community activities as a public relations asset to the company.

Title: Branch Manager

Organizational relationships
Reports to: District Manager
Supervises: Salesmen
Office and Warehouse Personnel

Primary responsibilities
He is directly responsible for maintenance and development of sales of company products in the areas assigned to him; for the development and maintenance of an effective, well-trained and efficient sales force to aggressively and profitably cover the areas assigned to them; for local interpretation of and compliance with company policy in the operation of the branch and representation of the company to present and prospective customers.

Duties
The duties of a branch manager are summarized as follows:

1. To recruit and select capable branch salesmen. Hiring and severance of salesmen shall be on authority and approval of the district manager and field sales manager.
2. To train branch salesmen in the sale of company products, policies, and procedures of the company, following appropriate sales methods and techniques found to be in good practice, and as developed and outlined by the sales training manager.
3. To maintain an adequate sales force needed to cover the branch areas, to anticipate replacement needs sufficiently in advance so as to have a suitable candidate available for consideration or hire, and to maintain current files of prospective candidates for sales positions. A branch manager may from time to time be requested to suggest the names of possible candidates for hire and assignment to other branches.
4. To assign salesmen to territories, predetermined and balanced for sales opportunities, sales coverage demands within available time, and in line with the salesmen's knowledge and skills.
6. To see that all company policies, programs, and instructions are put into effect and carried out in the branch assigned to him.
7. To review all salesmen's reports and schedules, and to counsel, advise, assist, and direct the salesmen in their activities.
8. To maintain an awareness of local market and competition conditions, of user preferences and desires, of industry trends, and to send such information promptly, with his recomendations to management.

9. To periodically analyze, jointly with the salesmen, sales objectives for both present and prospective customers, sales and service activity demands, and programs for effective sales coverage.

10. To aid the salesmen in arranging for, planning, and conducting instructive and stimulating meetings with customer personnel.

11. To make frequent and regular field trips with the salesmen for the purpose of inspecting activities, counseling with the, and generally supervising them.

12. To make field calls with the salesmen when advisable and thus to assist them by his managerial prestige. He is rarely to make calls by himself on customers, as this tends to depreciate the authority and usefulness of the salesmen in the customers' eyes.

13. To review expense reports of the salesman and to take such steps as are advisable for controlling expenses within company policies.

14. To maintain and review records and reports of calls on customers and sales results obtained.

15. To handle correspondence with present and prospective customers, and with company personnel as needful.

16. To supervise the activities of the branch office personnel and the operations of the branch warehouse.

17. To plan and hold regularly scheduled sales meetings.

18. To attend regularly scheduled branch managers' meetings as called by management.

19. To attend such conventions and trade meetings as may be designated by management.

20. To maintain, completely and carefully, all records requested by management, and to fill out and mail promptly all reports requested.

21. To maintain an awareness for promotability of salesmen to more responsible territories or positions in the branch or in the company as a whole, and to assist in the development of those men for such advancement.

22. To cooperate with all company executives, department heads, and other personnel as may be required to assure increased sales volume and satisfied customers.

23. To assume the obligations of good citizenship and to participate in worthwhile community activities as a public relations asset to the company.

Title: Market Research Manager

Organizational relationships

Reports to: Vice-President Marketing
Supervises: Clerical and Statistical Staff

Primary Responsibilities

He is responsible for the execution of economic studies that pertain to company's welfare and growth; for the interpretation of performance data as needed by management in establishing policies, directing marketing operations, and in correlating the planning of company activities; for maintaining data files and records available for company executive and management personnel; for conducting studies in cooperation with the merchandising manager, the product managers, and field sales organization personnel. He has no line authority over the field sales organization or other department; his is strictly a functional staff department.

Duties

His duties may be summarized briefly as follows:

1. To operate the market research department economically and effectively.
2. To consult with other company executives and personnel on performance, marketing, and sales problems.
3. To consult with marketing division personnel on methods best suited for use in dealing with specific statistical and research problems.
4. To study trade and government publications for indication of economic and industry trends and needs.
5. To direct correlation and other studies of company sales and production with available industry and economic data for the purpose of measuring company results, appraising foreseeable probabilities, and determining the company's position and progress.
6. To cooperate with the controller in preparing operating budgets.
7. To participate in industry and trade-association activities and studies on marketing and sales problems.
8. To receive sales, performance, and related reports, and to review and summarize them as required.
9. To prepare reports on sales, performance, products, markets, and economic conditions as requested.

10. To keep up-to-date files for reference as needed.
11. To assist in figuring commissions and bonuses as required.
12. To delegate work to other personnel as required and to supervise and direct their performance.
13. To cooperate with executives and departments as required to assure full use of available data, and to assist them in their problems of supervision, direction, and decision.
14. To assume the obligations of good citizenship and to participate in whorthwhile community and national activities as may be required for sound public relations for the company.

Title: Vice-President, Marketing

Organizational relationships
Reports to: President
Supervises: Field Sales Manager
Merchandising Manager
Customer Service Manager
Market Research Manager
Advertising and Sales Promotion Manager

Primary responsibilities
He is responsible for the general direction of short-range and long-range planning relating to product development and marketing policies; for providing general consultation and advice on all aspects of the company's marketing program; and for the compilation and maintenance of current and complete information on the company's marketing activities and on industry development. He is responsible for the general direction of distribution of the company's products in such a manner as to satisfy customer requirements; for building customer goodwill; for returning the required profit margins, and for providing sufficient volume to permit profitable use of the company's production facilities. His authority extends throughout the entire marketing division in all its varied activities, as required to fulfill the responsibilities assigned to him by the president of the company.

Duties
The duties of the vice-president, marketing, may be summarized briefly as follows:

1. To exercise general supervision over all marketing activities of the company.

2. To supervise the building and maintenance of an aggressive, well-trained, adequately compensated, and well-integrated organization.
3. To maintain equitable compensation and personnel development schedules which will attract and hold competent personnel.
4. To maintain good morale and develop loyalty in the personnel of the marketing organization.
5. To supervise the development of plans for the solicitation of orders and distribution of company products to all whorthwhile present and prospective customers.
6. To control selling costs and expenses, approve budgets of sales costs and expenses, and to strive to operate within approved budgets.
7. To approve traveling and selling expenses for all executives and managers in the marketing division, to review related monthly reports, and to institute remedial action when expense policies are violated.
8. To correspond with company personnel, and present and prospective customers, when required.
9. To guide personnel of his division in building goodwill with present and prospective customers.
10. To generally supervise the search for and the analysis of markets for company products.
11. To attain adequate profit margins and sales volumes as required to maintain profitable operations and to enhance the company's position and future growth in the industry.
12. To participate in marketing, distributor, and industry conferences and meetings as necessary to aid in product distribution.
13. To supervise the obtaining of data as to the sales plans, selling effort, markets, products, and prices of competitors to the extent that such data will be beneficial in determining satisfactory marketing policies, developing marketing plans and assisting in programming manufacturing for the company.
14. To give general supervision and approval in the proper development and execution of advertising and sales-promotion plans.
15. To serve on and constructively participate in such committee activities as may be assigned by the president of the company.
16. To supervise the preparation and interpretation of reports as to sales and markets, comparison of sales forecasts with actual sales, and the establishment of sales quotas, as may be needed for the guidance and use of company executives and sales-division personnel.

17. To participate in the review and approval of all requests for research and development projects concerned with new products or new models of old products, as they relate to development in the industry and to customer needs and usage.
18. To anticipate foreseeable marketing conditions and participate in the formation of company plans for future expansion or entrenchment programs.
19. To handle all marketing and distribution problems as assigned by the president and to be the president's advisor with respect to marketing management.
20. To cooperate with all other executives of the company and to require the cooperation of all marketing division personnel with other personnel throughout the company.
21. To assume the obligations of good citizenship and to participate in worthwhile community and national activities as may be required for sound public relations for the company.

Succession

Every sales manager should train a successor. He owes this not alone to his company, but to himself. In an untold number of instances, sales managers who had the qualifications for general executive responsibility have not been advanced to such positions because there was no one available to take over the sales department. The same thing applies, of course, to all sales executive positions. It is the responsibility of the sales head of the business to make sure that his entire second line is secure. There should not only be a good man in each position, but he should have a younger man coming along, qualified and trained to take over his job should the necessity arise. The policy makes for a flexibility of management highly desirable in sales administration. A well-organized sales department, like a well-organized military unit, should be so officered that there is always somebody "coming along" to replace the casualties.

The importance of building a strong second line of officer material has caused larger organizations to institute executive rating systems. These serve to spot men of outstanding leadership ability, and to evaluate them in terms of the proper sales jobs in the organization.

A sales executive who permits his subordinates to flood him with routine decisions is a weak executive; so, too, is one who must approve and sign all reports, letters, and bulletins. A strong executive is one who receives only condensed, summarized, and comparative reports that cover all the elements entering into his management. These summaries should have previously been carefully gone over by an assistant who notes on them all deviations from planned performance, good and bad.

Reprinted from Sales Manager's Handbook, *12th ed., Ovid Riso (Ed.), Copyright 1977 The Dartnell Corporation. Reprinted with permission.*

Appendix E   Principal business directories

(Prices subject to change at time of printing)

AB FUN RIDE SURVEY. Lists U.S. ride manufacturers showing type of unit, capacity, and price. Also includes importers and foreign manufacturers of the equipment. Arranged alphabetically. 40 pp. AMUSEMENT BUSINESS, 2160 Patterson St., Cincinnati, Ohio 45214. $1.00.

A.B.C. WORLD AIRWAYS GUIDE. Alpha-geographically arranged listing of all airports and airport services in the world, and other information. Twelve monthly issues published by ILIFFE-N.T.P., INC., 24 Central Drive, Farmingdale, N.Y.

ABD DIRECTORY. An alphabetical and geographical listing of 4,500 dealers, manufacturers and service firms in the aircraft and aerospace industries. 270 pp. Quarterly. AIR SERVICE DIRECTORY INC., 1 Bank St., Stamford, Conn. 06901. $20 annual subscription; $6 single issue.

ACCOUNTING INFORMATION SOURCES. Complete listing of current accounting literature. Three sections: background of modern accounting; associations which represent the entire profession; literature covering the regulation of accounting and auditing practices by U.S. Federal agencies. Alphabetically arranged by entry. Includes listing of Basic Accounting Library. Appendixes. Author and subject indexes. 420 pp. GALE RESEARCH CO., Book Tower, Detroit, Mich. 48226. $14.50.

AD CHANGE. Designed to give subscribers up-to-the-minute news of changes in the national advertising field. Issued weekly giving agency appointments and changes in personnel in the field. NATIONAL REGISTER PUBLISHING CO. INC., 5201 Old Orchard Rd., Skokie, Ill. 60076. $35.00 per year.

ADVERTISER COMMERCIAL CODE GUIDE. Lists over 2,000 TV advertisers coded on the basis of the ISCI (Industry Standard Commercial Identification) System which is the official system adopted by all major associations in the advertising field. Presented in two parts: Section One contains TV advertisers, advertising agencies and Part Two is a cross index of all listings in Part One. NATIONAL REGISTER PUBLISHING CO. INC., 5201 Old Orchard Rd., Skokie, Ill. 60076. $48.00.

ADVERTISERS ANNUAL. An alphabetical list of all British Firms engaged in advertising and selling, covering newspapers and magazines, outdoor publicity and posters, commercial television, radio, and cinema, advertising agents, consultants and public relations; direct mail agents; marketing specialist; etc.,

1,260 pp. Annually. INTERNATIONAL PUBLICATIONS SERVICE, 114 E. 32 St., New York, N.Y. 10016. $20.00.

ADVERTISING AGENCY EXHIBIT, ANNUAL. Describes outstanding advertising campaigns in Canada during the preceeding year, with name of agency, advertiser, creative and art directors and copy writers. Also includes an alphabetical listing of all Canadian advertising agencies, key officials and accounts served. "MARKETING" MAGAZINE, 481 University Ave., Toronto, Ontario M5W 1A7 Canada. $1.00.

ADVERTISING, EDITORIAL, AND TELEVISION ART AND DESIGN ANNUAL. Contains an alphabetically classified directory of products and services in the graphic field. Also other illustrated information is included. 576 pp. Annual. WATSON-GUPTILL PUBLICATIONS. One Astor Plaza, New York, N.Y. 10036. $22.50.

ADVERTISING SPECIALTY REGISTER. Directory contains entries of approximately 1,000 names and addresses of firms selling through advertising specialty distributors and jobbers—names of executives, products, and trade names. Published by ADVERTISING SPECIALTY INSTITUTE, 4730 Chestnut St., Philadelphia, Penna. 19139. Available to trade members only.

AERONAUTICAL ENGINEERING—A SPECIAL BIBLIOGRAPHY. A selected bibliography on aeronautical engineering. 132 pp. NATIONAL TECHNICAL INFORMATION SERVICE, Springfield, Va. 22151. $3.00.

AGENT, THE. Lists suppliers of fabrics, trimmings, services and equipment used in the garment manufacturing industry. Semi-Annual. Halper Publishning Co., 300 W. Adams St., Chicago, Ill. 60606.

AGING, DIRECTORY OF NATIONAL ORGANIZATIONS WITH PROGRAMS IN THE FIELD OF. An alphabetical listing of almost 300 private, non-governmental agencies representing a broad spectrum of organizations—social welfare, unions, professional groups, churches—whose programs directly or tangentially serve the interests of older people. 95 pp. NATIONAL COUNCIL ON THE AGING, INC., 1828 L St., N.W., Washington, D.C. 20036. 75 cents.

AGRI-BUSINESS BUYER'S REFERENCE. A listing of equipment and supplies used in grain handling and processing plants. Annual. AGRI-BUSINESS BUYER'S REFERENCE, Board of Trade Bldg., 141 W. Jackson Blvd., Chicago, Ill. 60604. $2.50.

AGRIBUSINESS ORGANIZATION DIRECTORY. A directory of all Government and private organizations concerned with international agribusiness. Includes name, address, phone numbers and functions for each. 50 pp. Sales and Distribution Branch, U.S. DEPT. OF COMMERCE, Washington, D.C. 20230. Free.

AGRICULTURE HANDBOOK 305, PROFESSIONAL WORKERS AND STATE AGRICULTURE EXPERIMENT STATIONS AND OTHER COOPERATING STATE INSTITUTIONS. Published by the UNITED STATES GOVERNMENT PRINTING OFFICE, Supt. of Documents, Washington, D.C. 20402. $2.75.

AIA GUIDE TO NEW YORK CITY. Describes thousands of architec- turally interesting buildings in New York City. Produced by the American Institute of Architects. 464 pp. MACMILLAN & CO., 866-3rd Ave., New York, N.Y. 10022. $6.95.

AIR CARGO GUIDE. An index of all cargo airlines, their routes, flights, freight charges, etc. 186 pp. Monthly. REUBEN H. DON- NELLEY CORP., 2000 Clearwater Dr., Oak Brook, Ill. 60521. $16.00 annual subscription, or $2.00 single copy.

AIR CONDITIONING, HEATING AND REFRIGERATION NEWS DI- RECTORY. Lists alphabetically, geographically, and by product and trade names, manufacturers of air conditioning, heating and refrigeration equipment. Also wholesalers, associations, and ex- porters are listed. 464 pp. Annually. BUSINESS NEWS PUBLISH- ING CO., P.O. Box 6000, Birmingham, Mich. 48012. $4.00.

AIR-CONDITIONING & REFRIGERATION WHOLESALERS DI- RECTORY. A list of 740 member air-conditioning and refrigera- tion wholesalers with their addresses, telephone numbers, and official representatives. Arranged alphabetically be region, state, and city. 52 pp. Annually. AIR-CONDITIONING & REFRIGERA- TION WHOLESALERS, 22371 Newman Ave., Dearborn, Mich. 48124. $2.50.

HEATING & AIR-CONDITIONING CONTRACTOR ANNUAL BUYERS GUIDE. Lists and describes heating and air-conditioning equip- ment, accessories, and shop and job equipment. Literature is listed for each. 60 pp.

HEATING & AIR-CONDITIONING CONTRACTORS PRODUCT AND TRADE LITERATURE DIRECTORY. Product and trade literature covering new products introduced during the preceding year in the heating, ventilating, air conditioning and sheet metal indus- tries. EDWIN A. SCOTT PUBLISHING CO., 522 N. State Rd., Briarcliff Manor, N.Y. 10510.

HEATING/PIPING/AIR-CONDITIONING MECHANICAL SYSTEMS INFORMATION INDEX. (HPAC Info-dex.) Listing of names and addresses of manufacturers of heating, piping, and air- conditioning equipment for industrial, commercial, institutional, and public buildings. All products listed by categories; all trade names identified. Also includes a listing of engineering societies, associations, and institutes; a compilation of city, county, state, regional, and federal code-making authorities; a listing of engineering reference books and manuals; and a five-year index to articles published in Heating/Piping/Air Conditioning magazine. Over 350 pages. Annually. REINHOLD PUBLISHING CO., INC., 10 S. LaSalle St., Chicago, Ill. $3.50, or free with subscription to Heating/Piping/Air Conditioning ($7 annually).

AIR FORWARDER. A listing of air freight forwarders and cargo agents. Annual. REUBEN H. DONNELLEY CORP., 211 E. 43rd St., New York, N.Y. 10017.

AIRLINE INDUSTRY DIRECTORY OF PUBLICATIONS. Lists members of the Air Transport Association of America, and bibliography of Association publications. 20 pp. Published by the AIR TRANSPORT ASSOCIATION OF AMERICA, 1000 Connecticut Ave., N.W., Washington, D.C. 20036. Free.

AIRPORT EQUIPMENT REDBOOK DIRECTORY. Information on airport ground support equipment, materials, supplies and services. Annual. AIRPORT SERVICES MANAGEMENT, 731 Hennepin Ave., Minneapolis, Minn. 55403.

AIRPORT REFERENCE. Describes manufacturers and their airport equipment products. Annual. OCCIDENTAL PUBLISHING CO., 3924 W. Sunset Blvd., Los Angeles, Calif. 90029.

AIR SHIPPERS MANUAL. Manual contains a list of American and foreign offices of domestic and international airlines; I.A.T.A.—authorized cargo agents and C.A.B.—registered air freight forwarders. Listing of airline services to all parts of the world, and including air freight statistics, tables, charts, and graphs pertaining to the air cargo industry. 164 pp. Annually. REUBEN H. DONNELLEY CORP., 211 E. 43rd St., New York, N.Y. 10017. $5.00.

AMERICAN APPAREL MANUFACTURERS' ASSOCIATION DIRECTORY OF MEMBERS AND ASSOCIATE MEMBERS. Contains data on approximately 800 member firms of the American Apparel Manufacturers' Association, listing personnel by title. Also provides information on purchasing agents, merchandise manufactured, number of plants, and lists suppliers to the trade. annually. AMERICAN APPAREL MANUFACTURERS' ASSOCIATION, INC., 1611 N. Kent St., Arlington, Va. 22209. $125-members, $300-non-members.

AMERICAN ARCHITECTS DIRECTORY. Alphabetically arranged biographical sketches of over 23,000 architects, including members of the American Institute of Architects, showing names, home and professional addresses, outstanding architectural achievements, education, and licensing. Information on A.I.A.

Competition Code procedures and basic schedule of architectural services; listings are geographically cross-indexed. 1,126 pp. R. R. BOWKER COMPANY, 1180 Avenue of the Americas, New York, N.Y. 10036. $38.95.

AMERICAN ARTIST ANNUAL ARTISTS' GUIDE TO ART MATERIALS. Directory presents entries of approximately 300 manufacturers of art supplies, exclusive national distributors, art book publishers, and graphic arts materials firms classified under approximately 350 product headings. 24 pp. Annually. "AMERICAN ARTIST," One Astor Plaza, New York, N.Y. 10036. $1.00.

AMERICAN ASSOCIATION OF MOTOR VEHICLE ADMINISTRATORS PERSONNEL DIRECTORY OF MEMBER JURISDICTIONS. Approximately 1,000 motor vehicle administrators, traffic law enforcement administrators; driver license, vehicle registration, vehicle inspection, financial responsibility, equipment approval administrators, etc. 100 pp. Biennially. AAMVA, 1828 L St., N.W., Washington, D.C. 20036. $10.00.

AMERICAN BANK DIRECTORY. Consists of an alphabetically arranged list of 14,000 national, state, savings, private banks and trust companies—telephone number, address, date established, transit number, officers, directors, principal correspondents, condensed statement of condition, and out-of-city branches. Semiannually. McFADDEN BUSINESS PUBLICATIONS, 6364 Warren Dr., Norcross, Ga. 30071. National edition $35.00 per copy; individual state editions, $5.00.

AMERICAN CRAFTS COUNCIL—DIRECTORY OF CRAFT COURSES. Contains geographic listings by state and universities, private workshops, museum schools and art centers which include craft courses in their programs. About 600 institutions are listed. Included is information regarding the specific courses taught and degrees given in crafts. 16 pp. AMERICAN CRAFT COUNCIL, 44 West 53d St., New York, N.Y. 10019. $3.00.

AMERICAN CRAFTS GUIDE. A nationwide directory listing 3,000 craft shops, studios, museums, galleries, workshops, supply houses, places of instruction and sources of Indian work and folk art. Also lists major crafts, fairs and festivals in the U.S. 222 pp. THE H. M. GOUSHA CO., 2001 the Alameda, P.O. Box 6227, San Jose, Calif. 95150. $3.95.

AMERICAN INSTITUTE OF AERONAUTICS AND ASTRONAUTICS ROSTER. 23,000 professional members, aerospace scientists and engineers, of the AIAA. Arranged alphabetically by names and organizations. 340 pp. Biannually. AMERICAN INSTITUTE OF AERONAUTICS AND ASTRONAUTICS, 1290 Avenue of the Americas, New York, N.Y. 10019. $50.00.

AMERICAN NEEDLE TRADES DIRECTORY. A classified list of manufacturers and suppliers of fabrics, machinery, trimmings and factory equipment for the men's and women's garment manufacturing industry. KOGOS PUBLICATIONS CO., 77 Maple Drive, Great Neck, N.Y. 11021.

AMERICAN SOCIETY OF APPRAISERS—DIRECTORY OF MEMBERS. Directory contains a complete roster of the approximate 3,000 certified regular and senior members of the American Society of Appraisers. Annually. AMERICAN SOCIETY OF APPRAISERS, Dulles International Airport, P.O. Box 17265, Washington, D.C. 20041. Free.

AMERICAN STOCK EXCHANGE, INC. DIRECTORY. Publication consists of entries of regular and associate members of the American Stock Exchange—officials. Member organizations, Exchange staff, and executives of member organizations. Semiannually. COMMERCE CLEARING HOUSE, INC., Quail Hill, San Rafael, Calif. 94903. $3.00.

AMEX DATABOOK. Provides a membership, company list, trading volume, administration and information services of the Exchange, with data on each. Also a list of publications is included. 60 pp. AMERICAN STOCK EXCHANGE, 86 Trinity Pl., New York, N.Y. 10006. $1.00.

AMUSEMENT BUSINESS BUYERS' GUIDE. Directory contains an alphabetically arranged, classified listing of approximately 2,500 amusement and recreation equipment manufacturers, suppliers and service firms. 64 pp. Annually. BILLBOARD PUBLISHING CO., 2160 Patterson St., Cincinnati, Ohio 45214. 75 cents.

AMUSEMENT BUSINESS, SPRING SPECIAL—COMPLETE FAIR AND RODEO DATES. Supplies listings of fairs and rodeos in the U.S. as a special issue of Amusement Business. BILLBOARD PUBLICATIONS INC., 2160 Patterson St., Cincinnati, Ohio 45214.

AMUSEMENT—RECREATION MARKET ANALYSIS AND DIRECTORY. Publication consists of a classified listing of manufacturers and suppliers of amusement equipment, supplies and services. Annually. An issue of "Amusement Business" Magazine, BILLBOARD PUBLISHING CO., 2160 Patterson St., Cincinnati, Ohio 45214. 50 cents.

ANNUAL BUYERS' GUIDE—COMMERCIAL ARTISTS. Consists of listings of approximately 1,000 commercial artists, photographers and studios. Annually. "ART DIRECTION." 19 W. 44th St., New York, N.Y. 10036. $150.

ANNUAL PRODUCTION REVIEW. A listing, partly in convenient chart format, of approximately 550 American, Canadian, and overseas specializing producers of motion pictures, slidefilms, television commercials and presentations, including staff personnel, recent references, facilities, and other useful data. Also includes listings of national and international distributors of sponsored motion pictures; specializing writers of business/television films and audio-visual communication media. Listings are arranged alphabetically by service offered. All United States Government audiovisual personnel are included in listings. Annually. "BUSINESS SCREEN," 1 East First St., Duluth, Minn. 55802, $2.00 each, $5.00 per year.

ANNUAL REGISTER OF CERTIFIED PUBLIC ACCOUNTANTS AND PUBLIC ACCOUNTANTS—STATE OF IOWA. Directory contains entries of c.p.a.'s registered in practice; c.p.a.'s registered as not in practice, holding Iowa c.p.a. certificates; c.p.a.'s registered as not in practice, holding Iowa reciprocal c.p.a. certificates; public accountants registered in practice; public accountants registered as not in practice; registered c.p.a. firm names; registered public accountant firm names; listing of practitioners in Iowa, arranged by location; also copy of Iowa Regulatory Accountancy Law & Board Policies; and Rules of Professional Ethics; related editorial material; appendix. 91 pp. pp. Annually. IOWA BOARD OF ACCOUNTANCY, 627 Insurance Exchange Bldg., Des Moines, Iowa 50309. Free.

A.O.P.A. AIRPORT DIRECTORY. Lists 11,500 airports, seaplane bases, heliports in the U.S. geographically and alphabetically. 475 pp. Annual. AIRCRAFT OWNERS AND PILOTS ASS'N., Air Rights Bldg., 7315 Wisconsin Ave., Washington, D.C. 20014.

APPAREL MANUFACTURER DIRECTORY. A list of about 5,000 suppliers of garment industry fabrics, trimmings, machinery and equipment. 100 pp. Annually, July issue of 'Apparel Manufacturer.' ASSOCIATION PUBLICATIONS, INC., 1075 Post Rd., Riverside, Conn. 06875. $5.00.

APPAREL MARKET IDENTIFIERS. Publication contains a grouping of entries providing a listing of approximately 130,000 retail and wholesale apparel enterprises, with financial ratings noted for each. Published by DUN AND BRADSTREET, INC., 99 Church St., New York, N.Y. 10007.

APPAREL TRADES BOOK. Publication contains a grouping of entries providing a listing of approximately 110,000 retail and wholesale apparel enterprises, with financial ratings noted for each. Published by CREDIT CLEARING HOUSE DIVISION of DUN AND BRADSTREET, INC., 99 Church St., New York, N.Y. 10007.

ARCHITECTS, MEMBERSHIP ROSTER—ASSOCIATION OF UNIVERSITY. An alphabetical list of members of the Association of

University Architects giving names, university and home addresses, and telephone numbers. Periodically. ASSOCIATION OF UNIVERSITY ARCHITECTS, Office of Campus Planning, Western Washington State College, Bellingham, Wash. 98225. Free circulation limited to items of interest to the membership.

ARCHITECTS, ROSTER OF THE AMERICAN INSTITUTE OF LANDSCAPE. An alpha-geographical roster of 360 landscape architects who are members of the Institute. 75 pp. Annually. Joseph J. Brazan, p.o. box 670, La Miranda, Calif. 90637. $60.00.

ARCHITECTURE, MEMBER AND ASSOCIATE MEMBER SCHOOLS OF THE ASSOCIATION OF COLLEGIATE SCHOOLS OF. Directory provides material on 95 American and Canadian schools that are members and associate members of the Association of Collegiate Schools of Architecture, noting name of school, address, and name of head or dean of each. ASSOCIATION OF COLLEGIATE SCHOOLS OF ARCHITECTURE, INC., 1735 New York Ave., N.W., Washington, D.C. 20006.

ARCHITECTURE, MEMBERSHIP DIRECTORY—ASSOCIATION OF WOMEN IN. A tabulation of the entire membership of the Association of Women in Architecture—1,000 members, with biographical sketches on each as to education and occupation. Published by THE ASSOCIATION OF WOMEN IN ARCHITECTURE, P.O. Box 1, Clayton, Mo. 63105. Available to members only.

ARMS COLLECTORS, DIRECTORY—AMERICAN SOCIETY OF. Provides listings of approximately 175 members of the American Society of Arms Collectors—names and addresses and specialties in arms collecting. Published by SAMUEL E. SMITH, Box 313, Markesan, Wis.

ART BIBLIOGRAPHIES. A new international reference service covering the literature published in Art and Design and is comprised of three bibliographical series: Art bibliographies Modern; Art bibliographies Current Titles; and Art bibliographies Historical, Consult publisher for further information, ABC-CLIO INC., 2040 A.P.S. Santa Barbara, Calif. 93103.

ART DIRECTION'S BUYERS GUIDE. An alphabetical list of 600 artists, photographes, and illustrators. 32 pp. Annually. ART DIRECTION, 19 W. 44th St., New York, N.Y. 10036. $1.50.

ASHRAE GUIDE AND DATA BOOK: EQUIPMENT. Information is provided on available types of heating, refrigerating, and air-conditioning equipment and their manufacturers. 225 pp. AMERICAN SOCIETY OF HEATING, REFRIGERATING, AND AIR-CONDITIONING ENGINEERS, INC., 345 East 47th St., New York, N.Y. 10017. $30.00.

ASSOCIATION DIRECTORY. Automotive service associations are listed alphabetically. Address and name of executives are provided for each. 65 pp. MOTOR AGE, Chestnut & 56th Sts., Philadelphia, Pa. 19139. $1.00.

ASSOCIATION OF DIESEL SPECIALISTS MEMBERSHIP DIRECTORY. A list of over 200 service and supply specialists in diesel parts. Listed alpha-geographically. Published in the September issue of FLEET MANAGEMENT NEWS, 300 W. Lake St., Chicago, Ill. 60606.

AUDIO-VISUAL CATALOG DIRECTORY. Information on motion pictures, film strips, slides, sound recordings and video tapes that the federal government produces and either sells or loans for educational purposes. NATIONAL AUDIO-VISUAL CENTER, National Archives and Records Service, General Services Administration, Washington, D.C. 20409.

AUDIO-VISUAL COMMUNICATIONS ANNUAL BUYING GUIDE TO AV EQUIPMENT AND SERVICES. An alphabetical listing of products and services to the audio-visual communications industry. Listed are still projects, silent and sound, motion picture supplies and equipment, color labs, etc. 118 pp. Annual. UNITED BUSINESS PUBLICATIONS INC., 750 Third Ave., New York, N.Y. 10017. $4.95.

AUDIO-VISUAL EQUIPMENT & PRODUCTION DIRECTORY. A list of over 500 manufacturers of audio-visual equipment and supplies; laboratories engaged in motion picture and custom color, slide and filmstrip services, 60 pp. Annually. James S. Watkins, AUDIO-VISUAL COMMUNICATIONS, 750 Third Ave., New York, N.Y. 10017. $5.00.

AUDIO-VISUAL EQUIPMENT DIRECTORY. A list of 2,200 items of audio-visual equipment, alphabetically by company within 67 categories. 512 pp. Annually. NATIONAL AUDIO-VISUAL ASSOCIATION, INC., 3150 Spring St., Fairfax, Va. 22030. $9.00 prepaid; $10.00 invoiced; $35.00 to nonmember companies commericially engaged in A-V business.

AUDIO-VISUAL MARKET PLACE. Provides company names, addresses, and key personnel and product lines for all active producers, distributors, and other sources of AV learning materials. Also includes: national, professional and trade organizations concerned with AV; educational TV and radio stations; manufacturers of AV hardware, with full address, key personnel, etc.; AV dealers, contract production services; a bibliography of reference works on AV materials; etc. 293 pp. R. R. BOWKER CO., 1180 Avenue of the Americas, New York, N.Y. 10036. $18.50.

AUDIO-VISUAL MATERIALS FOR TEACHING ECONOMICS. An annotated bibliography of selected audio-visual materials in economic education K-12. Also includes a listing of publishers and distributors. 56 pp. JOINT COUNCIL ON ECONOMIC EDUCATION, 1212 Avenue of the Americas, New York, N.Y. 10036. $1.75.

AUDIO-VISUAL MATERIALS IN MATHEMATICS. A bibliography of films, transparancies, videotapes and other AV materials including lists of supplies and producers. 90 pp. NATIONAL COUNCIL OF TEACHERS OF MATHEMATICS, 1906 Association Dr., Reston, Va. 22091. $1.80.

AUDIO-VISUAL RESOURCE GUIDE THE. Designed for use in religious education, this cumulative edition includes classified evaluations of more than 2,500 current church-related audio-visual materials. Materials include under such headings as The Bible—Old Testament background, history of the Scriptures, contents of the Old Testament, concepts of God, historical and narrative literature, ethics, mental health, parent training, intergroup relations, problems of war and peace. FRIENDSHIP PRESS, P.O. Box 37844, Cincinnati, Ohio 45237. $8.95.

AUTO SUPPLIES AND HARDWARE CHAINS. Publication names approximately 1,900 chain stores operating over 38,000 stores in the United States; includes listings of buyers' names, products handled, number of stores operated, and executive personnel. Annually. CHAIN STORE GUIDE, 2 Park Ave., New York, N.Y. 10016. $49.00.

AUTO TRIM NEWS DIRECTORY OF PRODUCT SOURCES. Lists manufacturers and their products servicing the auto trim industry. Annual. NATIONAL ASSOC. OF AUTO TRIM SHOP, 129 Broadway, Lynbrook, N.Y. 11563.

AUTOMOTIVE YEARBOOK, WARD'S. Contains 600 automotive equipment and accessory industry executives listed alphabetically by company. Included are company and product listings and other statistical information. 284 pp. Annually. WARD'S COMMUNICATIONS, INC., 28 West Adams St., Detroit, Mich. 48226. Free to subscribers to "Ward's Automotive Reports;" $25.00 to others.

BANK DIRECTORY, AMERICAN. Consists of an alphabetically arranged list of 14,000 national, state, savings, private banks and trust companies-telephone number, address, date established, transit number, officers, directors, principal correspondents, condensed statement of condition, and out-of-city branches. Semiannually. McFADDEN BUSINESS PUBLICATIONS, 6364

Warren Dr., Norcross, Ga. 30071. National edition $35.00 per copy; individualized state editions, $5.00.

BEAUTY AND BARBER BUYING GUIDE. A directory of manufacturers, their products and brand names, alphabetically according to categories. Also includes beauty and barber supply dealers and schools. Over 5,000 listings included. 186 pp. Annual. SERVICE PUBLICATIONS INC., 100 Park Ave., New York, N.Y. 10017. $30.00.

BEAUTY AND BARBER SUPPLY DEALERS, DIRECTORY OF. Contains listings of approximately 1,600 beauty and barber shop suppliers—owners' names, number of salesmen, territory covered, and type of customers. Maintained in current condition by issuance of Supplements every 3 to 4 months. NATIONAL BEAUTY AND BARBER MANUFACTURERS' ASSOCIATION, 45 Middleneck Road, Great Neck, N.Y. 11022. $16.00 per copy. Available only to members.

BIBLIOGRAPHY OF PUBLICATIONS OF UNIVERSITY BUREAUS OF BUSINESS AND ECONOMIC RESEARCH. A reference guide to those publications of schools of business and economics which do not appear in traditional library indexes. Lists books, bulletins, monographs, working papers and periodicals covering a wide range of subjects—from economics, pollution and environment, business management, etc. UNIVERSITY OF COLORADO, Business Research Division, Boulder, Colo. 80302. Annual. 200 pp., $7.50.

BIBLIOGRAPHY ON PHYSICAL DISTRIBUTION MANAGEMENT. An annual publication supplementing the 1967 bibliography with entries in nine categories such as physical distribution concept, legal and public policy sources, handbooks and general reference etc. NATIONAL COUNCIL ON PHYSICAL DISTRIBUTION MGT., 222 W. Adams St., Chicago, Ill. 60606. $6.00.

BLUE BOOK OF MAJOR HOMEBUILDERS. Information on more than 700 major homebuilders, home manufacturers, mobile home manufacturers and new town community developers—the leaders of the home building industry. Lists names of principals, corporate structure, financial data, areas of operation, etc. 500 pp. Annual. CMR ASSOCIATES INC., 1559 Eton Way, Crofton, Md. 21113. $74.50.

BOOK TRADE OF THE WORLD, THE. A three volume symposium provides an international and country-by-country survey of bookselling and publishing today. Lists important information such as: book clubs, literary agents, import-export, etc. Published by R. R. BOWKER, CO., 1180 Avenue of the Americas,

New York, N.Y. 10036. Vol. I, $18.75. See publisher for prices of Vols. II and III.

BOOKMAN'S YEARBOOK. Lists antiquarian book dealers, libraries with antiquarian collections, individual collectors and publishers. Annual. 470 pp. ANTIQUARIAN BOOKMAN, P.O. Box 1100, Newark, N.J. 07101. $5.00.

BRUSH MANUFACTURERS BUYING GUIDE. Lists manufacturers, distributors, importers and export agents of all types of materials, equipment and machinery used in the manufacture of all types of brushes. Brooms, Brushes and Mops, 407 E. Michigan St., Milwaukee, Wis. 53201.

BRUSHWARE'S BUYERS' GUIDE. Consisting of approximately 2,000 entries arranged alphabetically by product and by company, publication contains a listing of sources of all material, equipment and supplies used in the manufacture of brushes, brooms and mops. Listings are cross-indexed by name of supplier. 90 pp. Annually. BRUSHWARE PUBLICATIONS, INC., 330 Main St., Madison, N.J. 07940. Single copy: $2.00; included free as part of regular subscription to "Brushware."

BUILDERS' COMMERCIAL AGENCY CREDIT REFERENCE BOOK. Publication contains the names, financial ratings and classifications of 15,000 firms and individuals directly connected with construction in the Chicago, Illinois, area. Annually with supplements by BUILDERS' COMMERCIAL AGENCY, 105 N. Oak Park Ave., Oak Park, Ill.

BUILDING CONSTRUCTION INFORMATION SOURCES. Publication presents a group of approximately 1,000 sources of information on building industry topics: bibliographies, dictionaries, government publications, periodicals, management, research programs, libraries, associations, etc. 180 pp. Published by GALE RESEARCH CO., Book Tower, Detroit, Mich. 48226. $14.50.

BUILDING CONSTRUCTION SPECIFYING BUYING GUIDE AND DIRECTORY. Lists manufacturers of materials used by the building construction industry. Annual. 160 pp. BUILDING CONSTRUCTION, 5 S. Wabash Ave., Chicago, Ill. 60603. $3.00.

BUILDING DESIGN AND CONSTRUCTION SPECIFYING BUYING GUIDE AND DIRECTORY. Lists manufacturers in the U.S. of all building products. Annual. CAHNERS BOOKS, 89 Franklin St., Boston, Mass. 02110. $4.50.

BUILDING OFFICIALS AND CODE ADMINISTRATORS INTERNATIONAL — MEMBERSHIP DIRECTORY. An alpha-geographical list of architects, engineers, municipalities, code enforcement officials. Approximately 3,000 listings. 120 pp. Annually. BUILDING OFFICIALS AND CODE ADMINISTRATORS INTERNATIONAL, 1313 E. 60th St., Chicago, Ill. 60637. $6.00.

BULLINGER'S POSTAL AND SHIPPERS GUIDE FOR THE U.S. AND CANADA. Presents an alphabetically arranged listing of approximately 200,000 American and Canadian towns and counties and their post offices and railroad stations, and mailing and shipping information. Guide supplies zip code numbers for towns or villages that do not have a post office. 1,500 pp. Annually. BULLINGER'S GUIDES, INC., 63 Woodland Ave., P.O. Box 501, Westwood, N.J. 07675. "Rental only." $38.00.

BUSINESS BOOKS IN PRINT. Contains bibliographic information on virtually every in-print business book available in the U.S. Fields covered are banking, advertising, research and many other subjects. Arranged in three sections; subject, author and title. Annual. R. R. BOWKER CO., P.O. Box 1807, Ann Arbor, Mich. 48106.

BUSINESS INFORMATION SERVICES. Lists firms selling alphameric business information to more than one firm. Includes other information in the field. 50 pp. PREDICASTS, INC., 200 University Cr. 11001 Cedar Ave., Cleveland, Ohio, 44106. $150.00.

BUSINESS MEETINGS SELECTOR FOR MARKETING EXECUTIVES. A semi-annual insert in "Advertising and Sales Promotion" magazine, lists sites, services and techniques for upcoming business meetings. ADVERTISING AND SALES PROMOTION, 740 Rush St., Chicago, Ill. 60611. 50 cents copy.

BUSINESS PAMPHLETS AND INFORMATION SOURCES. Publication consists of an alphabetical arrangement of approximately 1,500 information and service sources in the United States, arranged under 600 subject headings—trade associations, professional societies, information bureaus, research organizations, and federal, state and foreign agencies; libraries, museums and periodicals; individual topical authorities and their books; 950 pamphlets available free of charge or at a nominal cost; unique, odd, hard-to-find services. 80 pp. EXCEPTIONAL BOOKS, INC., 888 Seventh Ave., New York, N.Y. 10019. $2.95.

BUSINESS SCREEN ANNUAL PRODUCTION REVIEW. Lists film producers, distributors, script writers, government audio-visual activities and organizations serving the business and industrial films field. Annual. HARCOURT, BRACE, JOVANOVICH PUBLICATIONS INC., 757 Third Ave., New York, N.Y. 10017.

BUSINESS TRENDS AND FORECASTING. Information sources and bibliography on the subject. 152 pp. GALE RESEARCH CO., Book Tower, Detroit, Mich. 48226. $14.50.

BUY BOOKS WHOLESALE GUIDE. Gives complete name and address along with details as to price, discounts, etc. of well over 125 different wholesale sources for books of every description. Also an exclusive list of over 14 sources for book remainders. This reveals suppliers of closeout, surplus and overstock books. 12 pp. WORLD WIDE TRADE SERVICE, Medina, Wash. 98039. $2.00.

CAMPS BUYERS' GUIDE AND CAMP DIRECTORY, ASSOCIATION OF PRIVATE. Publication contains approximately 1,500 alphabetically arranged listings of children's camps in the East. Information provided as to location, and names and addresses of camp directors. Also contains an advertisers' listing of suppliers of services, supplies and equipment. 250 pp. Annually in January by the ASSOCIATION OF PRIVATE CAMPS, INC., 55 W. 42nd St., New York, N.Y. 10036. $5.00.

CAMP BUYING GUIDE. Consists of entries of 200 major suppliers of 1,700 chidlren's camp products. Annually. The March issue of "Camping" Magazine by GALLOWAY CORP., 5 Mountain Ave., North Plainfield, N.J. 07060. $1.25.

CAMPS AND CONFERENCES. This volume contains information on associations connected with camps and camping in the United States; with a calendar of coming events on conventions relating to the same field. Also contains a classified products directory. Published four times a year at CHRISTIAN BOOKSELLER, Gunderson Dr., and Schmale Rd., Wheaton, Ill. 60187. $4.00 per year.

CAMPS AND CONFERENCES CATALOG DIRECTORY. Lists firms offering supplies, construction, food, sleeping and recreational equipment and other services to the camping field. Annual. CAMPS AND CONFERENCES MAGAZINE, Gunderson Dr., and Schmale Rd., Wheaton, Ill. 60187.

CATALOG FOR COLLEGE STORES, THE. A compilation of catalogs and catalog sheets of manufacturers selling non-book items to college stores. 2,000 pp. Annual. COLLEGE STORE CATALOG INC., 299 Madison Ave., New York, N.Y. 10017.

CEMENT DIRECTORY, AMERICAN. Publication provides an alpha-geographically arranged grouping of entries on approximately 300 North, Central and South American cement manufacturing companies; also includes listings of officers and operating personnel. 270 pp. Annually. BRADLEY PULVERIZER CO., 123 S. 3rd St., Allentown, Penna. 18105. $15.00.

CEMETERY DIRECTORY, INTERNATIONAL. A geographic listing of approximately 10,000 cemeteries including telephone numbers, type of corporations, and style of cemetery. Buyers' Guide section lists cemetery suppliers and type of merchandise handled. 260 pp. Published every six to eight years by the AMERICAN CEMETERY ASSOCIATION, 250 E. Broad St., Columbus, Ohio. 43215. Cloth, $25.00; paper $10.00.

CERAMIC COMPANY DIRECTORY. Publication presents alphabetical listings of approximately 1,600 companies in or allied to the ceramic field. Listings detail name, address, telephone number, TWX, Telex and cable numbers, company description, names of officials and their titles, and number of employees. 150 pp. Annually. American Ceramic Society "Bulletin" by THE AMERICAN CERAMIC SOCIETY, 65 Ceramic Dr., Columbus, Ohio 43214. $2.50.

CERAMIC DATA BOOK. Contains a list of approximately 3,000 ceramic equipment and raw materials manufacturers and suppliers. Annually. CAHNERS BOOKS, 89 Franklin St., Boston, Mass. 02110. $3.50.

CHEMICAL ENGINEERING CATALOG. Listings of 3,000 firms, with data on equipment, materials and special services used by the chemical processing industry. 1,500 pp. Annually. REINHOLD PUBLISHING CO., 600 Summer St., Stamford, Conn. 06904. $15.00-domestic, $35.00-foreign.

CHEMICAL GUIDE TO THE UNITED STATES. Directory consists of listings of approximately 600 major American chemical concerns, providing name, address, principal officers, representative annual sales figures, plant locations, and products; foreign subsidiaries and affiliates are noted, as well. Biennially. NOYES DATA CORP., Noyes Bldg., Park Ridge, N.Y. 07656. $24.00.

CHEMICAL INDUSTRY HANDBOOK. A guide to the chemical industry in the British United Kingdom and European industries such as paint, oil, plastics, pharmaceuticals, etc., with information on each firm listed. 390 pp. INTERNATIONAL PUBLICATIONS SERVICE, 114 East 32 St., New York, N.Y. 10016. $42.00.

CHEMICAL MARKET ABSTRACTS. Provides in-depth coverage of all domestic and foreign information significant for the chemical, plastics, paper, metals, fibers, rubber, petroleum and other process industries. Over 14,000 digests annually are obtained from more than 100 key foreign and domestic sources. Monthly. PREDICASTS INC. 200 University Circle Research Center, 11001 Cedar Ave., Cleveland, Ohio, 44106. $350.00 per year.

CHEMICAL WEEK BUYERS' GUIDE ISSUE. The complete guide to sources for chemicals and packaging. This Guide lists 1,600 manufacturers and distributors; home branch and district offices; telephone numbers; 6,500 office listings. It is made up of a

Catalog Section; Chemicals, Raw Materials and Specialties Directory with over 6,000 product listings and 50,000 individual listings of major producers and distributors. There is also included a Tradenames Directory of over 6,500 names. In the Packaging Area there is a Company Directory of manufacturers of all types of packaging containers, accessories and bulk shipping equipment; also a Packaging Catalog Section. Included are 400 different categories of packaging items with 4,000 listings of all major suppliers. In addition there is a Packaging/Shipping Trade names directory of over 300 names. Published annually in October by CHEMICAL WEEK, McGRAW-HILL, INC., 1221 Avenue of the Americas, New York, N.Y. 10021. Available only to subscribers of Chemical Week Magazine.

CHEM SOURCES-EUROPE. Lists names of chemical producers in Europe, and manufacturers representatives and sales agents for these firms around the world. 400 pp. Annual. DIRECTORIES PUBLISHING CO., P.O. Box 422, Flemington, N.J. 08822. $40.00.

CHEM SOURCES-U.S.A. Consists of an alphabetical and chemical listing of approximately 600 organic and inorganic chemical producers and suppliers' listings of 55,000 chemicals. 797 pp. Annually. DIRECTORIES PUBLISHING CO., P.O. Box 422, Flemington, N.J. 08822. $48.00.

CHRISTIAN BOOKSELLER BUYERS GUIDE. This volume contains a classified directory of publishers and their products arranged alphabetically by category, with a publishers and suppliers directory which gives addresses. Annually as part of a subscription to "CHRISTIAN BOOKSELLER," Gunderson Dr., and Schmale Rd., Wheaton, Ill. 60187. $6.00 per year.

CITY DIRECTORY CATALOG. Presents a listing of every city directory in North America. Contains a census, county list, listings of auto owners, farmers, householders, property owners, telephone numbers, rural routes, taxpayers; wives' names detailed in each listing. Annually. ASSOCIATION OF NORTH AMERICAN DIRECTORY PUBLISHERS, 270 Orange Street, New Haven, Conn. 06509. $1.00.

CIVIL RIGHTS: A GUIDE TO THE PEOPLE, ORGANIZATIONS AND EVENTS. An alphabetical guide to names of individuals and organizations prominent in the civil rights movement between 1954 and the present. Also a list of states with civil rights legislation and stage agencies with civil rights responsibilities, and a list of black elected officials in the United States. 194 pp. Published by R. R. BOWKER CO., 1180 Avenue of the Americas, New York, N.Y. 10036. $11.50.

COLLECTION AGENCIES, AMERICAN DIRECTORY OF. Lists professional collection agencies and collectors throughout the U.S., Canada and parts of Europe. 255 pp. Annual. THE SERVICE PUBLISHING CO., 639 Washington Blvd. 15th & New York Ave., N.W., Washington, D.C. 20005. $10.00.

COLLECTORS, DIRECTORY OF BONDED. Consists of a listing of approximately 2,500 collection agency members of the American Collectors Association, with name of individual owner or manager, address and telephone number. 596 pp. Annually. AMERICAN COLLECTORS ASSOCIATION, INC., 4040 W. 70th St., Minneapolis, Minn. 55435. Free to members; $25.00 to qualified nonmembers.

COLLEGE STORE BUYERS GUIDE. Contains entries of approximately 1,000 products sold in college stores, with names of manufacturers. Published by THE NATIONAL ASSOCIATION OF COLLEGE STORES. Oberlin, Ohio.

COLLEGE STORE PRODUCTS AND MANUFACTURERS DIRECTORY. Lists manufacturers of products sold in college stores, COLLEGE STORE NEWS, 735 Spring St., N.W., Atlanta, Ga. 30308. $1.00.

COMMUNICATION DIRECTORY. Lists communication associations, communication centers, meetings, data sources, career sources, education sources, books and other publications and other sources and data on the communications field. COUNCIL OF COMMUNICATION SOCIETIES, P.O. Box 1074, Silver Spring, Md. 20910. $4.00 prepaid; $8.00 invoiced.

COMMUNICATION IN ORGANIZATIONS. A bibliography and sourcebook of information on all aspects of organizational communications, arranged by topics of interest. 286 pp. GALE RESEARCH CO., Book Tower, Detroit, Mich. 48226. $14.50.

COMMUNICATION RESEARCH IN U.S. UNIVERSITIES: A DIRECTORY. An alphabetical list of 109 universities and colleges which teach communications or journalism. 30 pp. INSTITUTE OF COMMUNICATIONS RESEARCH, University of Illinois, 1207 West Oregon, Urbana, Ill. 61801. $1.00.

COMMUNICATIONS GRAPHICS. This directory features a bibliography listing 300 books, periodicals, directories, suppliers, manufacturers, and articles dealing with communications graphics. Also includes a "how-to" guide and a point-by-point coverage of facilities-planning. 240 pp. VAN NOSTRAND REINHOLD CO., 450 West 33d St., New York, N.Y. 10001. $25.00.

COMMUNICATIONS/SOURCE. Describes the politics, activities, and how to get in touch with more than 500 groups at work reinventing the social and humane uses of printing, publishing, art, music, theatre, libraries, film, newspapers, television, and computers. Also includes descriptions of 400 books, periodicals, films, and tapes useful as communications resources in social change. 125 pp. THE SWALLOW PRESS, INC., 1139 S. Wabash Ave., Chicago, Ill. 60605. $1.50.

COMMUNICATIONS, SOURCE NO. 1. A guide to 1,000 print and media groups, books, films, periodicals useful as communications resources for initiating social change. 120 pp. THE SWALLOW PRESS, INC., 1139 S. Wabash Ave., Chicago, Ill. 60605. $1.75.

COMMUNITIES, SOURCE NO. 2. A bibliography of reference material on tenant housing problems, active groups, community programs, etc. 256 pp. THE SWALLOW PRESS, INC., 1139 S. Wabash Ave., Chicago, Ill. 60605. $7.00—$2.95 paper.

COMPUTER AND INFORMATION SYSTEMS. Devoted to complete and comprehensive coverage of the world literature in this field. CAMBRIDGE SCIENTIFIC ABSTRACTS INC., 6611 Kenilworth Ave., Suite 437, Riverdale, Md. 20840.

COMPUTER-ASSISTED INSTRUCTION: A SELECTED BIBLIOGRAPHY. A computer print-out bibliography of articles and books on computer-assisted instruction. 235 pp. ASSOC. FOR EDUCATIONAL COMMUNICATIONS AND TECHNOLOGY, 1201-16th St., N.W., Washington, D.C. 20036. $3.50.

COMPUTER DISPLAY REVIEW. Contains in four volumes information on cost, availability and application of all types of Display terminal equipment. 2,000 pp. Annual with supplements. G. L. M. CORPORATION, 594 Marrett Rd., Lexington, Mass. 02173. $450.00.

COMPUTER EQUIPMENT SPECIFICATION REFERENCE MANUAL. An alphabetical by category listing of companies that produce computer hardware, with equipment specifications. About 300 listings are included. 300 pp. Annually. APPLIED LIBRARY RESOURCES, 1343 H St., N.W., Washington, D.C. 20005. $9.95.

COMPUTER SEMINAR DIRECTORY. An alphabetical by organization listing of over 200 institutions, companies, universities, etc. that offer workshops, short courses and home study programs in 165 subjects related to data processing and computer technology. 60 pp. Biennially. EDUCATION AND TRAINING ASSOCIATES, P.O. Box 304-AD, Dunellen, N.J. 08812. $5.00.

COMPUTER SYSTEMS HOUSES CONTINUE TO THRIVE. MULTIPLY. Lists over 100 systems engineering firms, with their addresses, phone numbers, number of employees, and specialties.

70 pp. Published by CONTROL ENGINEERING, 466 Lexington Ave., New York, N.Y. 10017. $2.00.

COMPUTER VOICE (AUDIO) RESPONSE INDUSTRY, THE. Voice or audio response is applied to computer systems that have the capability of answering an input inquiry by using a human voice. Presented is a comprehensive analysis of the industry and names and addresses of equipment suppliers are appended. 154 pp. ALL-TECH COMPUTER SYSTEMS INC., 5434 King Ave., Pennsauken, N.J. 08109. $495.00.

COMPUTER YEARBOOK AND DIRECTORY. Publication contains entries on manufacturers of data processing equipment and services, colleges and universities offering data processing courses, private business schools, private and public institutes, associations with interest in data processing, computer-user organizations, audio-visual aids. Also provides information on flow charting symbols and techniques, computer manufacturers, computer and computer systems, insurance companies' data processing usage, federal government ADP installations inventory, and a list of data processing abbreviations. Annually. AMERICAN DATA PROCESSING, INC., 134 N. Thirteenth, Philadelphia, Pa. 19107. $22.50.

COMPUTERS, ALL ABOUT USED. Contains sources of supply for used computers—Federal Government, leasing companies, private owners, manufacturers. Also information on valid markets for used computers. 330 pp. Boston Computer Group, Inc., Available from FROST & SULLIVAN INC., 106 Fulton St., New York, N.Y. 10038. $275.00.

COMPUTERS AND DATA PROCESSING INFORMATION SOURCES. Ten sections cover: General Orientation, Planning and Organization, Personnel (staffing), Equipment, Supplies, Facilities, Communication and Records, Comptrollership, Operating, Directing, Front Office References. The Future, broken down into 79 subheads. Appendixes. Author and Title index. Subject index. 275 pp. Published by GALE RESEARCH COMPANY, Book Tower, Detroit, Mich. 48226. $14.50.

COMPUTERS DIRECTORIES. A series of seven volumes—each provides the name and address of firms with computer installations and describes their equipment. Each volume covers a different geographical area. Contact publisher for full details and prices. C. W. ASSOCIATES, P.O. Box 144, Babson Park, Mass. 02157.

CONCRETE INSTITUTE DIRECTORY, AMERICAN. Directory's approximately 15,000 listings provide a complete membership ros-

ter of the American Concrete Institute. Biennially. AMERICAN
CONCRETE INSTITUTE, P.O. Box 4754, Detroit, Mich. 48219.
$10.00; distribution limited.

CONCRETE INSTITUTE—MEMBERSHIP DIRECTORY, PRESTRES-
SED. Directory contains information on approximately 2,100
company members (producers), associate professionals and
students (architects and engineers) in the field, affiliated with the
Prestressed Concrete Institute. All technical and other committee
personnel listed by committee. Annually. 96 pp. PRESTRESSED
CONCRETE INSTITUTE, 20 N. Wacker Dr., Chicago, Ill. 60606.
$10.00.

CONFERENCE CALENDAR, INTERNATIONAL. Intended for De-
partment of Commerce internal use, material in this publication
has been extracted from the Library of Congress publication,
"World List of Future International Meetings," prepared by the
International Organizations Section. General Reference and Bib-
liography Division, Reference Department, Library of Congress.
Published by the UNITED STATES GOVERNMENT PRINTING
OFFICE, Supt. of Documents, Washington, D.C. 20402. $1.25.

CONSERVATION DIRECTORY. Arranged alpha-geographically, this
directory lists over 1,500 organizations and agencies in the U.S.
and Canada concerned with the conservation and management
of natural resources. 210 pp. Annually. NATIONAL WILDLIFE
FEDERATION, 1412 16th St., N.W., Washington, D.C. 20036.
$2.00.

CONSERVATION YEARBOOK. Directory contains listings of approximately 6,000 individuals and 1,000 state, federal and private
agencies, commissions and societies engaged in natural resources conservation. Description of forest conservation practices; water, soil, wildlife, range and grasslands conservation.
Published by "CONSERVATION YEARBOOK," 2918 29th St.,
N.W., Washington, D.C. 20008.

CONSULTANT & RESEARCHER'S DIRECTORY, WORLD. All international technical and management consultants and research organizations by countries and fields who are prepared to be re-
tained by the various Japanese enterprises and organizations
are listed. Published by THE INTERNATIONAL TECHNICAL IN-
FORMATION INSTITUTE, Rion Bldg., 1-6-5 Nishishimbashi,
Minatoku, Tokyo, Japan. $30.00.

CONSULTANTS AND CLIENTS MANAGEMENT. An annotated bibliography including books, monographs, directories and articles
covering the management consultant field, divided into subject
headings. 542 pp. MICHIGAN STATE UNIVERSITY, Division of

Research, 5-J Berkey Hall, East Lansing, Mich. 48823. $12.00.
CONSULTANTS AND CONSULTING ORGANIZATIONS DI-
RECTORY. Publication contains descriptive material about 5,000
firms and individuals conducting consultation servies. Directory
is divided into three main sections, the first alphabetically, the
second arranged under subjects—listing firms in geographic
areas which are engaged in particular fields of consultancy—
the third, an alphabetical index of officers and principals of organizations listed in the first section. 835 pp. GALE RESEARCH
CO., Book Tower, Detroit,Mich. 48226. $45.00. New Consultants,
a periodic supplement service, $45.00.
CONSULTANTS, DIRECTORY OF ENVIRONMENTAL. Lists over 400
Environmental Consultants, their specialties and affiliations.
Many will provide free free services to government, industry and
citizen organizations. 78 pp. Annual. DIRECTORY PRESS, P.O.
Box 8002, St. Louis, Mo. 63108. $9.95.
CONSULTANTS, DIRECTORY OF TRAINING. Lists 365 training con-
sultants and their specialties, with address, phone numbers,
areas served and clients of some consultants are included. Part
of special issue of "Sales Meetings" magazine. SALES MEET-
INGS, 1212 Chestnut St., Philadelphia, Pa. 19107. $3.00 copy.
CONSULTANTS, ENGINEERING. Provides entries on approximately
500 consulting engineers—biographical and professional information on each, with information on engineering services offered. Periodically. AMERICAN INSTITUTE OF CONSULTING
ENGINEERS, 345 E. 47th St. New York, N.Y. 10017. $3.50
CONSULTING, WHO'S WHO IN. A reference guide to professional
personnel engaged in consultation for business, industry and
government. 900 pp. GALE RESEARCH CO., Book Tower, Detroit, Mich. 48226. $45.00
CONSUMER COMPLAINT DIRECTORY. Lists over 2,000 consumer
agencies, governmental and private throughout the U.S. that can
offer help or guidance in consumer complaints. Also a precise
step-by-step guid showing how to complain to the right at the
right time in the way that will command response and action.
PETER H. WYDEN, PUBLISHER, 750 Third Ave., New York, N.Y.
$7.95 hardcover, $2.95 paperback.
CONSUMER COMPLAINT GUIDE. Contains names addresses and
chief executive officer of all major manufacturers and service
companies to be used as an aid for consumer complaints,
C.C.M. INFORMATION CORP., 866 Third Ave., New York N.Y.
10022. $8.00 cloth, $1.95 paper.
CONSUMER DISCOUNT PRICE GUIDE. Information on over 10,000
products: automobiles, appliances, hi-fi stereo equipment, tele-

visions, air conditioners, etc. 386 pp. Annually. PUBLICATIONS INTERNATIONAL, LTD., 7954 N. Karlov, Skokie, Ill. 60076. $1.95

CONSUMER PRODUCT INFORMATION. Lists federal publications aimed at assisting the consumer in the purchasing, usage and care of products. Areas covered include appliances, automobiles, chold care, health, food, housing, etc. 16 pp. PUBLIC DOCUMENTS DISTRIBUTION CENTER, Pueblo, Colo. 81009. Free

CONVENTION FACILITIES DIRECTORY, INTERNATIONAL. Contains a listing of meeting facilities and rates of leading hotels, motels and auditoriums throughout the world; also included is a directory of speakers, suppliers and sources for meetings. Annually. "SALES MEETINGS," Directory Dept., 633 Third Ave., New York, N.Y. 10017. $5.00

CONVENTIONS, DIRECTORY OF. A geographical list of over 18,000 meetings held throughout the United States and Canada. It is cross indexed by 86 different industries, businesses and professions. All events are listed chronologically by dale within each city and state. For each convention listed, the name of executive in charge, his title and address are given. Annually. SALES MEETINGS. Directory Dept., 633 Third Ave., New York. N.Y. 10017. $22.00 with supplement.

EEM-ELECTRONIC ENGINEERS MASTER. Contains entries of approximately 6,300 electronics manufacturers—names, addresses, telephone numbers, sales managers, sales office locations; 3,000 product headings with manufacturers included. Annually, 1,500 pp. UNITED TECHNICAL PUBLICATIONS, 645 Stewart Ave., Garden City, N.Y. 11530. 02110. $7.50

ELECTROMECHANICAL BENCH REFERENCE. Lists alphabetically, geographically and by products, manufacturers and distributors of electrochemical equipment, materials, supplies and services. 64 pp. Annual. BARKS PUBLICATIONS INC., 400 N. Michigan Ave., Chicago, Ill. 60611. $5.00

ELECTRONIC INDUSTRIES ASSOCIATION MEMBERSHIP LIST AND TRADE DIRECTORY. Presents a listing of 300 member companies of the Electronic Industries Association, their products, key personnel, trade names and source-code numbers. Annually. ELECTRONIC INDUSTRIES ASSOCIATION, 2001 Eye St., N.W., Washington, D.D. 20006. $5.00.

ELECTRONIC MARKET IN THE U.S.A., CENSUS OF THE. Provides a statistical summary of The Electronic Engineer Census of the Electronic Market in the U.S.A. Included are data presented by state, county, and metropolitan area on the number of electronic plants, total employment, number of electronic engineers employed and dollar volume of those plants. Also listed is the number of electronic plants within each state, county and metropolitan area by fifteen electronic product categories; 5,032 listings. 100 pp. Triennially. CHILTON PUBLICATIONS, The Electronic Engineer, Chestnut and 56th Sts., Philadelphia, Pa. 19139. $50.00.

ELECTRONICS, DIRECTORY OF. An alpha-geographical listing which provides addresses, number of employees, local executives, and areas of activity. It covers electronics, communications, cyrogenics, design, engineering, photography and others. Also includes listings of government procurement centers, related educational institution and their specialties. Biennially. Research and Development Department. GREATER BOSTON CHAMBER OF COMMERCE. 125 High St., Boston, Mass. 02110. $7.50.

ELEVATOR WORLD—ANNUAL ISSUE. Presents an alphabetical compilation of manufacturers and suppliers to the elevator industry in the United States and foreign countries, giving company name, address, telephone number, name of executive, and description of product or service. Includes an alphabetical index of advertisers with page references. Contains articles and features and is illustrated with pages of color photographs. 125 pp. October issue of "ELEVATOR WORLD," 56½ St. Michael St., Mobile, Ala. 36601. $2.00, each issue.

ENGINEERING BUYERS' GUIDE, FIRE. D rectory of equipment for fire department is provided alphabetically. Some of the equipment listed includes air horns, alarm systems, ambulances, axes, boots, etc. Under each category, the manufacturers of the product are given. 115 pp. FIRE ENGINEERING, 466 Lexington Ave., New York, N.Y. 10017. $2.50

ENGINEERING INDEX MONTHLY. Contains more than 5,000 items of significance, annually covering some 3,500 journals, conference proceedings, standards, monographs, etc. Alphabetically arranged in more than 12,000 main headings and subheadings. Also an author index is provided. Published monthly by ENGINEERING INDEX, INC., 345 E. 47th St., New York, N.Y. 10017. $540.00

ENGINEERS AND ARCHITECTS IN THE VETERANS ADMINISTRATION. Describes immediate and continuing employment opportunities in the Veterans Adminstration for mechanical, civil, electrical, and general engineers and architects. 24 pp. Published by the UNITED STATES GOVERNMENT PRINTING OFFICE, Supt. of Documents, Washington, D.C. 20402. 35 cents.

ENVIRONMENTAL ENGINEERING DESKBOOK. An up-to-date listing of suppliers of equipment, materials and services to the pollution control field. Also articles from experts in the field. 100 pp. Annually in June by Chemical Engineering, McGRAW-HILL, INC., 1221 Avenue of the Americas, New York, N.Y. 10020. $2.50

EXECUTIVE CLUB INTERNATIONAL BUSINESS DIRECTORY, AMERICAN. The club is especially designed to give recognition to women in the business world. The directory provides a listing of the name, business or profession, address, phone, services or products offered, of the members of the club, plus brief biographical descriptions of many. The club offers travel opportunities, travel services, etc. AMERICAN EXECUTIVE CLUB INC., 520 Fifth Ave., New York, N.Y. 10036. Consult club for membership fees and requirements.

EXECUTIVE RECRUITERS DIRECTORY. Describes executive recruiting firms and their services. BETTER/QUICKER CORP. Box 2012, Princeton, N.J. 08540. $2.00

EXPORTERS AND IMPORTERS. AMERICAN REGISTER OF. Listing includes over 30,000 importers and exporters and products handled, cross-indexed by product classification and name of firm. Register notes export officials, bank, managers of firms, freight forwarders; aircraft, airlines. Annually. AMERICAN REGISTER OF EXPORTERS AND IMPORTERS, INC., 90 W. Broadway, New York, N.Y. 10017. $20.00 per copy, postpaid, both U.S. and Foreign shipped against prepayment only.

FINANCE COMPANIES, NATIONAL DIRECTORY OF. Contains a listing of approximately 35,000 finance and small-loan companies in the United States. Published biennially by INTERSTATE SERVICE CO., INC., 714 Neosho Blvd., P.O. Box 1, Neosho, Mo. $12.00

FLOORING DIRECTORY AND BUYING GUIDE. Directory includes listing of floor covering and interior surfacing products, with brand names, manufacturers' addresses; distributors of floor coverings and related products; installation services and independent sales agents, 330 pp. Annually. HARCOURT, BRACE, JOVANOVICH PUBLICATIONS, 757 Third Ave. New York, N.Y. 10017. $10.00

FLORIST BUYERS DIRECTORY ISSUE. Products for the florist industry are listed alphabetically by category with names of sources. Suppliers are listed also alphabetically by company name with address, telephone number and contact. Companies include manufacturers, wholesalers or growers. 60 pp. FLORIST, 900 W. Lafayette, Detroit, Mich. 48226. 67 cents.

FOREIGN AFFAIRS RESEARCH, A DIRECTORY OF GOVERNMENT RESOURCES. A discriptive listing of the many government resources accessible to the scholar who is engaged in social and behavioral science research on foreign areas and international affairs. 50 pp. Supt of Documents, GOVERNMENT PRINTING OFFICE, Washington, D.C. 20402, 55 cents.

FOREIGN INFORMATION SOURCES, GUIDE TO. Provides a listing of approximately 200 foreign embassies and legations in the United States, other organizations and services relating to major areas of the world, and selected references. 31 pp. International Group, CHAMBER OF COMMERCE OF THE UNITED STATES, 1615 H St., N.W., Washington, D.C. 20006. 30 cents.

FOUNDATION DIRECTORY, INTERNATIONAL. Information of foundations around the world. 500 pp. GALE RESEARCH CO., Book Tower, Detroit, Mich. 48226. $22.00

FOUNDATION DIRECTORY, THE. List consists of approximately 5,300 foundations, including name, address, donor, officers, and trustees; statement of general purposes, fields of interest, and specific limitations; assests, new gifts, and total expenditures, including grants for the most recent year. 642 pp. COLUMBIA UNIV. PRESS, 136 S. Broadway, Irvington, New York, N.Y. 10533. $15.00

FOUNDATIONS GRANTS INDEX, THE. Lists American philanthropic foundations and the recipients of their grants. 257 pp. COLUMBIA UNIVERSITY PRESS, 562 W. 113 St., New York, N.Y. 10025. $7.50

FOUNDATIONS, LIST OF ORGANIZATIONS, FILING AS PRIVATE. Records the names of more than 29,000 foundations which file information returns (Forms 990 and 990 AR) with the Internal Revenue Service. Arranged geiographically by state in alphabetical sequence. 167 pp. Biennial. COLUMBIA UNIVERSITY PRESS, 562 W. 113 St., New York, N.Y. 10025. $7.50

GLASS FACTORY DIRECTORY. List of approximately 450 American and Canadian glass manufacturing firms and their personnel, tank capacity and main products, containing a list of mirror manufacturers. Arranged alpha-geographically. 180 pp. Annually. NATIONAL GLASS BUDGET, 443 S. Pacific Ave., Pittsburg, Pa. 15224. $4.00

GLASS INDUSTRY DIRECTORY ISSUE. International listings of thousands of suppliers to and manufacturers of glass products. Gives names of corporate officers, phone numbers, equipment at plants, etc. 182 pp. Annual. THE GLASS INDUSTRY, Magazines For Industry, 777 3rd Ave., New York, N.Y. 10017. $7.00

GLASS/METAL CATALOG, INTERNATIONAL. Lists several thousand manufacturers and suppliers, by product classification, dealing with fiat glass, architectural metal and allied products. 268 pp. Annual. ARTLEE CATALOG, INC., 15 E. 40 St., New York, N.Y. 10016. $15.00

GOVERNMENT PUBLICATIONS AND THEIR USE. A basic guide to Government publications, indicating uses, limitations of available indexes, catalogs, bibliographies etc. 502 pp. THE BROOKINGS INSTITUTION, 1775 Mass. Ave., N.W. Washington, D.C. 20036. $8.95

GOVERNMENT REFERENCE BOOKS. Reviews over 1,000 titles including bibliographies, directories, indexes, statistical works, handbooks and guides, almanacs, and catalogs of collection. Also corporate bodies and personal authors are included. Entires are grouped in some 100 subject categories. 203 pp. Biennially. LIBRARIES UNLIMITED, INC., P.O. Box 263. Littletown, Colo. 80120. $8.50.

GOVERNMENT REPORTS ANNOUNCEMENTS (GRA). An abstract journal announcing all NTIS documents as they become available for release to the public. Semi-monthly. U.S. DEPT. OF COMMERCE, National Technical Information Service, 5258 Port Royal Rd., Springfield, VA. 22151 $30.00 per year. $3.00 single copy.

GOVERNMENT REPORTS INDEX (GRI). Companion publication to the GRA indexing each issue by subject, corporate and personal author, and contract and report numbers. Semi-monthly. U.S. DEPT OF COMMERCE, NTIS, 5258 Port Royal Rd., Springfield, Va. 22151. $22.00 per year, $3.00 single copy.

HAM REGISTER. Directory of approximately 11,000 American, Canadian and foreign amateur radio (ham) operators—personal sketch on education, background, interests and other hobbies. Published every four or five years by the HAM REGISTER INC., 37 S. 6th St., Indiana, Pa. $.500

HANDBOOK OF HOBBIES AND CRAFTS. A guide to hundreds of leisure time activities with a description of each, related associations, clubs and organizations as well as a bibliography of pertinent books, pamphlets and periodicals. 700 pp. R. R. Bowker Co., P.O. Box 1807, Ann Arbor, Mich. 48106.

HARDWARE AGE DIRECTORY ISSUE. Every product distributed through the hardware trade is listed and indexed; every manufacturer is listed under the product heading of every product he makes. Product index and manufacturer-wholesaler index included. 670 pp. Annually. "Hardware Ag," CHILTON CO., Chilton Way, Radnor, Pa. 19089. $2.00

HARDWARE AGE DIRECTORY OF HARDLINES DISTRIBUTORS. An alphabetical listing by state, city and type of 594 American and Canadian full line hardware wholesalers, and 968 specialty distributors—their branches, territory covered, number and kinds of lines carried, and buyers' names. Also approximately 1,300 manufacturers', agents, 1,760 chain buying headquarters with buying responsibility for 64,500 reaail stores. 588 pp. Triennially. "Hardware Age." CHILTON CO., Chilton Way, Radnor, Pa. 19089. $60.00

HOBBY INDUSTRY ANNUAL DIRECTORY. A complete listing of hobby/craft products by category, and approximately 1,000 majufacturers and wholesalers of craft, model, and hobby merchandise, and their executives. Annually. HOBBY PUBLICATIONS, INC., 229 W. 28th St., New York, N.Y. 10001. $5.00

HOME APPLIANCE BLUE BOOK. List of all types of Refrigerators, Freezers, Electric Ranges, Gas Ranges, Washers, and Dryers, giving list prices, brief description of each and current trade-in value. Annually, E. C. RANKIN, 114 N. Carroll St., Madison, Wis. 53703. $10.00

HOME ECONOMICS IN BUSINESS. Names, titles, companies, addresses, cities and states of 2,600 home economists in business. Alphabetically and geographically arranged. 123 pp. Annually. HOME ECONOMISTS IN BUSINESS, 1100 17th St., N.W., Washington, D.C. 20036. $6.00.

HOSPITAL ASSOCIATION GUIDE TO THE HEALTH CARE FIELD, AMERICAN. The AHA guide contains health care data available for adminstrative planning in the hospital complex. Lists approximately 7,000 hospitals in the United States registered by the American Hospital Association, with information on the name of the hospital's administrator, number of beds, census, membership and approvals, admissions, expenses, personnel, facilities and services. Also contains lists of accredited extended care facilities, lists of institutional, personal and associate members of the American Hospital Association; as well as officers, offices and historical data. Provides listings of Blue Cross and Blue Shield plans, professional schools, public and private organizations having working relationship with hospitals. In addition, this section lists international, national, regional, state and local hospital associations and councils. Includes a guide for hospital buyers in more than 1,000 categories of products and services important to hospital procedures. 585 pp. Annually. AMERICAN HOSPITAL ASSOCIATION, 840 N. Lake Shore Dr., Chicago, Ill. 60611. $14.00 per copy for casebound edition.

HOSPITAL CONSULTANTS DIRECTORY, AMERICAN ASSOCIATION OF. An alphabetically arranged biographical listing of professional and nationally recognized hospital consultants; description of the various fields of service engaged in by members; code of ethics and principles of relationship of the American Association of Hospital Consultants. 32 pp. Annually. AMERICAN ASSOCIATION OF HOSPITAL CONSULTANTS, 1 Wyoming St., Dayton, Ohio 45409. Distributed free of charge.

HOUSE MAGAZINE DIRECTORY, GEBBIE PRESS. Publication consists of a guide to approximately 4,000 major house organs, listed in editorial detail; gives editors' names, company names, addresses, circulation figures, and description of free-lance material or publicity releases sought by each. Triennially bu Gebbie Directory. NATIONAL RESEARCH BUREAU, INC., 424 N. Third St., Burlington, Iowa 52601. $34.95.

HOUSEWARES DIRECTORY ISSUE. An alphabetical by category listing of 11,000 products, brand names, etc. by houseware manufacturers in the United States. 150 pp. Annually. BOB McCLAIN, 43 E. Ohio St., Chicago, Ill. 60611. $15.00 with annual subscription.

INDUSTRIAL AND SCIENTIFIC INSTRUMENTS. A survey of facts and figures for exporters of industrial and scientific instruments. Information supplied for 22 countries on export opportunities for each country. Includes a bibliography, a list of personnel contacts and other data also supplied. 94 pp. Supt. of Documents, GOVERNMENT PRINTING OFFICE, Washington, D.C. 20402. $1.25.

INDUSTRIAL DESIGNERS SOCIETY OF AMERICA—MEMBERSHIP DIRECTORY. Consists of an alphabetical listing of all members of the Industrial Designers Society of America, showing company, school, and other affiliations and giving complete addresses. Consultants noted. Board of directors, regional and chapter offices listed geographically without addresses. Lists 725 industrial designer, consultants, company design department heads and staff designers located mainly in five major areas of the United States—the northeast, the mideast, the midwest, the west coast and the south. Also lists business affiliations. Notes purpose of the society. 25 pp. Annually. INDUSTRIAL DESIGNERS SOCIETY OF AMERICA, 1750 Old Meado Rd., McLean, Va. 22101. $100.00

INDUSTRIAL DISTRIBUTORS, DIRECTORY OF. Lists 9,000 industrial distributors and their product information. Biennially. Industrial Distribution, MORGAN-GRAMPIAN INC., 16 W. 61 St., New York, N.Y. 10023. $150.00

INDUSTRIAL RESEARCH "NEW PRODUCT" ANNUAL. A three-part annual containing descriptions of the 1,000 most significant new techinal products—primarily laboratory instruments, materials, and equipment—developed during the past year. Arranged alphabetically by product subjects. 150+ pp. Annualy. INDUSTRIAL RESEARCH, INC. Industrial Research Bldg., Beverly Shores, Ind. 45301. $5.00

INDUSTRY'S GUIDE TO GEO-ECONOMIC PLANNING. Lists by states and Canadian provinces, industrial development organizations and prepared industrial sites. Also includes statistics on U.S. and Canadian industrial growth factors, financial assistance and tax incentives etc. 200 pp. Annual. CONWAY RESEARCH INC., Peachtree Air Terminal, 1954 Airport Rd., Atlanta, Ga. 30341. $10.00

INSTRUMENTS AND CONTROL SYSTEMS BUYERS' GUIDE. Contains listings of approximately 4,500 manufacturers of over 1,000 instrument and control products—systems, devices, components and accessories used in measurement, inspection, testing analysis, computing, data handling and automatic control. Includes complete address and phone number, names, addresses and phone numbers of district sales offices and representatives. Annually. 304 pp. CHILTON CO., Chilton Way, Radnor, Pa. 19080. $5.00

INSTRUMENTS SPECIFIER ANNUAL. Lists approximately 40 different types of laboratory instruments and services with data on each. Companies are arranged alphabetically with instruments currently available listed. Provides addresses, phone numbers, contract persons, etc. 130 pp. INDUSTRIAL RESEARCH, Beverly Shores, Ind. 46301. $2.00

INSULATION/CIRCUITS DIRECTORY/ENCYCLOPEDIA ISSUE. Publication consists of compilation of manufacturers listed by products—materials, parts, components, wirwire, cable, circuits, instruments, testers, processing equipment, accessories. Converters, fabricators, distributors, sales agents, and testing companies supplying eletrical/electronic manufacturers also listed. Annually. LAKE PUBLISHING CORP., Box 159, 700 peterson Rd., Libertyville, Ill. 60048. $15.00

INSURANCE ALMANAC, THE. Publication presents alphabetical and alphageographic entries of approximately 7,000 insurance firms and organizations. Almanac also notes agents, adjusters, companies, officers, state insurance department executives and officials. 798 pp. Annually. THE UNDERWRITER PRINTING AND PUBLISHING CO., 291 South Van Brunt St., Englewood, N.J. 07631. $25.00

INSURANCE BAR, THE. Publication provides entries of approximately 3,000 selected American and Canadian insurance defense lawyers. Annually. THE BAR LIST PUBLISHING CO., 550 Frontage Re., Northfield, Ill. 60093. $10.00

INSURANCE BROKERS DIRECTORY. Contains an alphabetical listing of approximately 32,000 licensed New York State insurance brokers, companies, agencies, supervisors, general agents; trade names list and excess lines brokers section; non-resident brokers listed in seperate sections. Published with three annual supplements by THE INSURANCE ADVOCATE, 136 William St., New York, N.Y. 10038. $13.00

INSURANCE COUNSEL, HINE'S. Contains listings of approximately 1,900 law firms and attorneys specializing in the defense of insurance companies and sel-insurance, with material on personnel and major clients represented. Annually. HINE'S LEGAL DIRECTORY, 443 Duane St., P.O. Box 71, Glen Ellyn, Ill. 60137. $5.00

INSURANCE INFORMATION SOURCES. A bibliography covering books, periodicals, libraries; professional organization and educational institutions concerned with insurance study. 332 pp. GALE RESEARCH CO., Book Tower, Detroit, Mich. 48226. $14.50.

INTERNATIONAL BUSINESSMEN'S WHO'S WHO. Privides biographical information about thousands of people in international commerce and industry throughout the world. It records the important detains of the personal and career history of directors, executives, businessmen and businesswomen concerned with overseas transactions in industry and commerce. Available from INTERNATIONAL PUBLICATIONS SERVICE, 114 E. 32nd St., New York. N.Y. 10016. $23.00 per copy.

INTERNATIONAL INDEX AND NEW PRODUCTS DIRECTORY. Alpha-geographically arranged directory contains full descriptions and preview of all new products and inventions exhibited in the Annual International Inventors and New Products Exposition. Also contains worldwide patent laws; a complete source of New Products Expositions overseas; and a complete source of inventors associations worldwide. Over 5,000 new inventions and new products shown at eight new product expositions abroad are

previewed, authenticated and reported to give advance information on all new products available for immediate licensing. 250
pp. Annually. INTERNATIONAL NEW PRODUCT CENTER, LTD.,
135 Avenue of the Americas, New York, N.Y. 10036. $2.50.

INTERNATIONAL TRADERS DAY BOOK AND REFERENCE GUIDE,
Lists contries and data on each, such as: principal exports and
imports, banks, hotels, etc., that will aid the international trader.
270 pp. PAN-TERRA DIRECTORIES, INC., P.O. Box 181, Forest
Hills, N.Y. 11375.

LUMBERMEN'S NATIONAL REFERENCE BOOK. Directory contains
listings of approximately 45,000 lumber and woodworking concerns in the United States, arranged geographically, with credit
ratings for each. 1,200 pp. Published semiannually by LUM-
BERMEN'S CREDIT ASSOCIATION, INC., 608 S. Dearborn St.,
Chicago, Ill. 60605. $325.00 each.

MAIL LIST RATES & DATA DIRECT. Approximately 22,000 mailing
lists available for rent. Arranged alphabetically by class/type of
market. Each listing gives description of list, list sources, rental
rates, quantity, commission, restrictions, test arrangement,
method of addressing, etc., all arranged under 12 uniform, numbered headings, included are listings of brokers, managers and
compilers, and a directory of suppliers and services. Semiannually. STANDARD RATE & DATA SERVICE, INC., 5201 Old Orchard R., Skokie, Ill. 60076. Single copy $35.00. One year $50.00
(2 issues).

MAJOR MASS MARKET MERCHANDISERS. An alpha-geographical
listing of approximately 1,700 discount, variety, drug, supermarket chains, as well as rack jobbers and leased department
operators; mens, womens and childrens wear buyers and merchandise managers and lines handled; telephone numbers, buying headquarters, and New York resident buying offices are given, 374 pp. Annually. THE SALESMEN'S GUIDE, INC., 1140
Broadway, New York, N.Y. 10001. $40.00

MANUFACTURERS' REPRESENTATIVES, DIRECTORY OF. Lists representatives of manufacturers selling plumbing, heating and
cooling equipment, components, tools and related products, to
this industry through wholesale channels. Gives addresses and
telephone numbers as well as information on areas served,
warehouses, sales staff, specialization of product lines and lines
carried. About 1,800 listings arranged geographically and alphabetically. 32 pp. Annually. SCOTT PERIODICALS CORP., 522
N. State Rd., Briarcliff Manor, N.Y. 10510. $10.00

MARKET AND MEDIA EVALUATION. A bibliography of sources of information including trade organizations, periodicals, books and directory—foreign and domestic. Also provides other information on markets and media. 435 pp. THE MacMILLAN CO., 866 Third Ave., New York, N.Y. 10022.

MARKET DATA AND DIRECTORY ISSUE—CHAIN STORE AGE. Consists of a listing of 7,500 firms selling resale goods to variety-general merchandise chains. Firms are listed under 6,000 categories arranged in 18 product divisions; market data section details variety chain trends; brand-name index gives ownership of 15,000 brand names. Annually. "CHAIN STORE AGE," Variety Edition, 2 Park Ave., New York, N.Y. 10016. $2.00 per single issue, when available.

MARKET DATA ISSUE. Lists 1,500 available market data issued by media, trade associations and other groups. 75 pp. ADVERTISING AGE, 740 Rush St., Chicago, Ill. 60611. $1.00

Reprinted from Sales Manager's Handbook, *12th ed., Ovid Riso (Ed.).*
Copyright © 1977 The Dartnell Corporation. Reprinted with permission.

Glossary

account analysis	Account analysis involves the determination of purchasing patterns and profitability for each account.
account management	Account management entails the classification and analysis of accounts according to past and future projected sales to determine how much time and effort should be invested in a particular account.
added incentive	An added incentive is a bonus offered to customers to encourage them to buy now rather than later, e.g., "for today only, buy one shirt get another free."
adoption factors	Product features that either speed or retard sales.
advertising	Any paid form of nonpersonal communication by an identified sponsor.
agent	A person with authority to represent another in conducting business. Agents are used commonly by firms that do not have a large enough volume to support its own salesforce.

appeals	Product features that are presented as benefits to the customer.
approach	The manner in which a salesperson opens a sales presentation.
assumptive close	The sale is closed nonverbally when the salesperson begins the mechanics of paperwork, wrapping, order writing, and so on.
beeper	A beeper or "pager" is a device that signals a person with an electronic tone sent from a base unit. To respond to the signal the person must telephone the base unit.
benefit-centered presentation	A benefit-centered presentation is one which the product features are presented as customer benefits, e.g., "people want holes, not drill bits."
breakdown method	The breakdown method is a process of analysis and goal setting. The major sales goal is analyzed into its constituent parts (territories, products, accounts, etc.) and subgoals are established.
broker	A person who arranges transactions between two parties. Real estate and stocks are sold in this manner.
budget	A budget is an estimate of costs to perform certain functions during a specified period of time.
bulk mail	Pieces of mail that are presorted by Zip Code and are in lots of 200 or more can be sent as bulk mail. Such mailing requires a federal permit.
build-up method	The build-up method is a process of analysis and goal setting. The smaller constituent parts are combined to provide an overall picture.
buyer conditioning	Using the first minutes of a presentation to develop a friendly and comfortable relationship with the customer.
call frequency	Call frequency refers to the number of times a customer is contacted during a specified time period.
call rate	The number of sales calls that find a customer in and willing to meet with the salesperson. This rate may be improved by making appointments beforehand.
card dialer	A type of telephone that accepts a plastic card with a recorded number for rapid dialing.
career goal	A job or position a person seeks to attain in the future.
cash flow	Actual cash income minus actual cash expenditures during a specified period of time.
closing	The completion of a sale, i.e., when money is paid or an order is written.

cognitive dissonance Conflicting feelings about a situation, e.g., a purchasing decision.

cold canvas A sales call made without any prior contact.

collusion An agreement between two or more parties to obtain illegally or unfairly something from another party. Price fixing is an example of collusion.

company knowledge Every salesperson must have a thorough knowledge of his or her firm's history, organizational structure, financial policies, personnel, facilities, product lines, etc.

consideration In legal terms, consideration refers to the amount of money or other value given by one party in return for the act or promise of the other party. For example, I promise to mow your lawn every week for a fee of $5.00. This agreement is a contract; the $5.00 is the consideration.

consumer behavior Consumer behavior refers to the behavior exhibited during the purchasing process.

Consumer Protection Act The Consumer Protection Act (also known as the Truth-in Lending Act) was passed in 1968. It requires disclosure to the customer of interest, service, or other finance charges included in a credit sale. You can find this information on the back of most major credit cards.

contests Contests serve as incentives to both the customer and salesperson. At the retail level, contests are used to encourage the customer to buy. At the commercial and industrial level, contests are used to motivate the salesforce.

contract A legal contract is an agreement between two or more parties to do or not to do a particular thing. See *consideration*.

convention A convention is a meeting of a group of people with similar business or educational interests.

cooperative advertising Cooperative advertising is a means of advertising in which the costs are shared by the manufacturer and the wholesaler or retailer.

credit sales A credit sale is made on the basis of the customer's promise to pay for the good or service at a future date.

cross-selling Cross-selling refers to the practice of providing references for other departments or divisions. It also can refer to team selling by people from different departments.

CRT CRT is a piece of equipment used to display data on a screen. It is similar to a television screen.

custom tailor	Custom tailor means to adapt a presentation to the customer's unique requirements.
customer file	A salesperson's file containing information about each customer and purchases.
demand creation	The use of advertising and sales promotion increases or creates demand for a product or service.
demography	The statistical study and analysis of human population with reference to size, distribution, income, education, sex, occupation, etc.
detail selling	Selling to a third party that specifies a good or service.
direct denial	A direct denial occurs when the seller states that a customer's objection is false by directly challenging the assumed facts.
direct mail	Direct mail pieces require a customer response, usually by telephone or return mail.
direct marketing	Sales made in a customer's home or place of business. The sales may be brought about through customer response to advertisements, telephone solicitation, or placement of an order through a catalog.
distribution	Distribution involves transportation, storage, materials, handling, and inventory control of physical goods.
EDP	Electronic equipment used to handle and store information about a company's business.
emotional close	An emotional close includes the use of fear, love, vanity, or other emotional appeals.
emotional motive	An emotional motive buying is one that is based on sociological and psychological criteria.
empathy	The ability to understand another person's situation and feelings.
EOQ	It is a means of reordering that has the lowest total costs associated with it. The orders can be transmitted automatically via a computer.
ethics	Ethics is a code of accepted and established principles of conduct.
exposition	An exposition is a large show with many exhibitors displaying goods or services.
external environment	The social, economic, and political factors that affect a company's method of selling, potential market, sales volume, and profits.
extraverted	An outgoing personality; at the extreme, overly aggressive and domineering. *Cf. introverted.*

Federal Deposit Insurance Corporation	The FDIC was established in 1933. It insures 97 percent of all banks in the United States. If an insured bank closes, the FDIC will pay up to $40,000 to each depositor.
fairs	A show in which exhibits are primarily agriculture in nature. The state and county fairs do draw a large urban crowd.
Federal Trade Commission	An independent, federal agency established in 1914 to protect consumers from unfair business practices and to oversee competition within the market place.
feedback	Information received from a customer that indicates how he or she has received your message and his or her reaction to that message.
filmstrips	A filmstrip is a single strip of film with many frames. It is often synchronized with an audio tape.
financial close	A sales close in which the focus is on size and frequency of payments rather than on product benefits.
financial information	Financial information refers to a firo's or customer's ability to pay for a purchase.
flip book	A flip book is a bound book which is part of a planned sales presentation.
follow-up	To call on the customer, either personally or over the phone, to make sure the product was received and the customer is satisfied.
frame of reference	Past experiences that are used for comparison and evaluation in making purchasing decisions.
Gestalt	Gestalt is a psychological term meaning "whole" or "total". In psychological terms it refers to viewing the person as a "whole" rather than as a composite of impulses and needs.
impulse buying	Purchases made without prior planning.
informal organization	Informal organization refers to a company's "grapevine"; it also relates to decision making—knowing who really exerts influence on the decision making process.
in-home selling	Selling consumer goods or services in the customer's home, e.g., interior decorating services.
introverted	A person who is shy and withdrawn. *Cf. extraverted.*
inventory control	Inventory control is responsible for recording stock on hand, tracking incoming and outgoing shipments, and analyzing the cost factors for each item.

knowledge about competitors	A successful salesperson must be fully informed about his or her competitors (organization, pricing policies, etc.) and their products.
knowledge gap	The difference between a sales person's knowledge of a product and what the customer knows about the product.
listening	Listening is a learned skill. One must be aware of the spoken words, voice pattern, intonation, etc. All of these elements convey a message.
manufacturer's rep	A person or company that sells for a manufacturing firm that does not maintain its own fulltime salesforce.
marginal account	A marginal account is a small account that produces little profit or costs too much in relation to the volume of sales.
market research	Market research involves the collection and analysis of data concerning attitudes, opinions, and buying behavior, which are relevant to the marketing mix.
market segmentation	Division of a market into submarkets. Each submarket is different from the other in one or more significant respects.
marketing	The flow of goods and services from the producer to the consumer. Marketing is profit-oriented, although it always begins from the consumer's perspective.
marketing mix	The marketing mix is the strategy adopted for particular market segment. It includes the price, promotion, and distribution of a product. For example, the marketing mix for a product directed at the 25 to 30-year-old market would differ significantly from the marketing mix for a product directed at the 55-year-old market.
Maslow's hierarchy	Maslow's hierarchy is a classification of human wants and needs as a basis for analyzing behavior. It was developed by Abraham Maslow (1908–1970), the founder of the school of humanistic psychology.
merchandise mart	A market center is a building where many competing firms maintain sales and display offices. It is essentially a shopping center for retailers.
merchandiser	A sales support person who aids several salespeople in servicing existing accounts. The main function of a merchandiser is to allow the salesperson more time to sell to new accounts.
micropublishing	Micropublishing refers to the recording of documents in miniature on film. A 4″ x 6″ film card can hold up to 98 color frames.
minor-point close	A sales closing in which the assumption of a sale has been made and the focus is on minor points such as delivery, options, etc.

missionary sales	The introduction of a company or product into new markets or different distribution channels.
motivation	A need or desire that causes a person to act in a particular manner. For example, the desire for money is a great motivation for some people.
need recognition	The awareness of an unsatisfied need.
nonverbal communication	Sending a message by body clues such as posture, gestures, and eye contact, rather than by the spoken word.
nonverbal objection	Those objections that are communicated by body language rather than by words.
objections	A buyer's reasons for not making a purchase.
objective	A goal or desired result.
optical scanner	An input device that reads magnetic codes on products; it also reads graphic marks.
order processing	Work associated with processing an order: sales, accounts receivable, order packing, transportation, insurance, and inventory control.
orientation	A period immediately following hiring when new employees are given a general introduction to and information about the company and their respective jobs.
outside sales	Retail sales made in the customer's home by an established firm such as a department store.
paired-choice close	A closing technique for situations in which the customer cannot decide between several offerings. The salesperson should help the customer to narrow down the choices to two items and then discuss them with the customer.
personal assessment	In this text, an evaluation of one's strengths and weeknesses as they relate to a career.
personal space	The actual space a person wishes to keep between self and another person. Personal space is culturally determined. In Latin cultures, the personal space is less than in Anglo-American cultures.
P.O.P. materials	Displays and packaging designed to create a desire to buy.
positive affirmation	A planned series of questions about a product designed to elicit "yes" answers.
premium	An item given to the customer as an incentive to place an order.

pricing policy	A policy decision based on the financial and long term objectives of the company.
probing	Asking questions of a potential customer to determine that person's needs and wants.
product demonstration	Demonstrating a product in use in a retail setting.
product knowledge	Knowledge of the history of a product and its benefits.
product life cycle	The cycle every product passes through: innovation, growth, decline, and death. The duration of each stage varies according to the product and market conditions.
promotion	Activities used by a firm to stimulate sales.
prospect	A person or firm within a market segment to which a firm's products are directed.
prospecting	Those activities involved in finding and qualifying prospects.
qualifying	Determining if a firm is within a particular market.
qualitative analysis	Judging a person or an activity according to subjective criteria.
quantitative analysis	Judging a person or an activity according to objective criteria.
rack jobber	Salespeople who restock racks in local retail stores. They often own both the merchandise and the display rack. See *route sales.*
radiophone	A mobile telephone that uses a radio signal for communication with a regular telephone.
rational motives	Motives based on economics, availability, or some other practical factor.
referral	A name of a person or firm in a particular market segment. The referral is provided by a customer, friend, or other salesperson.
route sales	Sales made by people who have assigned routes and regular accounts. See *rack jobbers.*
sales manager	A person whose primary responsibility is the supervision of the salesforce.
sales support	The work of engineers, artists, technicians, or other specialists who aid in the preparation of presentations, take part in presentations, or work in the home office to provide information and service to customers.
secondary data	Published information from sources outside the company, e.g., business directories, membership rosters.

Securities Exchange Commission	The SEC is an independent, federal agency. It was established in 1934 to govern the sale and purchase of stocks and bonds.
self-concept	The image a person has of his or her self and one's relationship with other people and the environment.
selling-through	To provide services on behalf of an intermediary customer to one of their customers.
showmanship	Adding drama or flair to a presentation.
SIC	A widely used method of categorizing business by numerical codes (Standard Industrial Classification).
slides	Color transparencies that are viewed on a large screen. Some slide projectors are available with audio synchronization.
spatial object	A desk, chair, or other object that is used to control the distance between two people.
specialty item	Items imprinted with the company name or trademark and given to customers.
SRO closing	The SRO closing (standing-room-only) is used when the product is unique or demand is greater than supply. The salesperson implies that this opportunity is a one-time-only deal.
synergism	Closely coordinated activities produce a greater response than they would if pursued independently. "The whole is greater than the sum of its parts."
target group	A market segment that a particular seller concentrates on.
team selling	Sales presentations made by several specialists to provide thorough coverage of benefits offered. It is usually coordinated by a sales engineer or an account executive.
territory analysis	Determining the best method for covering accounts in a geographic area.
tickler file	A portable file of current customers and prospects.
time management	Planned allocation of time to different activities.
trade mart	An office building in which many related firms maintain sales and displays offices. See *merchandise marts.*
trade publication	A magazine or journal for professionals in a particular field, e.g., *Publisher's Weekly.*
trade shows	Expositions limited to wholesalers, retailers, or other qualified buyers.

trial close	A method to determine the intentions of the customer. It is not really a closing technique.
underling barrier	Lower-level personnel who can block access to the decision maker, e.g., secretaries, assistants.
valid objection	A solid reason for not purchasing an item.
vertical promotion	A coordinated selling effort by a manufacturer and wholesaler or retailer.
vestibule training	A training program relating to job skills that is given to new employees.
videodisc	Similar to a videotape but uses a disc instead of a tape cassette for recording.
videotape	A television recording system that can be played back immediately after recording.
visual selling	The use of media and print materials in a sales presentation. For example, an architect would bring a model of the building being discussed.
WATS	A service provided by the telephone company in which a monthly rate is charged for all long-distance phone calls. (Wide Area Telephone Service)
wholesaler	A firm that buys and stores goods for the purpose of reselling them to other firms.
win-win	A situation in which both the buyer and the seller receive satisfaction from a completed transaction.

Index